THE LIFE

IN THE

HEREAFTER

(Translation of Jahan e Farda)

WHAT DOES THE QURAN SAY?

GHULAM AHMAD PARWEZ

1969

Tolue-Islam Trust ®

(Intentionally left blank)

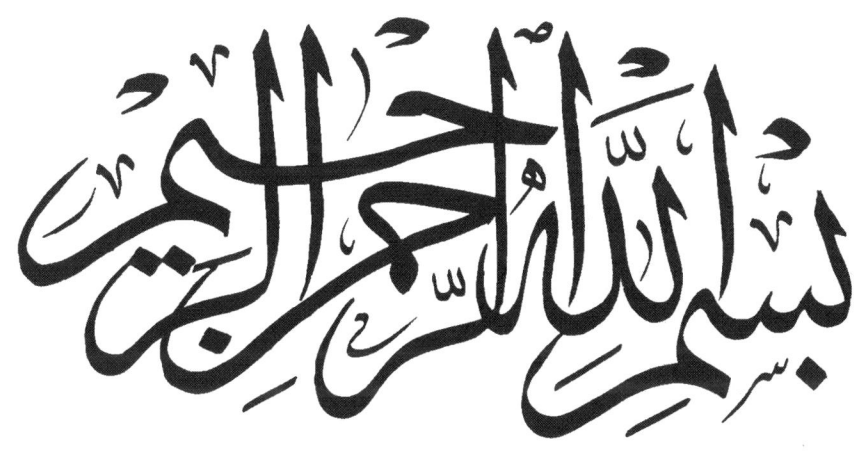

ALL RIGHTS RESERVED.

Title : **The Life in the Hereafter**

Original Title : **Jahan-e-Farda**

Author : **Ghulam Ahmad Parwez**

Translator and editor : **Ejaz Rasool. (Glasgow, UK)**

Published by : **Tolu-e-Islam Trust ®**

ISBN : **978-1514773154**

25-B, Gulberg II,
Lahore-54660 PAKISTAN.
www.islamicdawn.com

(Intentionally left blank)

About the Author

Ghulam Ahmad Parwez was born in Batala, Punjab, in British India on 9th July 1903 into a profoundly religious family. His grandfather, who was deeply religious and belonged to the Hanafi school of thought, was a renowned religious scholar who intended to make the author inherit his knowledge and religious understanding. As a consequence, his education and training was carried out under the direction of his grandfather. While he studied the traditional religious teachings, he also had the desire and inkling to question its content using his intellect and reasoning. This led to his inner conflict with the external religious environment and he continued to question the prevalent religious concepts and practices. He noticed that whatever was being taught as part of the religion was being referred to some Imam or religious scholar for authority. It was also noted in the religious literature, that whatever the forefathers had followed should be obeyed without any question, and this was considered to be a requirement of Islam.

For Parwez, this did not satisfy his desire to seek reason and logic in every claim and statement made within the religious literature. However, he could not express these doubts and reservations initially due to his respect for his grandfather, and the constraints of the religious environment which prevailed at the time in his town. Later due to his employment, he moved to Lahore (now part of Pakistan), and found a degree of freedom to question some of these religious concepts and beliefs. After the death of his grandfather, he found complete freedom to pursue his line of enquiry and research into the prevalent Islamic beliefs, doctrines, ideologies, and religious practices. This led to his discovering that most of these have been acquired from others. He tried to study the Quran using the traditional religious approach but was unable to find the answers to all his doubts, which required satisfaction from a logical point of view. He also studied the life of the last messenger, and the establishment of the Islamic State in the 7th century, and his quest to determine the cause which contributed to this greatest revolution, based on the Quran. He especially paid attention to the statement from the last messenger, 'the Quran is not a product of my thinking or that of any other human being' and that this is the message from Allah. He soon learnt the procedure to understand the Quran.

Through his contact with the famous philosopher and poet, Allama Iqbal, who had a deep interest in the Quran, Parwez concluded, that to understand the Quran, one has to understand three fundamentally important points:

1) The Quran calls itself Light (*Nur*) and a light does not need any external source or aid to make itself visible. It makes itself evident, and also exposes the reality of those things which are within its domain.
2) The Quran is revealed in the Arabic language, and to understand it correctly one needs to understand the Arabic context which was prevalent at the time of its revelation.
3) The Quran has guided us by saying that through '*Tasreef ul Ayat*' (through cross reference within the verses of the Quran) it makes its guidance clear e.g. see (6:106).

In order to meet the second requirement regarding the precise meaning of the Arabic words in the Quran, he researched and compiled a *'Lughat ul Quran'* (now translated into English), which is a dictionary of all the words and terms used in the Quran which includes the meanings which were prevalent among the Arabs at the time of the Quranic Revelation. For the third requirement of *'Tasreef ul Ayat'*, the Quran is different from books written by human beings, where the latter are usually divided based on various subjects: the Quran is based on mentioning a reality in one verse or verses and then its further explanation is noted in another place or places. For example in *Surah Inaam* the Quran states:

> And thus do We explain the signs by various verses, so that they acknowledge 'You have explained them', and We make the Qur'an clear for a people who know. (6:106)

In order to meet this requirement, Parwez felt the need to compile all the verses under one subject as referred in various verses of the Quran and he compiled a book in Urdu entitled *'Tabweeb ul Quran'* i.e. Classification of the Quran. This made it easy to refer to various subjects and look at all the verses mentioned in the Quran relating to a subject.

Along with writing and producing literature on the Quran, Parwez also held a regular weekly meeting in Lahore to deliver a *'Dars'* (lecture explaining the Quran) in Urdu, and these are also available in audio and video recordings. He dedicated most of his life to researching the Quran and its significance in relation to presenting an alternative solution to human problems, and answering questions relating to human creation, its purpose and the question of death and the next life.

He also participated in the struggle for Independence during the period 1938-1947, and the creation of Pakistan, which was based on the ideology of the Quran, with a view to establishing an Islamic State for the Muslims of the sub-continent. He worked very closely with the founder of Pakistan, Muhammad Ali Jinnah (*Quaid e Azam* or 'Great Leader') and had regular discussions with him on various aspects of the message of the Quran. In order to support the movement for a separate state for the Muslims of India and to counter the arguments put forward by some of the religious lobby who opposed the creation of Pakistan, he published a monthly journal called *'Tolu-e-Islam'* commencing in 1938.

Parwez joined the Indian Civil Service in the Home Department in 1927, and after the creation of Pakistan, he migrated to Karachi, and continued to serve in the same department till 1955, when he took early retirement, and devoted the rest of his life fully to his work on the Quran. He moved to Lahore from Karachi and settled there.

He left this life on 24th February, 1985 in Lahore and his body was laid to rest in Lahore.

(Intentionally left blank)

(Intentionally left blank)

Foreword

The aim of my life is to understand the Quran and then to pass on this understanding to mankind. The series called '*Maarif ul Quran*' (Introducing the Quran) was started in the 1930s and as a consequence many books have been published including the following:

1) *Mano yazdaan* - The Quranic concept of God – the relation between God and man. The book has now been translated into English.
2) *Iblees-o-Adam* - The Quranic concepts about Adam (man), Iblees (Satan), the angels, revelation and Risalat (messenger hood). This book has now been translated into English.
3) *Joo-e-noor* - The narratives in the Quran from the messenger Noah to the messenger Shoaib.
4) *Barq-e-toor* - The narrative in the Quran about the messenger Moses and describing Bani Israel.
5) *Shola-e-mastoor* - detailing the life of the messenger Jesus.
6) *Mairaaj-e-insaniat* - The challenges and struggles of the last messenger Mohammed as detailed in the Quran.
7) *Insan nae kia socha?* - (Urdu for What did man think?). In the absence of Revelation, what did human intellect and reasoning consider about human problems and their solution?
8) *What is Islam?* - An introduction to *Deen* (Way of Life) as expounded in the Quran

In addition to the above publications, other books are available and should also be included in this list. *Kitab ul taqdeer, Lughatul Quran* and *Mafhoom ul Quran*.

In this series, life in the hereafter is an important concept, and there was a demand from those people who had a strong desire to understand this aspect of the Quranic message. I am glad that with the blessings of Allah, I am discharging this duty in the form of this book.

As is evident, issues relating to the next life belong to metaphysics, and with our present level of consciousness we cannot understand the reality of the next life in the same way as we do the visible life around us in the physical world. The Quran has discussed these realities using metaphors and similes. As we understand, this is the correct way to refer to these realities. Metaphors can be understood with reference to the existing level of understanding of available human knowledge at a particular time and according to the educational and intellectual level of the reader. This is the reason why the explanations given regarding these realities at any point in time is likely to change as human knowledge and understanding progress in the future. So this can never be the last word and subsequent generations will draw their own conclusions from their study of the Quran. I have interpreted the metaphors and similes used in the Quran by this method, and my purpose is to present this understanding to others, and to invite them to reflect on these realities.

If others study the Quran in detail and reach a different conclusion concerning any of the aspects discussed, then I will be pleased to ponder again on these issues.

I am grateful to Allah for the positive response I have received from people with regard to Quranic understanding, and the interest it has generated to examining the matters discussed in the Quran. I remember when I had initially begun this work, that there were very few people with the same degree of interest in the Quran and its guidance to mankind. Now, with the blessing of Allah, interest in the Quran is developing in many countries across the world. This has also helped the younger generation who are unhappy with the prevalent traditional religious beliefs, to turn to the Quran on finding their questions answered in my work. This is all because of the Quran.

I have now reached the latter part of my life where I am closer to the other side of the river. It is my strong desire that the last days of my life are spent in the pursuit of studying the Quranic message which has been an objective of my life.

... Our Sustainer, accept this from us: for You are the All-Hearing and the All-Knowing
(2:127)

G. A. Parwez
25 B Gulberg 2
Lahore
October 1969

(Intentionally left blank)

(Intentionally left blank)

Editor's Note

Death is an important part of life as it is something every human being will have to face and the Quran has covered this aspect in great detail. This book entitled *'Jahan e Farda'* (The Life of Tomorrow), written by G. A. Parwez in 1969, was originally written in Urdu, and it was felt that there was an urgent need to translate it into English to make it accessible to a much wider audience in the world.

This translation covers all of the aspects which are discussed in the original Urdu version; however, the Arabic text of the verses from the Quran has not been included, and readers can refer to the Quran for these details. The translations used for the verses of the Quran are mainly from the translation of the Quran by Abdullah Yusuf Ali, with some alterations made using the 'Exposition of the Quran', published by Tolu-e-Islam, to elaborate the meanings where required. The relevant references for these verses have been noted, the first figure indicating the relevant chapter and the second figure after the colon referring to the verse number e.g. (2:214) indicates Chapter 2, verse 214.

As is the case with all translations, it is difficult to translate everything literally, as this can affect the flow and meaning of the original text. In order to clarify some of the words and terms, explanations have been provided as footnotes at the bottom of the page and (Ed) is written against these additions indicating this is from the editor. Footnotes without (Ed) are to be considered as being from the author himself.

The Quran is a book which deals with the human mind, and frequently refers to the subject of human accountability. When reading this book, the following points should be noted:

- Human beings have free will, allowing them to make choices in life: they are free to make a choice, but they cannot alter the results of this choice.

- Because of this free will, they do not have any internal guidance, unlike other creatures on earth.

- Every human being wishes to increase his personal happiness and minimise his pain and also wishes to obtain quick results from his deeds in this life – this is the condition of man without Quranic guidance.

- The Quran cites the purpose of human life as being the accountability of each individual, which works through the effects on the human self of its own actions, known as the Law of Requital.

- The Quran asks us to take a projected view of our actions in the present life, and the effects of these actions on our life after death, repeatedly reminding us about the working of the Law of Requital.
- The Quran draws our attention to the significance of human beings, who can make sense of the world around them and the implication of man's ability to make

choices. The Quran invites us to its guidance and to the Permanent Values (Divine Laws)[1].

- The Quran provides an objective concept of God which is unique and based on the Divine Attributes[2]. This serves as a model for man at the thinking level, which then helps to develop the human self for the next stage of evolution, beyond the physical existence in this world i.e. for the life in the hereafter. So, this concept of God as per the Quran is a necessity for the human self if it wishes to develop further. The Quran leaves it to us to make this choice and then explains the changes which a developed self-experiences in this life once it begins to follow the path defined by the Quran. The Quran invites us to use our intellect and reasoning to analyse its message and the Permanent Values – it lays emphasis on the use of the human mind (i.e. intellect and the ability to reason) which it calls a 'new creation' (23:14) and which places us above other all known creations in the universe. So it serves as a tool for our intellect, reflection and reasoning, with which to look at human creation and then help to become what Allah wishes us to become i.e. to 'live' this life and then be able to move on to the next one for further development.

- Since our thinking precedes whatever we do, this means that behind every visible act there is a thought which can be viewed as an invisible 'act'. The motive behind this thought decides what type of impact this will have on our self. So being aware of our thinking processes in all our decision making and thus enhancing our self-consciousness, and referring back to the Permanent Values, is the central focus of the Quranic guidance. This increase in our cognitive consciousness through the study of the Quran is what it terms as 'life' in this world (8:24).

We have also used the term 'Allah' throughout the book when referring to the Quran, and the term 'God' is only used when it is not referring to any specific parts of the Quran. 'Allah' as used in the Quran is a very comprehensive attribute which encompasses all of His other Divine attributes[3] and refers to His complete sovereignty in the universe. The Quran explains the relationship of Allah with the human world, and the purpose of human creation i.e. the accountability process and its functioning according to the Law of Requital (45:22).

The Quran makes use of metaphors to make things clear. Metaphors are an important means of understanding the world around us and in communication. In their book, 'Metaphors We Live By', Lakoff and Johnson (1980)[4] explain the role of metaphors in human understanding:

---

[1] I have included some examples of the Permanent Values in Appendix 1. (Ed)
[2] The Divine Attributes include some which are only in reference to Allah and others which human beings can emulate – please refer to the book titled 'Man and God' by the author.
[3] For further details on the concept of God, please refer to the book titled 'Man and God' by the author. (Ed)
[4] 'Metaphors We Live By' by George Lakoff and Mark Johnson (1981), p 3.

'…we have found that metaphor is pervasive in everyday life, not just in language but in thought and action. Our ordinary conceptual system, in terms of which we both think and act, is fundamentally metaphorical in nature'.

With regard to the human self, in his book titled 'Man for Himself', Fromm (1947)[5] has noted the following:

'Birth is only one particular step in a continuum which begins with conception and ends with death. All that is between these two poles is a process of giving birth to one's potentialities, of bringing to life all that is potentially given in the two cells. But while physical growth proceeds by itself, if only the proper conditions are given, the process of birth on the mental plane, in contrast, does not occur automatically. It requires productive activity to give life to the emotional and intellectual potentialities of man, to give birth to his self. It is part of the tragedy of the human situation that the development of the self is never completed; even under the best conditions only part of man's potentialities is realised. Man always dies before he is fully born'.

Erich Fromm obviously had no access to the Quranic concept of life in the hereafter which would have answered his concluding remarks in the above quoted paragraph i.e. that man will get a chance to realise his potentialities as life does continue beyond his physical death. However, as the Quran explains, this will only be available to those who make a deliberate choice in this direction while living in this world by following the Permanent Values.

The book is divided into 20 chapters which cover various aspects of the subject. Chapters 1-5 cover the topics which come under the subject of the Law of Requital. This explains the process of human accountability in this life and its working in our daily life. Chapters 6-7 discuss the aspects of Repentance (*Tauba and Maghfirat*) and the Day of Judgment in detail. Chapters 8-11 cover the consequences of the Law of Requital both at an individual and a collective level and their effects on human life in this world with some reference to the life in the hereafter. This also reflects on the conduct of nations and their rise and fall in this world. Chapters 12-15 deal with the life in the hereafter in relation to the life in this world. Chapters 16-19 deal with the consequences of human deeds individually as well as collectively and discusses various forms of punishments which are applicable in this life. Chapter 20 gives details on the concept of paradise (*Jannat*) and covers various metaphorical terms used in the Quran in relation to this life.

---

[5] 'Man for Himself' by Erich Fromm (1947), pp 66-67.

Finally, if after reading this book, readers have any questions, please feel free to contact us at the address, e-mail or Tolu-e-Islam website as given above.

Finally, this work is a translation, and as such any ambiguity in the text in the English version which is not present in the Urdu version, is my responsibility as a translator and not of the original author.

Ejaz Rasool
Glasgow, UK
May 2015

(Intentionally left blank)

(Intentionally left blank)

1   The Law of Requital

The basis of *Deen*[6] is centred on the Law of Requital – the reality is that the whole system of the universe is based on this Law. The meanings of the Law of Requital are:

1)   Allah has ordained a fixed outcome for every cause e.g. if a pot of water is put on a fire, then after a while the water will first become warm, and then will start boiling, or if a poison is eaten in a particular quantity, this will kill a man. This is an established Law of Allah.
2)   Man's every deed gives birth to its own result or consequence

This is an immutable Law in which there can never be any change. The Quran has declared:

> *This has been Allah's Sunnat (Law) and there will never be a change in this*
> *(48:33, 17:77, 35:43)*

This is also referred to as:

> *... the scales fixed by Allah...(33:38)*

These are clearly defined scales[7] established by Allah and in common terminology these are known as the Divine Laws.

When we say that there can be no alteration of Allah's Laws, ordinary thinking people will raise the objection that, because of this, 'this restricts the powers of Allah, Who is supposed to be All Powerful'. He can only be considered All Powerful if we think that He can do everything. There is no doubt that He can do anything, but He has intentionally through His free will and choice, created and implemented these Laws and then declared these to be immutable. This does not go against His being All Powerful as He has by choice put a restriction on Himself and despite having the choice to change these laws, He does not do this[8].

His being All Powerful could have been questioned, if someone else had put this restriction on Him. The choice of not breaking this self-imposed restriction comes under taking a principled stand and is part of being self-disciplined. This is what is referred in the Quran as fulfilling the promise:

> *Allah's promise is true (Haqq). (28:13)*

---

[6] *Deen* is a complete system of life which is based on the Permanent Values given in the Quran. For further details please refer to the book entitled 'The Quranic System of Sustenance' by the author. (Ed)

[7] Our thoughts and deeds have scales of measurement – this aspect requires further research. (Ed)

[8] This is why He invites us to follow these Laws which will not favour one over another, but will remain the same for everyone (50:29). According to the Quran, changing of laws is injustice and we can see this injustice being done to human beings across the globe. (Ed)

And:

Allah does not go against His promise. (3:8)

At some other places, He has referred to these self-imposed restrictions in different contexts e.g.:

...He has inscribed for Himself (the rule of) Mercy... (6:12)

Thus it is fitting on Our part that We should deliver those who believe! (10:103)

From this it is clear that these self-imposed restrictions do not curtail the powers of Allah and reflect on His Omnipotence – therefore, the fact that the Laws which He has established are immutable does not go against His being All Powerful. The Law of Requital is also one of His immutable Laws established by Him. He has stated further in the Quran that the whole universe is entirely focused and working to the end that every self can find the recompense of the deeds it has done in this life:

Allah created the heavens and the earth for just ends, and in order that each self may find the recompense of what it has earned, and none of them be wronged (45:22). See also (53:31)

1.1   The Law Working in the Physical Universe

The physical universe and its mesmerising and awesome system is within the grip of the Law of Cause and Effect. In common language this is known as the laws of Nature. Nothing whatsoever in the universe can escape obedience to these Laws, e.g. in *Surah An Nahl* it is stated:

And to Allah do obey all that is in the heavens and on earth, whether moving (living) creatures or the universal forces (angels): for none are arrogant (before their Sustainer). They all revere their Sustainer, high above them, and they do all that they are commanded. (16:49-50)

Since the question of the working of the physical universe is not part of the current discussion in this book, which is about the issues relating to human life, we will not dwell further on this aspect.

1.2   Functioning of the Law of Requital in Human Life

Human life has two parts – one part is physical which follows the physical laws established by Allah. In this respect there is no difference between a human being and an animal e.g. eating, drinking, sleeping, awakening, health, disease, and finally death – all are subject to the physical laws. In this, man's choice or intention and knowledge is not a condition. For example, if someone puts his finger into fire, his finger will burn and he will suffer pain. For this:

1) It is not essential that man should know that if he puts his finger into fire, it will burn, or that if he does not know this, then his finger will not burn. The finger will burn irrespective of any knowledge about the burning power of the fire.

2) Nor is it essential that if a man puts his finger intentionally through his own choice into the fire that the fire will burn it or if his finger is pushed into the fire by someone else then it will not burn. The fire will burn the finger in both cases.

This law is strict to such a degree that if it is my finger which is burnt then I will have to bear the pain, and another will not bear the pain. It is also not possible that on the intervention or recommendation of someone else, the pain can be reduced or removed or shared to a degree. The only solution to be free of this pain is that one has to refer to another of Allah's laws i.e. applying a medicine which can deal with the burn. So under one law the finger is burnt by the fire, while through another law, the pain can be relieved and the burn can be treated by using a specific medicine.

When we went against the first law, then the resultant pain was Justice (*Adl*). By following the second law of Allah we can get relief from the pain, and this is called His Mercy (*Rehmat*). This is the Quranic concept of Mercy. Obviously, both of these laws relating to Justice and Mercy are equally applicable to every human being. There is no distinction in these laws between whether one is a Muslim or a non-Muslim. In fact, in this aspect there is no difference between human beings or animals. These physical laws are equally applicable to all in the world.

1.3   Human Life

Human life is not only a physical one (or an animal life), as it has another aspect which is beyond the animal level. Here we come across two ideologies of human life – one ideology is that human life is a physical life, but because man is a social being, his life is not lived as an individual isolated life, but is lived as a collective life within a society. It is therefore important that Laws should be formulated to prevent conflicts and clashes between individual interests, and should bring order within a society. Everyone should live a peaceful and prosperous life. For this aim, society makes laws and regulations, and obedience to these laws is compulsory. Those who break these laws are declared by society as criminals and punished. This is known as the system of justice within a society. This is also in reality a form of the Law of Requital, but in this and in physical laws there is a difference, and that difference is very significant. According to the system of justice established by a society it is possible:

1) That a person can break a law, but may not be caught by the system of justice.

2) That a person even if he is apprehended, may escape punishment as a result of deceit, a bribe or intervention etc.

If a person breaks a law and escapes punishment in this way, then there will be no difference between him and a person who has not broken a law. Both will be viewed as peaceful citizens in the eyes of society. If lawlessness becomes commonplace in a society, then the people who break the laws live a more pleasurable life compared to those who obey the laws, as the former exploit the system using both lawful and unlawful means to their advantage to live a more luxurious life.

1.4   The Second Concept of Life

In contrast to the above, the other concept of human life is that it is not merely a physical existence but in addition to this it has another existence, which is called the human self[9]. Every act which a human being does, affects its self - good deeds have a good effect, while bad deeds have a bad effect. Man cannot escape from these effects through his own schemes and tricks. For these effects to take place, there is no need for an eye witness to be present, or the need for someone to arrest, nor is there a need for a decision from a court of justice, or the need for an administrating authority to carry out this decision. This effect results automatically in the same way that a finger is burnt by putting it into fire. With the physical death of man, his self does not finish, instead this self with all the effects collected during its worldly life imprinted on it, moves forward after death to the next stage. The types of effects and their total sum determine the future of the self – this concept of life is called *Deen*.

Deen also shapes and establishes a society, because outwith a society, an individual who lives an isolated life within which he does not interact with other human beings, for him the question of good and bad does not arise. This means that the laws given in *Deen* have an effect on society. These laws however do not only have an effect on the society but also on the self of individuals who obey these laws or go against them.

---

[9] Human self here means the personality which we develop by using our thinking processes, and it resides in our memory – this includes our strong sense of identity, education, training, experiences, beliefs, attitudes, values, outlook, intentions, motives, decision making and its effects, etc. This is what influences our day to day living and keeps changing as we live our lives. (Ed)

For example:

1) An individual forms an intention to commit theft somewhere, but does not get an opportunity to do this. This individual will not be declared a criminal according to the system of justice of a society. However, there will be a result of this intention of his in that it will leave an effect on his self.

2) If the same person succeeds in carrying out a robbery but is not caught, or otherwise escapes punishment from the system of justice of the society, then though he may not get punished as per the laws of the society, this action of his will however have an impact on his self.

3) If the same individual is caught and punished according to the laws of the society, then after he has served his time he will no longer be considered a criminal by the society. However, the effect this criminal activity has had on his self will not be absolved, despite being punished by society's laws.

4) The impact of the effect of his wrong action on his self can only be removed when he acts according to the Divine Laws, which are established for this purpose.

5) If he fails to remove the effects on his self, then these will remain part of his self and will be carried forward to the life in the hereafter.

In this connection we need to understand two further important matters: firstly, only those acts will affect the self about which the individual is aware that these were good deeds or bad deeds. If someone was not aware of this law, or his intellectual level is not sufficient to understand this law, then these deeds will not affect his self. Secondly, if he was forced to carry out an act and was unwilling, but could not avoid doing so, then this also will not affect his self. The Quran has clarified this point by stating:

On no self does Allah place a burden greater than it can bear. It gets every good that it earns, and it suffers every ill that it earns... (2:286)

One interpretation of this is that an individual is only responsible for those of his acts which he carried out with his intention and knowledge.

Now we come to the case of a society and nation states. One fundamental point we need to understand in this connection is that *Deen* is the name of harnessing the forces of nature and resources and using these for the good of mankind. These forces of nature can only be harnessed if the established physical laws created by Allah are followed. For the correct use of these resources, we will need those laws which relate to 'human life'. We will call these the Permanent Values in order to differentiate them from the physical laws.

It is evident here that:

1) If a nation does not harness the forces of nature according to the physical laws, its worldly life cannot be prosperous. Since it did not harness these forces of nature, the question will not arise regarding the use of these forces according to the Permanent Values. Therefore this nation cannot live its life according to the *Deen* - consequently this nation's life on this earth will be dark and its future will be dark as well. However, if among this nation there are individuals who are dissatisfied with this way of life, and make efforts so that changes can take place in the society, within which they would then be able to live their lives according to *Deen*, then for these people this worldly life will generally be difficult and unsatisfying, but their next life will be prosperous.

2) The nation which harnesses the forces of nature, even though it does not utilise them within the domain of the Permanent Values, its present life can be prosperous. However, the later part of the life of its people will be dark. But if there are some people in this nation who try to organise life according to the Permanent Values, the later life of such individuals will be bright.

3) The nation which harnesses the forces of nature and then brings them into use within the domain of the Permanent Values, its present life will be prosperous and bright, and its later life will also be successful. This nation will then possess an Islamic System. However, if some people among this nation are unhappy to live within this system, but continue to live under constraint, their later life will be dark.

The Quran has described in detail the collective consequences of the working of the Law of Requital and states:

1) The nation which does not make use of the natural resources or forces of nature may live for a short time on its inherited wealth, but ultimately will be destroyed.

2) The nation which exploits the natural resources but does not use them within the remit of the Permanent Values, will obtain the immediate benefits and pleasures of this life, but ultimately its system will weaken, decline, and be destroyed.

The Quran terms this destruction as '*Al-sa'at*', which means a great revulsion which takes place in the life of a nation. Such events have different forms e.g.:

a) Sometimes it happens that due to following a wrong system, a nation starts developing an inner downward trend and the people lose the ability to face natural calamities and gradually the nation loses its identity and effectiveness and becomes irrelevant in the world.

b) Or another more powerful nation overwhelms the weaker nations and subjugates them directly or indirectly and the nation loses its freedom and independent identity.

If this powerful nation possesses *Deen* as a system, then it can transform the existing wrong system of the former nation with the correct *Deen*, and in this way the people of the weaker nation can attain the respectable position which is due to humans. However, if the new powerful nation does not follow *Deen*, and has a self-destroying system in place which is anti-humanity, then this nation too, will gradually lose its power and identity and become irrelevant with the passage of time.

The Quran calls the life of these nations which lose their identity as being a state of 'worldly hell', whereas the society which is based on the Permanent Values, it calls its life a 'paradise society'. The life of paradise and hell in this life will convert into a life of paradise and hell in the hereafter respectively. The Quran has referred to the life in the hereafter metaphorically, as the reality about the next life cannot be conceived within the present level of human consciousness.

This is a bird's eye view of the working of the Law of Requital, which the Quran has explained in detail. To describe this, the Quran, which is in Arabic, has used terms and phrases commonly used in human society. For example, it says that all your deeds are written and records are being kept, you will be held accountable, your deeds will be weighed according to the balance of justice, criminals will be presented in a court, there will be 'policemen' with them to bring them to a court, plaintiff and witnesses both will also be present. In this court there will be no intervention, no bribes and none else will be able to share the punishment meted out. Similarly, the punishments which are referred to in hell are illustrated by examples based on the human world. For example, imprisonment, fire and spilling of blood in a battlefield are like facing hell. As far as the references to hell and paradise in this life are concerned, these are in physical terms, but the reference to the hereafter is explained using metaphors.

Regarding the Law of Requital as explained in this introduction, we have now to see how the Quran has explained these details. Keeping the introduction in mind, we now need to look at these details further. With this in mind, understanding will be easier and we will not have to go over the same point repeatedly.

(Intentionally left blank)

2 Each is Recompensed for His Deeds

As discussed in the previous chapter, the system of *Deen* revolves around the Law of Requital. This means:

1) Every individual gets a result for his work.

2) The return is only for the work one has done, whether individually or as part of a team.

3) No-one's work remains unrecompensed – constructive work will have a pleasant result, while destructive work will have an unhappy result.

The Quran very comprehensively explains this basic reality, in a few concise words in the following verse:

…Can they expect to be rewarded except as they have wrought? (7:147). See also (52:16, 37:39, 45:28)

The Quran declares that the results of our deeds are given promptly:

…for what they do, they will soon be requited. (7:180)

In *Surah Yunus* it states:

…you get but the recompense of what you earned! (10:52)

The recompense will only be for what we do:

That Allah may requite each Self according to its deserts… (14:51)

It is further elaborated that the system works for all without any exception or favour:

And, of a surety, to all will your Sustainer pay back (in full the recompense) of their deeds: for He knows well all that they do. (11:111) See also (29:7)

Also stated in *Surah Nehl*:

..and every self will be recompensed (fully) for all its actions, and none will be treated unjustly (16:111). See also (40:17, 39:70)

Everyone will be fully recompensed for their deeds and none will be treated unjustly - nothing will be taken away from their due.

As for the people who live their lives with balanced and righteous deeds, the Quran has declared:

They shall have all that they wish for, in the presence of their Sustainer... (39:34)

And then adds:

...such is the reward of those who do righteous deeds... (39:34)

The next verse clarifies this further:

So that Allah will turn off from them (even) the worst in their deeds and give them their reward according to the best of what they have done. (39:35)

In *Surah Ahqaf*, the Quran states that these righteous people will have paradise because of their righteous conduct:

...a recompense for their (righteous) deeds (46:14). See also (52:19)

About the people who do wrong, the Quran states that their lives will be hell because of their evil deeds - see (66:7) i.e. recompense according to deeds (78:26).

2.1   The Evil Doer Destroys His Own Self

In any society people who follow the wrong path think that by exploiting others they are benefitting themselves. In reality, they are doing damage to their own self and this loss to their self is far greater than the benefit they draw physically by doing evil deeds. They do not destroy others by their actions but destroy their own future and their life in the hereafter. The Quran states:

... those who have lost their own self ... (6:20). See also (7:53)

In it is concealed their own destruction:

...but they only destroy their own self, and they perceive it not... (6:26)

They know they are cruel and unjust to others but in reality they are doing injustice and wrong to themselves:

...and wrong their own self. (7:177)

When the destruction comes on them, they cry that Allah has been unjust to them, but the reality is as per the Quran:

...But Allah wronged them not: nay, they wronged their own self. (16:33)

They do wrong to their own self and these wrongs build up over a period of time and become the cause of their self-destruction:

> ...it was not Allah Who injured (or oppressed) them: They injured (and oppressed) their own self. (29:40). See also (16:112, 30:9)

2.2   The Recompense is Non-Transferable

We know that when we go for a walk this exercise benefits us, and if our brother does not go for a walk then he does not get the advantages. Even if you wished a thousand times to transfer the benefits of your morning walk to your brother, you cannot do it. He will only get this benefit when he himself goes for a walk. This is called the individuality of the human self. That is, that every human self is different from every other, and any recompense of any deeds cannot be transferred to another person nor can another snatch this away. Nor can it be that some other person does a bad deed and you get the bad result of it. Whichever person puts his finger into the fire, his finger will burn. No other can stop his suffering. This is the basic principle of the Law of Requital about which the Quran declares:

> ...(every Self) gets every good that it earns, and it suffers every ill that it earns. (2:286)

At another place it is stated:

> And if any one commits a crime, he earns it against His own self... (4:111)
> See also (30:44, 41:46)

If anyone does those deeds which promote harmony and good in a society, then he benefits his own self. According to the Law of Requital:

> .. those who receive guidance, do so for the good of their own self; those who stray, do so to their own loss..(10:108) See also (17:15, 39:41)

The same point is emphasised again in that whoever proceeds with his eyes open will get the benefit to himself of that, and the one who walks with his eyes closed, will fall into the well himself.

> Now have come to you, from your Sustainer proofs (to open your eyes): if any will see, it will be for (the good of) his own self; if any would like to remain blind, it will be to his own (loss)... (6:104) See also (27:92, 29:6)

The issue is further elaborated in the same Surah:

> ...Every self draws the meed of its acts on none but itself: no bearer of burdens can bear the burden of another... (6:165)

Therefore this belief that we can pass on the recompense of our good deeds to someone else, or that someone can remove the bad effects of their sins and crimes by taking on the recompense of the good deeds of someone else - this is against the basic teaching of the Quran:

If you did good deeds, you did these for yourselves; if you did evil, (you did it) against yourselves ... (17:7)

...And whoever purifies himself (by doing righteous deeds) does so for the benefit of his own self... (35:18)

If there is someone who is struggling under his burden, he cannot call out and ask someone else to lift his burden, as another will not be able to remove any part of his burden even if he is a very close relation (39:7). Every person will come with his own burden (6:31, 53:38).

Those who are responsible for misguiding others, will carry this burden also, over and above the burdens of their own deeds:

Let them bear, on the Day of Judgment, their own burdens in full, and also of the burdens of those without knowledge, whom they misled. Alas, how grievous the burdens they will bear! (16:25) See also (29:13)

This does not mean that for those who were misguided, their responsibility will be mitigated and they may have reduced responsibility - the Quran declares that they will carry the burden of their own deeds and this will not reduce. However, those who misguided them, their burden will increase due to the crime of leading others astray.

The basis of the Law of Requital is that whoever does a wrong deed, he will get the recompense of this deed, and whoever does a good deed, he will get its reward and none will be dealt with unjustly.

If any do deeds of righteousness, be they male or female - and have conviction (Eimaan), they will enter Heaven, and not the least injustice will be done to them. (4:124)

In this regard, the greatest human being in the universe, Muhammed, the last messenger himself, as quoted by the Quran, declared:

Say: 'I would, if I disobeyed my Sustainer, indeed have fear of the penalty of a Mighty Day'. (6:15) See also (10:15, 39:13)

The last messenger was further told that if supposing you had gone against the guidance and the Quranic Values, then you too would have had to face the consequences in both the present life and the next life:

In that case We should have made you taste an equal portion (of punishment) in this life, and an equal portion in death: and moreover you would have found none to help you against Us! (17:75)

The one who has greater responsibility will be subjected to higher accountability. This announcement is a reflection of a great reality. Looking at the different religions in the world, the followers of these religions have grossly exaggerated the status of the founders of their religions. Some declared him God and the son of God and said that he died for their sins. Another belief which exists in all religions in some form or another, is that their founders and elders will be able to intercede on their behalf, to save them against any punishment from God for their sins.

Contrary to this, the Quran states that the last messenger has said, how could he save someone from the punishment for their sins, when if he himself goes against the Divine Laws, he is unable to save himself from the punishment. Instead, he states that he would be subjected to double punishment as compared to others.

From this we can understand the Law of Requital cannot be better expressed than this example. This is why the Quran has told the followers of the last messenger, do not think by merely associating yourself with him, that you will enter paradise this way and will thereby avoid the need to go through the life threatening stages which are on the path to heaven:

> *Or do you think that you shall enter the Garden (of bliss) without such (trials) as came to those who passed away before you? They encountered suffering and adversity, and were so shaken in spirit that even the Messenger and those of faith who were with him said: 'When (will come) the help of Allah?' Ah! Verily, the help of Allah is (always) near! (2:214).*

By passing through these stages, there will be an assessment to find out which among you by persistent endeavour and continuous action attains paradise by right, see verses (3:142, 9:16). This right is not obtainable by simple verbal means i.e. just saying that you accept *Eimaan* - for this one has to go through many trials and tribulations:

> *Do men think that they will be left alone on saying, 'We believe', and that they will not have to go through the challenges of life? (29:2)*

Every human being desires to enter paradise but the paradise defined by the Quran is the natural outcome of one's righteous deeds (70:38-39). This cannot be received either as a free gift nor can it be gained as a favour. This is a result of:

> *... an excellent reward for those who do (good) (29:58). See also (32:17, 37:61)*

This is the reason that those who enter paradise will be clearly informed:

> *...Behold! The Garden before you! You have been made its inheritors, in return for your deeds of righteousness. (7:43)*

And since you have achieved it by your own efforts and deeds, you are the owners of this paradise. Now no-one can turn you out of it, and you will live in it forever:

They will dwell therein for ever. Verily in Allah's presence is a reward, the greatest (of all). (9:22)

Recompense from your Sustainer, a gift sufficient. (78:36)

2.3   Scales of Justice

For this accountability, Allah has set in motion the balances for doing justice. The following verse from *Surah Anbiya* points to this fact:

We shall set up scales of justice for the Day of Judgment, so that not a self will be dealt with unjustly in the least, and if there be (no more than) the weight of a mustard seed, We will bring it (to account): and enough are We to take account. (21:47)

On the Day of Judgment, We will erect the scales of justice and in this way there will be no injustice or wrong done to anyone. These scales will be such:

Then shall anyone who has done an atom's weight of good, see it! And anyone who has done an atom's weight of evil, shall see it. (99:7-8)

As mentioned earlier, every human being's action leaves a mark on his self so there is no question of any deed going wasted. In this regard, at one place it says[10]:

... Allah does not allow the reward of Momineen to be lost. (3:170)

At another place:

We do not waste the reward of those who do righteous deeds. (12:56)
See also (12:90, 18:30, 2:277)

Everyone will get the reward from Allah for each of their deeds, and on no-one will any wrong be done, because not giving full reward for the work done is unjust, and Allah does not approve of those who do injustice:

Then shall every self be paid what it earned, and none shall be dealt with unjustly. (2:281)
See also (3:24, 3:56, 3:160)

Far from doing injustice, under Allah's Law of Requital in fact, the return gained for doing righteous deeds will far exceed human expectations:

But to those who believe and do deeds of righteousness, He will give their (due) rewards, and more, out of His bounty... (4:173). See also (3:135)

---

[10] Our deeds are preceded by our thoughts and these thoughts become stored in our memory where the self-concept forms. (Ed).

However, this is a certainty, that no-one will get anything without putting in efforts or actions, because this is the basic principle of the Law of Requital:

That man can have nothing but what he makes effort for. (53:39)

The grades within paradise will be according to the scales of the deeds, there being higher grades for those who have done a greater number and better deeds:

To all are degrees (or ranks) according to their deeds: for your Sustainer is not unmindful of anything that they do. (6:133). See also (46:19)

Allah knows everything about what deeds each one of us has done.

2.4   Human Life is an Arena for Deeds

The purpose of the present level of human life in this physical world is to develop the self to such a degree that it can be made ready for the next evolutionary stage of further development. Death is in reality a test for the human self to determine as to what extent it has attained strength enough to move to the next stage for its further progress. The Quran states:

He Who created Death and Life, that He may provide you opportunity to do righteous deeds…(67:2)

Therefore in this arena of action and deeds:

To any of you who wishes to go forward, or wishes to lag behind. (74:37)

In the next verse, the Quran puts the whole philosophy of the Law of Requital in a nutshell in one short sentence:

Every self will be (held) in pledge for its deeds. (74:38)

In another verse:

…each individual is in pledge for his deeds. (52:21)

Whatever a person does, he has to face the consequences of his actions. This means that he will curtail part of his freedom of action depending upon the consequences of his previous actions. From this no other person can release him. In order to explain this, the Quran has explicitly declared that the Law of Requital is so effective that one cannot escape its grip even by leaving one country and moving to another part of the world. Even by trying to war against this in order to try and defeat it, you cannot get away from its hold as this is not within the realms of possibility:

But we think that we can by no means frustrate Allah throughout the earth, nor can we frustrate Him by flight. (72:12). See also (96:15-16)

It is possible that if you are in a bad society you may save yourself from the consequences of your crimes. But you can do this while in this worldly life only, which has a fixed duration. After this, the Quran says that even if you have a life lasting a thousand years, you will not escape the grip of the Law of Requital:

…Each one of them wishes He could be given a life of a thousand years: But the grant of such life will not save him from punishment (consequences of their deeds). For Allah sees well all that they do. (2:96)

2.5   What Have You Sent Forward for Tomorrow?

Since what we do comes before its results manifest themselves, the Quran has therefore used the term 'tomorrow' or *'Farda'* to refer to this process. In *Surah Hashr* it is stated:

… and let every self-look to what (provision) He has sent forth for its tomorrow… (59:18)

The term 'sending forward' points to the significance of the results of our deeds. This term has been repeated at other places in the Quran (73:20, 75:13, 78:40, 18:14, 82:5). In *Surah Al-Fajr*, another word has been added which clarifies this reality. It is said that the inhabitants of hell, when they see the destruction, will cry out stunned:

He will say: 'Ah! I wish I had sent forth (good deeds) for (this) my (Future) Life!' (89:24)

This makes it clear that the next life will be solely based on the results of our deeds and conduct in this life by each one of us. The negative consequences of our wrong deeds will affect our abilities even in this world, like rust coating the human abilities and as a result these abilities do not flourish:

But by no means! But on their hearts is the stain of the ill which they do! (83:14)

These results will become impediments in the path of the next life to come.

2.6 Concern about Our Deeds

If this is the reality that each one of us is responsible for his own conduct in this life, and this is how our 'paradise' and 'hell' gets created, then man should hold himself accountable on a continuous basis. By wasting our time in prying into what others do, how does that help to improve our own lives? This is the reason that the Quran emphasises to the *'Momineen'* (Believers) not to argue unnecessarily with their opponents but to tell them in forthright terms:

> *... we are responsible for our deeds and you for yours ...(2:139). See also (28:55)*

In *Surah Kafiroon*, by referring to deeds as the 'results of deeds' instead (called *Deen*), it is made even clearer:

> *To you be your Deen, and to me my Deen. (109:6)*

In *Surah Saba* the Quran says to tell them:

> *Say: 'you will not be questioned as to our crimes nor shall we be questioned as to what you do'. (34:25) See also (10:41)*

2.7 Conduct of Forefathers

Not only should you not get into arguments with your opponents, the Quran also points out that there is no advantage in getting into unnecessary arguments over the conduct of forefathers, whether they were good or evil and whether they are in paradise or in hell. You should remember:

> *That was the people that have passed away. They shall reap the fruit of what they did, and you of what you do! Of their merits there is no question in your case. (2:141) See also (2:134)*

If we keep this great principle in front of us, then we can escape all the complications in which the *'Ummah'* (the Muslims as a community) is involved for the last 1300 years, as a consequence of which time, work, energy, and wealth have been wasted and still are being wasted. Also as a result of this, mutual hatred and distrust will disappear and unity will be born. Allah has stated plainly that it will not be asked of you, what your forefathers did. But we insist, no, we will be asked this question first, therefore we need to 'investigate and research' this in detail in order to prepare ourselves.

And we also need to clearly understand that if our forefathers did good deeds, the benefit of these will be apportioned to them. We cannot get any benefit from these. As has been explained previously, no result of any deed by another can be transferred to anyone else.

2.8   No-One will be of Benefit to Another

This value is repeatedly referred to in the Quran i.e. none can affect the outcome of our deeds. In *Surah Baqra* it is stated:

Then guard yourselves against a Day when one self shall not avail another nor shall intercession be accepted for him, nor shall compensation be taken from him, nor shall anyone be helped (from outside). (2:48) See also (2:123)

At another place:

O you who believe! Spend out of (the bounties) We have provided for you, before the Day comes when no bargaining (Will avail), nor friendship nor intercession... (2:254) See also (14:3, 34:42)

This day even friends will become enemies to each other. However, the righteous will be exempted from this state:

Friends on that Day will be foes, one to another, except the Righteous. (43:67)

However, despite being a friend, none will be able to interfere or intervene on another's behalf:

The Day when no protector can avail his client in aught, and no help can they receive. (44:41) See also (86:10)

The following verses and references further emphasise the effectiveness of the functioning of the Law of Requital:

... never would be accepted from any as much gold as the earth contains, though they should offer it for ransom... (3:91) See also (5:36, 13:18, 39:47, 34:37, 57:15, 6:70)

Those who reject Eimaan, neither their possessions nor their (numerous) progeny will avail them aught against Allah. (3:116) See also (57:15, 31:33)

Of no profit to you will be your relatives and your children on the Day of Judgment: He will judge between you: for Allah sees well all that you do. (60:3)
See also (69:28-29, 92:11)

A Law is that which cannot be interfered with from outside, both the functioning and the consequences of the Law are inherent within it, and are unchangeable and equally applicable to all. Everyone will be handcuffed with the consequences of their own various deeds and be present in the court. There, the state will be such that:

That Day shall a man flee from his own brother, and from his mother and his father, and from his wife and his children. (80:34-37) See also (70:10-14)

In order to escape punishments in the human system, many interventions and intrigues can work; however, under the Law of Requital no-one can escape the consequences of their deeds (52:46). This is because every consequence of an action has an impact on the human self. This is why, what is there that an external power can do to remove the effect?

Regarding this truth which the Quran has comprehensively explained, the more attention one pays to this process and reflects on it, the more one is awed regarding its rigorous working.

The human self is that entity which is referred to as 'I'. We call ourselves 'I' or 'Me' and the rest we call as 'mine' or 'my'. For example, my property, my friends, my wife, my children, my body and even my life. Human actions affect this 'I', and at the time of death, whatever comes under the category of 'my' or 'mine' is left behind and the 'I' proceeds alone to the next life.

See how this reality is explained by the Quran:

> And behold! you come to us bare and alone as We created you for the first time: you have left behind you all (the favours) which We bestowed on you: We see not with you your intercessors whom you thought to be partners in your affairs: so now all relations between you have been cut off, and your (pet) fancies have left you in the lurch! (6:94) See also (18:48)

In *Surah Maryam* this fact is stated again very succinctly in the following words:

> And every one of them will come to Him singly on the Day of Judgment. (19:95)

Everyone will come to Allah individually, i.e. no additional baggage will be with them - their self will go forward with the results of their deeds (19:80).

(Intentionally left blank)

3 Accountability

The natural and logical outcome of the Law of Requital is that each human being becomes responsible for all of his own conduct and actions, or it can be said that the natural outcome of a man's deeds are that he should face the consequences of these deeds. In both cases it is the same, we say about the person who is responsible for something, that he will be held accountable for this. This is called accountability. The Quran has declared this to be 'giving account'. In *Surah Al-Hijr* it is stated:

Your Sustainer is a witness, that We will, of a surety, call them to account, for all their deeds. (15:92-93)

In another verse:

Then, you will be questioned that Day about the blessings (or favours) of life. (102:8)

The question that will be asked is, 'how did you earn it and where did you spend it'? Man thinks that since in his business transactions he is totally independent and has control, he can do as he wishes. It is correct that man is free to make choices and has the freedom to do as he wishes, but he has to face the consequences of his deeds i.e. he is free in this context to make his choices, but he is not able to change the consequences of his choices. For this, he is chained to the Law of Requital:

...and his reckoning will be only with his Sustainer!... (23:117)

...and Allah will pay him his account: and Allah is swift in taking account. (24:39)

The messengers of Allah used to give warning about the Law of Requital, stating this in clear terms to the people:

Their account is only with my Cherisher, if you could (but) understand. (26:113)
See also (88:26)

Allah clearly informed the messengers that their responsibility was only to pass on this message, while holding the people accountable for their deeds was with Allah:

...your duty is to make (the Message) reach them... (13:40).

And

...But all-sufficient is Allah in taking account...(4:6) See also (33:39, 4:86)

There is nothing that can escape from Allah's system of accountability:

We shall set up scales of justice for the Day of Judgment, so that not a self will be dealt with unjustly in the least, and if there be (no more than) the weight of a mustard seed, We will bring it (to account): and enough are We to take account. (21:47)

In the human system of justice, accountability is restricted to visible deeds and intentions and inner thoughts are outside the purview of this system. This is not the case with the functioning of the Law of Requital, where both human deeds and thoughts affect the self and thus are within the grip of Allah. The Quran states:

…Whether you show what is in your minds or conceal it, Allah calls you to account for it… *(2:284).*

A *'Momin'* (believer)[11] is convinced of this and this is how he saves himself from taking any wrong steps. That is why when the time comes for the results of his deeds to become manifest, he is able to say:

I did really understand that my account would (One Day) reach me. (69:20)

Contrary to this, those who are heading towards hell, on seeing the outcome of their deeds will wail:

And one who will be given his Record in his left hand, will say: 'Ah! Would that my Record had not been given to me!' And that I had never realised how was my account! (69:25-26)

Since the deeds of the inhabitants of paradise will be in line with the Divine Laws, their accountability will be easy:

Soon will his account be taken by an easy reckoning. (84:8)

Contrary to this, the evil-doers will have a difficult reckoning:

…For them will the reckoning be terrible… (13:18)

Therefore it is important that each individual should keep in mind that everything which is done in this life has an accountability attached to it.

---

[11] A *Momin* is a believer as per the Quran (plural – *Momineen*) e.g. see (2:177) (Ed)

3.1   Man is His Own Warden

So far we have seen that Allah is said to be 'the One who takes account' of everything. This is only to help understanding, and the aim is to tell us that human accountability is based on the Law of Requital and this accountability is inbuilt in each one of us. The self is its 'book of deeds' and it can read its book of deeds and hold itself accountable. In *Surah Bani Israel* the Quran has explained this succinctly:

Every man's fate We have fastened on his own neck: On the Day of Judgment We shall bring out for him a scroll, which he will see spread open. (It will be said to him:) 'Read your (own) record: Sufficient is your self this day to make out an account against you'. (17:13-14)

3.2   Swift Accountability

As soon as an individual carries out a deed, its effect starts immediately, though its visible effect may appear sometime later in his life. This process whereby the impact of a deed commences immediately on the commission of an act, is declared by Allah in the Quran to be '*Saree ul hisaab*' i.e. One Who is quick in accountability. The following verse illustrates this:

...But if any deny the Signs of Allah, Allah is swift in calling to account. (3:19) See also (5:4, 13:41, 14:51, 24:39, 40:17)

At another place Allah has noted that He is the quickest in accountability:

... and He is the swiftest in taking account. (6:62)

3.3   The Day of Account

When the results of human actions manifest themselves, whether in this life or in the life in the hereafter, the Quran defines this Day as the Day of Account or '*Yaum ul hisaab*'. For example, after mentioning the blessings of paradise in *Surah Saad*, it is then stated:

Such is the Promise made to you for the Day of Account! (38:53).

As it will be explained later, the results of human actions show up in this life as well. In this regard, the Quran states:

Closer and closer to mankind comes their Reckoning: yet they heed not and they turn away. (21:1)

The degree of disorder in the world and dishonesty of people is continuing because these very people do not believe in the Day of Reckoning or in the Law of Requital. These are the people from whom all peace loving and considerate people wish to seek protection. When Moses saw the reaction of Pharaoh against Allah's message, he instinctively stated as noted by the Quran:

Moses said: 'I have indeed called upon my Cherisher and your Cherisher (for protection) from every arrogant one who believes not in the Day of Account!' (40:27).

As has been written earlier, everyone is responsible for his own deeds. This is made clear by the Quran - so much so that even in the case of the last messenger the Quran states unequivocally:

... you are not accountable for them, and they are not accountable for you ... (6:52).

3.4 Without Measure

At various places in the Quran, it is stated that people will be given reward for their deeds beyond measure. For example in *Surah Zumar* it is stated:

...good is (the reward) for those who do good in this world. Spacious is Allah's earth! Those who patiently persevere will truly receive a reward without measure. (39:10)

People who remain steadfast in the face of the difficulties and challenges of life, are recompensed without measure e.g. in the matter of supply of '*Rizq*' or sustenance, it is stated:

...for Allah Provides sustenance to whom He pleases (as per His Law) without measure. (3:36) See also (24:38, 40:40)

It does not mean that with Allah there is no Law or procedure established, and He gives without any measure, as this is against the teaching of the Quran. These verses mean that when you work within the Permanent Values, then by your own standards the reward you get is far beyond what you could imagine. This point is reiterated in *Surah Talaq*, where it is emphasised that outward circumstances may appear unfavourable, but:

And He provides for him from (sources) he never could imagine. And if any one puts his trust in Allah, sufficient is (Allah) for him. For Allah will surely accomplish his purpose: verily, for all things has Allah appointed a due proportion (65:3).

Contrary to this, regarding those people of the Book who did not fulfil their pacts and rebelled against the Muslims after ratifying treaties, the Quran states:

It is He Who got out the Unbelievers among the People of the Book from their homes at the first gathering (of the forces). Little did you think that they would get out: And they thought that their fortresses would defend them from Allah. But the (Wrath of) Allah came to them from quarters from which they little expected (it), and cast terror into their hearts, so that they destroyed their dwellings by their own hands and the hands of the Believers, take warning, then, O you who have vision! (59:2)

In the verses where it is stated that Allah bestows without measure, it should be noted that this means beyond human expectation - Allah's measuring of scales is different from human scaling.

3.5   Accountability of Nations

Accountability under the Law of Requital is not limited to individuals only - nations are also held accountable collectively on a continuous basis. In *Surah Talaq*, the Quran states:

> *How many populations that insolently opposed the Command of their Sustainer and of His messengers, did We not then call to account - to severe account? And We imposed on them an exemplary Punishment. (65:8)*

3.6   The Grip of Allah

In some verses, the result of this accountability is termed as Allah's grip. In *Surah Baruj*, it is stated:

> *Truly strong is the Grip (and Power) of your Cherisher. (85:12) See also (44:16)*

If an individual after committing a crime manages to escape, the police follow him and sometimes are successful in apprehending him and sometimes the suspect manages to remain at large. The Quran has used this example as a simile and called accountability under the Law of Requital as '*Auqaab*' or chasing a prey like an eagle. The Quran states that the nations which were destroyed due to their transgressions were given a term of respite as part of the working of the Law of Requital:

> *Mocked were (many) messengers before you: but I granted respite to the unbelievers, and finally I punished them: Then how (terrible) was my requital! (13:22)*

And look at the pages of history, and see how was Our pursuit of the criminals:

> *But (there were people) before them, who denied (the Signs),- the People of Noah, and the Confederates (of Evil) after them; and every People plotted against their messenger, to seize him, and disputed by means of vanities, therewith to condemn the Truth; but it was I that seized them! and how (terrible) was My Requital! (40:5) See also (41:43, 6:166, 7:167, 2:196, 2:211, 3:10, 5:2, 5:98, 8:52, 13:6, 40:22, 59:4)*

Since every deed's end is its final outcome (or every outcome has a deed behind it), the term '*Aqaba*' has been used to mean the final outcome as well. For example:

> *There, the (only) protection comes from Allah, the True One. He is the best to reward, and the best to give success. (18:44) See also (13:24, 13:35, 13:42)*

3.7   Holding Accountable ('*Zunti-Qaam*')

In Arabic, the term '*Inteqaam*' means recompensing for a crime and this is why one of the Divine Attributes is *Zunti-qaam* i.e. Allah ensures that as per the Law of Requital, criminals get their due punishment:

Then those who reject Faith in the Signs of Allah will suffer the severest penalty, and Allah is Exalted in Might, Sustainer of Retribution. (3:4) See also (5:95, 14:47, 39:37)

In places the Quran states that Allah took 'revenge' on the nations committing crimes, thereby meaning that they were punished for the crimes they committed:

So We exacted retribution from them: We drowned them in the sea, because they rejected Our Signs[12] and failed to take warning from them. (7:136) See also (15:79, 30:47, 32:22, 43:41, 43:25, 44:16)

In this regard, the Quran states that this punishment meted to the nations in the past should serve as an example for those coming after them:

So We exacted retribution from them: now see what was the end of those who rejected (Truth)! (43:25)

---

[12] The Quran repeatedly invites our attention to the physical universe and its creation and asks us to use our intellect and reasoning to reach the conclusion that all this is created for man who with his free will has a higher purpose. (Ed)

(Intentionally left blank)

(Intentionally left blank)

4   Scroll of Deeds

As has been mentioned earlier, the results of man's deeds leave a mark on his self, and this self stores all of these effects. In this way, the sum total of these effects on his self becomes a 'book of record' of his deeds. We should understand that this process is such that every deed (including passing thoughts), is continually saved just like a video film. When the time comes for the manifestation of the results of our deeds, this video film is played back to us. The Quran uses similes from the human justice system in a court as examples to describe the functioning of this Law:

- Since no human deed remains hidden from the 'eyes' of Allah, this means that there is an eye witness to all that we do, therefore when there is such a trustworthy witness to a crime, there is no difficulty regarding proof.

- It is also said that 'Our secret police' keep noting what each individual is doing throughout his life and that these (policemen) are extremely honest and do not omit anything from their documentation i.e. they make a note of everything which people do. This way a diary is compiled which will then be used as evidence in the Divine court of law to prove the case against man.

In this connection, first of all the matter of Divine knowledge arises, which can be regarded as having the status of an eye witness.

4.1   Allah is Cognisant of Your Deeds

The Quran initially addresses the fundamentally erroneous thinking of humans which leads to the committing of a crime. It states:

Does he think that none sees him? (90:7)

After this it says that man is mistaken when he thinks that he is alone and that no-one is watching him. Even then there is 'someone' with him and this other is Allah Himself:

...He (Allah) is with you wherever you are... (57:4)

And He sees whatever man does:

...And Allah sees well all that you do. (57:4)

The point to note here is that, if a man is convinced that wherever I am, Allah is watching, then such an individual can never deliberately break the 'Law'. Most crimes are usually committed only because of the assumption that no-one is watching[13]. The Quran plainly states that Allah has surrounded man from all directions:

… for Allah compasses round about all that they do. (3:119)

But Allah does encompass them from all directions. (85:20) See also (89:14)

Not only does He see you when you perform some visible deed, He even knows the thoughts which are crossing your mind. In *Surah Qaaf* it is stated:

It was We Who created man, and We know what suggestions his self makes to him: for We are nearer to him than (his) jugular vein. (50:16)

At another place:

(Allah) knows of (the tricks) that deceive with the eyes, and all that the hearts (of men) conceal. (40:19)

No matter how secretive man's consultations, he cannot hide these from Allah[14]. This is why when there are three persons present, He is the fourth one – when there are five, He is the sixth one; He is always present irrespective of the number of people conferring among themselves:

See you not that Allah does know (all) that is in the heavens and on earth. There is not a secret consultation between three, but He makes the fourth among them, - Nor between five but He makes the sixth, nor between fewer nor more, but He is in their midst, wheresoever they be: In the end will He tell them the truth of their conduct, on the Day of Judgment. For Allah has full knowledge of all things (58:7).

Therefore there is nothing hidden from Him:

That Day you will be brought to Judgment: not an act of yours that you hide will be hidden. (69:18)

This is the reason that Allah has called Himself the Knower of things:

---

[13] This is especially true at the level of nation states, when the more powerful nations, following the view that 'might is right', carry out all types of crimes against the weaker states in order to promote their own interests. (Ed)

[14] For everything we do in life, we first have to think about it and form decisions before turning these into visible actions – some decisions we make are never carried out and simply remain in our inner self for a long time. Once a thought has arisen it is up to us whether we take it further or ignore it or act upon it at a later stage The Quran makes it very clear that the moment a thought arises in the human mind, Allah knows about it. (Ed)

Say: 'The Death from which you flee will truly overtake you: then will you be sent back to the Knower of things secret and open: and He will tell you (the truth of) the things that you did'. (62:8)

It is the same (to Him) whether any of you conceal his speech or declare it openly; whether he lie hid by night or walk forth freely by day. (13:10)

His seeing is such that:

No vision can grasp Him, but His grasp is over all vision: He is above all comprehension, yet is acquainted with all things. (6:103)

This is why He will reveal every iota of human deeds even if it is hidden within the stones of the rocks or anywhere in the heavens or earth. See verses (31:16, 25:6, 24:64, 33:54, 65:12, 13:42, 2:74, 2:96, 2:234, 3:153).

4.2 The Written Record

This reality is referred to in many places:

… We shall record what he says… (19:79)

Every deed is written down:

Whoever works any act of righteousness and has Eimaan (conviction), His endeavour will not be rejected: We shall write it down. (21:94)

Verily We shall give life to the dead, and We record that which they send before and that which they leave behind, and of all things have We taken account in a clear Book (of evidence) (36:12). See also (78:29)

Man may forget it, but Allah does not omit even a word as everything is recorded:

On the Day that Allah will raise them all up (again) and show them the Truth (and meaning) of their conduct. Allah has reckoned its (value), though they may have forgotten it, for Allah is Witness to all things. (58:6)

In some verses this fact is explained by stating that there are guardians appointed for every individual who record everything:

For each (such person) there are (guardians) in succession, before and behind him: They guard him by command of Allah. Verily never will Allah change the condition of a people until they change it themselves…(13:11)

No word leaves his tongue that is not recorded like a tape recorder:

Not a word does he utter but there is a sentinel by him, ready (to note it). (50:18)

In *Surah Infitar* these recording guardians are called:

Very honest and respectable, writing down (your deeds). (82:11) See also (86:4)

In other words, the recorders are extremely trustworthy and honest. These are those guardians from whom no deed of man remains secret. This record or register is not kept hidden nor are its entries written in such an obscure language that none can read it. This register is an open book:

In whatever business you may be, and whatever portion you may be reciting from the Quran - and whatever deed you (mankind) may be doing, We are witnesses thereof when you are deeply engrossed therein. Nor is hidden from your Cherisher (so much as) the weight of an atom on the earth or in heaven. And not the least and not the greatest of these things but are recorded in a clear record. (10:61) See also (27:75, 34:3)

All that they do is noted in (their) Books (of Deeds); every matter, small and great, is on record. (54:52-53)

When Pharaoh asked Moses as to what is the state of the forefathers who have gone before, the reply given by Moses was:

(Pharaoh) said: 'What then is the condition of previous generations?' He replied: 'The knowledge of that is with my Sustainer, duly recorded: my Sustainer never errs, nor forgets'. (20:51-52) See also (23:62)

This is that book (record of deeds), which when presented to the 'right hand', they will be the owners of a life of bliss and success (69:19), and when presented to the 'left hand', they will beat their heads in despair and lament:

'Eat you and drink you, with full satisfaction; because of the (good) that you sent before you, in the days that are gone!' And he that will be given his Record in his left hand, will say: 'Ah! Would that my Record had not been given to me!' (69:25-26) See also (84:7-11)

This is the time when all human secrets will be exposed:

The Day that (all) things secret will be tested. And that which is (locked up) in (human) breasts is made manifest. (86:9).

Let us pause for a moment here. In this life we meet thousands of people. Character-wise we are internally something different from the external persona which we present to others. In this way, we can remain very trustworthy in the sight of others. We continue to reassure our friends about our sincerity and honesty, while in our hearts we can harbour contrary opinions about them. In the eyes of those with whom we interact we remain very sacred and saintly, because our reality is not exposed or made apparent to them. In this way, while retaining an outwardly trustworthy and reliable persona we leave this world.

Now bring this scene to mind, that all the people are sitting in front of us to whom we had presented ourselves as honest, sacred, pure, sincere and truthful, and in their presence our true reality is exposed in such a way that no doubt remains. Then ponder what would be our state of mind? Can there be a bigger punishment than this, that one is exposed in front of those before whom he appeared very trustworthy? This is what man's record of deeds will do[15]. As mentioned earlier, this record of deeds is not external:

> *(It will be said to him:) 'Read your (own) record: Sufficient is yourself this day to make out an account against you.' Who receives guidance, receives it for his own benefit: who goes astray does so to his own loss: No bearer of burdens can bear the burden of another...*
> *(17:13-14)*

This record of deeds is man's own self, on which every one of his actions leaves a stamp. This is why man is essentially the writer of his own deeds, and also holds himself accountable. This is that record of deeds, on the exposure of which the criminals will shriek in terror:

> *And the Book (of Deeds) will be placed (before you); and you will see the criminals ('Mujrimoon') in great terror because of what is (recorded) therein; they will say, 'Ah! woe to us! what a Book is this! It leaves out nothing small or great, but takes account thereof!' They will find all that they did, placed before them: And not one will your Cherisher treat with injustice. (18:49)*

---

[15] Some of the recent disclosures through WikiLeaks and Edward Snowden's revelations have exposed the hypocrisy of politicians across the world; in fact, the use of the internet, Facebook and Twitter have exposed many events and continue to do so. This provides evidence to support what is stated in the Quran in (45:22). (Ed)

In this life the state of man is such that he tries to hide the truth, and if there is a threat that some weakness of his is in danger of being disclosed, he produces such witnesses of his who will vouch for his integrity and honesty. He does this to deceive others. As far as his own self is concerned, his own self-deceiving intellect produces scores of justifications for all his wrong deeds in order to keep him satisfied in his state of deceit. But when the consequences of his deeds are exposed, the whole situation will be reversed:

Nay, man will be evidence against himself; even though he were to put up his excuses.
(75:14-15)

This is the way all individual and collective deeds will bear results:

And you will see every sect bowing the knee: Every sect will be called to its Record: 'This Day you will be recompensed for all that you did!' (45:28)

We will discuss the nations later.

(Intentionally left blank)

(Intentionally left blank)

5 Meeting With The Sustainer ('*Rabb*')

When a criminal commits a crime and realises there is a possibility of punishment, he escapes so that he does not have to face the court - the police calls such a criminal a fugitive. Another example is of an individual who says something wrong behind another person's back and after this when he realises his error he feels reluctant to face that person.

The Quran, while explaining the effectiveness of the Law of Requital, has stated unequivocally that after committing a crime you cannot run away. You will of a certainty be presented in front of your *Rabb* (the Sustainer). For this, the Quran has used the term '*Liqae Rabb*'[16] (meeting *Rabb*) i.e. meeting 'face to face' with Allah. In this connection, this point is important to understand that *Liqae Rabb* does not mean that human beings are not currently in the presence of Allah and that the meeting will only occur in the hereafter. The concept of 'going to Allah' after death will be addressed later. At this stage, it is important to understand only that this 'meeting Rabb' is like going to court within the human system. The Divine system of accountability as per the Law of Requital means that it is everywhere in front of man and in this respect man is in Allah's court with every breath that he takes. To understand the meaning of *Liqae Rabb*, it is important to keep this in mind.

In some places the Quran also uses another term, '*Rijaat il lillah*' (return to Allah). This term does not mean that before birth we were residing with Allah and then we emerged into this worldly life and after death we will return to Him. This concept is not correct. As previously written, Allah is with us constantly and He is closer to us than our jugular vein and we do everything in His presence. So the idea of coming to this life with birth after parting with Him, and then meeting Him again after death is a non-Quranic concept. This also means that wherever you are, your every step is moving inexorably towards Allah's Law of Requital, and you cannot avoid it. Another term '*Ilaa hae rajeoon*' (going to Him) also means the same.

Since the consequences of human actions can appear during this life and will without doubt appear in the life to come, the terms *Liqae Rabb* and *Rijaat il lillah* mean that this accountability of human actions is effective throughout this life as well as in the life to come.

---

[16] After observing and reflecting on the wonders of creation and reaching this reality that this whole universe is according to Allah's wisdom, true and in the grip of immutable laws, in some verses the Quran has called this *Liqae rabb* e.g. (13:2). In other words, it can be understood in such a way as if man is standing in front of Allah Himself and seeing everything. However, at this point we are presenting *Liqae Rabb* as part of the Law of Requital.

5.1 *'Eimaan'* (Conviction) in *'Liqae Rabb'* (Meeting With Allah)

In *Surah Inaam* it is stated that *Bani Israel* received Divine Guidance:

Moreover, We gave Moses the Book, completing (Our favour) to those who would do right, and explaining all things in detail, and a guide and a mercy, that they might believe in the meeting with their Sustainer. (6:154). See also (32:23)

In *Surah Ra'ad*, the Quran states that the Divine Laws and their purpose have been made clear:

Allah is He Who raised the heavens without any pillars that you can see; is firmly established on the throne (of authority); He has subjected the sun and the moon (to his Law)! Each one runs (its course) for a term appointed. He does regulate all affairs, explaining the signs in detail, that you may believe with certainty in the meeting with your Sustainer. (13:2)

The Quran has referred to the fundamental characteristic of *Momineen* (Believers) as being that they always keep in mind that they will be going in front of Allah, therefore their every step is geared in this direction:

Who bear in mind the certainty that they are to meet their Sustainer, and that they are to return to Him. (2:46)

The day that they will go in front of Allah, or in other words the day that the consequences of their deeds will bear results, they will hear the great news of their success:

Their salutation on the Day they meet Him will be 'Peace!'; and He has prepared for them a generous Reward. (33:44)

Contrary to the above, those who do not believe in *Liqae Rabb*, will be destroyed:

Lost indeed are they who treat it as a falsehood that they must meet Allah - until on a sudden the hour is on them, and they say: 'Ah! woe unto us that we took no thought of it'; for they bear their burdens on their backs, and evil indeed are the burdens that they bear. (6:31) See also (10:45)

For example, if someone does not even believe that poison can cause death, then he will keep using it and will ultimately die of poisoning[17]. Such people keep an eye on the immediate benefits of life and their belief is that by obtaining these benefits by whatever means they can, they will have achieved the purpose of their lives. The Quran sums it up by saying:

---

[17] We see this being practiced by many people e.g. people smoke and drink alcohol, both of which affect their health negatively and can also impact adversely on family life. Though they are aware of the negative effects of these on their health, they persist, in denial that these will affect them. (Ed)

Those who rest not their hope on their meeting with Us, but are pleased and satisfied with the life of the present, and those who heed not Our Signs. (10:7)

The Quran states that these people are intoxicated by their selfish interests and blindly continue to persist in this path:

If Allah were to hasten for men the ill (they have earned) as they would fain hasten on the good, then would their respite be settled at once. But We leave those who rest not their hope on their meeting with Us, in their trespasses, wandering in distraction to and fro. (10:11)

They find it disgusting to be advised of the difference between what is legitimate and what is illegitimate. They say they are not ready to follow this Quran as it interferes with their unchecked vested interests, and say if in the place of this Quran you can bring a different Quran or make changes in this Quran according to their desires, then they will listen to your invitation:

But when Our Clear Signs are rehearsed unto them, those who rest not their hope on their meeting with Us, Say: 'Bring us a reading other than this, or change this,' Say: 'It is not for me, of my own accord, to change it: I follow naught but what is revealed unto me: if I were to disobey my Cherisher, I should myself fear the penalty of a Great Day (to come)'. (10:15)

They are told that these are Divine Laws which are immutable and nothing can be changed in them. Nor can there be any compromise with them whereby man's laws can be mixed with Allah's laws and consequently they may be saved from the destructive effects of their deeds. Can we alter the effects of poison by mixing it with sugar? Therefore, he who believes in the Law of Requital will have to follow the Divine Laws:

…whoever expects to meet his Cherisher, let him work righteousness, and, in the following of his Cherisher, admit no one as a partner. (18:110)

As noted earlier, man will only be able to follow the righteous path when he knows that following the wrong path will destroy him. If this conviction does not exist, then man will produce thousands of justifications in order to not abandon his wrong path. These are the kind of people about whom the Quran says, they ask 'why Allah Himself does not come before them' or 'why angels do not descend on them directly'? (25:21). This is despite the fact that they pass by the ruins of people gone before, who were destroyed because they did not believe in the Law of Requital (25:40). If they had believed in it, they would not have hesitated to accept the reality that following the wrong path would lead to destruction (29:5).

The person who believes in the Law of Requital, if he ever steps in the wrong direction, believes that by turning and taking the right direction he will be able to compensate for the loss – this is called the mercy of Allah. Contrary to this, an individual who does not believe in the Law of Requital and thinks that the events which take place in the world occur by chance, if he takes a step in the wrong direction, he has no recourse of saving himself from the results of his wrong deed:

Those who reject the Signs of Allah and the Meeting with Him, it is they who shall despair of My Mercy: it is they who will (suffer) a most grievous Penalty. (29:23)

Just reflect here for a moment, that an individual who has no hope of getting out of the difficulties of his life, what a painful and miserable life he spends. The Quran says about these people:

Say: 'Shall we tell you of those who lose most in respect of their deeds?' Those whose efforts have been wasted in this life, while they thought that they were acquiring good by their works? They are those who deny the Signs of their Cherisher and the fact of their having to meet Him (in the Hereafter): vain will be their works, nor shall We, on the Day of Judgment, give them any weight. (18:103-105) See also (30:16, 32:14)

Those who reject the existence of the Law of Requital actually deny the existence of life beyond physical death. In fact these two concepts are mutually inclusive and linked. The argument of the people who deny the hereafter is 'how can we get another life when our body after death is dust'? The Quran states:

And they say: 'What! When we lie, hidden and lost, in the earth, shall we indeed be in a creation renewed?' Nay, they deny the Meeting with their Sustainer. (32:10)

Actually these people do not believe in the Law of Requital, otherwise if man believes in the Law of Requital and that his every deed will not remain without a result, then regarding those deeds which have not resulted in a consequence in this life, he will categorically understand that their results will show up after death. This is where belief in the Law of Requital and the next life are interconnected and essentially part of one reality.

The discussion of life in the hereafter will take place later in the book. As far as the Law of Requital is concerned, the Quran invites our attention to the physical world and the universe around us. What conclusions does man draw from the universe and its functioning? What conclusion does man reach? Is it not that every particle in the universe is tied up in the chains of the law of cause and effect. This system which enthrals human intellect, is only functioning on the basis that here in this universe each movement of everything produces an effect, and it is these effects which are the natural and immutable laws of nature. So when nothing in this universe can venture outwith these laws, how can man who is the last link in the chain of evolution, be exempt from these laws?

In Surah Rum, it asks, do people not pay attention to their own life and to the system of the universe around them? Allah has created this intellect baffling universe in truth. In truth means this, that the universe is created with a purpose and it is working under a special system. But this is not for an infinite time. Instead it will continue for a defined period of time. After reflecting on this universal system, what conclusion do you reach? Do you not reach this conclusion that there are immutable Laws governing this system:

Do they not reflect in their own minds? Not but for just ends and for a term appointed, did Allah create the heavens and the earth, and all between them, yet are there truly many among men who deny the meeting with their Sustainer (at the Resurrection)! (30:8)

After this it is stated that regarding those kind of people who do not wish to reflect on the working of the universe, say to them then do you not see the ruins of previous populations in which there were nations residing who were more prosperous and powerful than you. The stories of those are written all over in the signs of the ruins they left behind. They provide evidence of the functioning of Allah's Law of Requital. They will communicate to you that such a nation followed a certain path and so this was the result of following that path. And another nation followed another kind of path, another system, and its result was different. In this way the reality will become clear to you:

Do they not travel through the earth, and see what was the end of those before them? They were superior to them in strength: they tilled the soil and populated it in greater numbers than these have done: there came to them their messengers with clear (Signs). (Whom they rejected, to their own destruction): It was not Allah Who wronged them, but they wronged their own self. In the long run evil in the extreme will be the end of those who do evil; for that they rejected the Signs of Allah, and held them up to ridicule. (30:9-10)

This fact was addressed to men who lived 1400 years ago, but along with this the Quran states that this technique of reflection to find out knowledge and the reality of the working of the Law of Requital was applicable not only to them, but to all of mankind for all times: atonement

Soon will We show them our Signs in the (furthest) regions (of the earth), and in their own self, until it becomes manifest to them that this is the Truth... (41:53)

Whatever Allah has stated, is a sure thing, but in spite of this, they repudiate their meeting with Allah:

Ah indeed! Are they in doubt concerning the Meeting with their Cherisher (Liqae Rabb)? Ah indeed! It is He that does encompass all things! (41:54)

5.2 *'Yaum Talaaq'* – The Day of Mutual Meeting

The day the results of our deeds manifest themselves and the day of going in front of Allah is also known as *'Yaum Talaaq'*:

...that it may warn (men) of the Day of Mutual Meeting. (40:15)

In *Surah Zumr* it states that when the people destined for hell reach its door, they will be asked:

The Unbelievers will be led to Hell in crowd: until, when they arrive there, its gates will be opened. And its keepers will say, 'Did not messengers come to you from among yourselves, rehearsing to you the Signs of your Sustainer, and warning you of the Meeting of This Day of yours?' The answer will be: 'True: but the Decree of Punishment has been proved true against the Unbelievers!' (39:71)

That day nothing will remain secret or hidden. The deeds which man thought are unknown to others and lay hidden within his self, will all be exposed:

That Day you will be brought to Judgment: not an act of yours that you hide will be hidden. (69:18)

This will be the day of the Meeting. The Quran has explained in various ways that each individual will then find what he has sent forward for his next life:

For to Us will be their return; Then it will be for Us to call them to account. (88:25-26) See also (43:38, 75:30, 36:51, 67:15, 67:24)

5.3 *'Rijaat Il Lillah'* – Going Towards Allah

We have earlier explained that in relation to the Law of Requital, the universe has not been created without a purpose. Regarding this, about man it is declared:

'Did you then think that We had created you in jest, and that you would not be brought back to Us (for account)?' (23:15)

The meaning of a creation with a purpose is that human life has a future. There is a destination for the pageant of life - every individual will determine his place in this future through his own deeds and this is declared as being *Rijaat il lillah*.

We have already written and wish to reiterate that the term *'Il lillahae Rajeoon'* (going back to Allah), does not mean that we were first with Allah and then we parted from Him and came into this world and that we will then go back to Him. This belief or doctrine is from the Hindu philosophy of *'Vedant'* (reincarnation) and from there has been imported to mysticism (Sufism). The philosophy of *Vedant* is that the human soul (*Atma*) is part of the Divine soul called *'Parmatma'* which after becoming detached from its own origin, has become ensnared in the temptations of the material world (*Prakarti*).

According to this philosophy, the aim of human struggle is to free this soul from the material attractions of life, so that it can re-join with the Divine soul. This way the pain of separation can again become the pleasure of union with its origin. So in this way the human self is absorbed into the Divine self and disappears and this is the purpose of its life. This same philosophy is known as '*Wahdat e wajood*' – 'one body' in mysticism.

This is a non-Quranic concept. According to the Quran, the human self is not a part of the Divine Self. This human self is a great asset which has been given to man and none else in the universe. This is what gives man his freedom to choose, and consequently makes him responsible. Man has been given this self in an undeveloped form on earth, and the purpose of human life is that his self should develop to such a degree that he should be able to reach the next evolutionary stage of life. (Further details will be available about this aspect in the chapter on Life in the Hereafter). At this stage it is only necessary to explain that the term *Rijaat il lillah* means that as a consequence of doing deeds in this life he is subject to the Law of Requital. Regarding this, the word *'Rijaat'* is used to relate the real life event where a criminal after committing a crime escapes the crime scene and is then brought back to the area as part of the investigation. Wherever you run to, Allah's Law of Requital will confront you. So, understand that your escaping is also taking you towards this Law, whereas you are thinking in your mind that by running away from your crime scene, you are heading in some other direction, but in reality you are coming back to meet those very consequences of your crime:

> *Verily, to your Sustainer is the return (of all). (96:8)*

5.4 '*Rijaat il Lillah*' - as it Works Within this Life

This return to Allah with every step of man, like the return of an escaped criminal to court, happens in this life as well as after death. The term '*Alayna rajioon*' (21:93) does not only mean that you will come back to Us after death; it actually means that at every step of your life you are returning to Us. This is the meaning of *Rajioon*. The following verses make this clear:

> *To Him will be your return - of all of you. The promise of Allah is true and sure. It is He Who begins the process of creation, and repeats it, that He may reward with justice those who believe and work righteousness... (10:4)*
>
> *...and to Him you will (all) be brought back[18]. (28:70)*
>
> *And to our Sustainer surely, must we turn back. (43:14)*

---

[18] This term is also used in the following verses – (10:46), (11:4), (19:40), (21:35), (28:88), (29:17), (29:21), (30:11), (36:83), (39:44), (40:43), (41:21), (43:13), (43:85), (45:15), (10:4), (28:79).

In relation to this it is also important to understand that in *Surah Baqra* it is stated that those people who in life rise up in the path of Divine revolution, for them at every step there will be very hard opposition and strong resistance which they will have to struggle against. They do not become fearful at these times, but whenever a new stage comes in front of them, which requires perseverance and patience, then with unity of heart and great courage they say:

Who say, when faced with the challenging and difficult tasks: 'To Allah We belong, and to Him is our return'. (2:156)

Our every step will aim for this objective which we have set up according to Divine guidance. If a multitude of difficulties arise, let them; the storm of difficulties will come and we will, without fear of danger, continue to move towards our goal.

So, as we were saying, in life man with his every breath is doing *Rijaat il lillah* i.e. his every step is in the direction of the Law of Requital, so that the results of his deeds can be evident. The Quran has said this in the following verse:

O you who believe! Guard your own self: If you follow (right) guidance, no hurt can come to you from those who stray. The goal of you all is to Allah. It is He Who will show you the truth of all that you do. (105:5) See also (6:60, 5:48, 6:165, 10:23, 24:64, 29:8, 31:15, 31:23, 39:7)

5.5   *Rijaat Il Lillah'* - As it Applies After Death

This concept of returning to Allah is not confined to this life; indeed it continues beyond the event of physical death. This is why according to the Quran the results of human actions manifest both in this life as well as in the life in the hereafter. This is why the Quran mentions *Rijaat il lillah* in various verses dealing with death. For example in *Surah Baqra*:

How can you reject the faith in Allah, seeing that you were without life, and He gave you life; then will He cause you to die, and will again bring you to life; and again to Him will you return. (2:28)

How can you deny the existence of Allah? Reflect on your condition. Allah began your creation from inert matter, then by going through various evolutionary stages you arrived at your present form. After completing this physical life you then die, and after this He gives you life. In all of these stages you are confined within the boundary of His Laws, so after death how do you expect to get out of this boundary of Laws? Even now your every step is taking you towards Him and after death it will be the same. This is noted in *Surah Inaam*:

Those who listen (in truth), be sure, will accept it: as to the dead, Allah will raise them up; then will they be turned unto Him. (6:36)

This aspect is further elaborated in *Surah Tauba*:

And say: Work (righteousness): Soon will Allah observe your work, and His Messenger, and the Believers: Soon will you be brought back to the knower of what is hidden and what is open: then will He show you the truth of all that you did. (9:105)

This makes the meaning of *Rijaat il lillah* clear. It has been covered in a number of other places in the Quran – see (9:94, 10:70, 21:35, 24:64, 30:11, 32:11, 36:22, 36:83, 50:43, 62:8, and 64:3)

5.6   All Matters are Referred Back to Allah

The verses we have mentioned so far regarding the above matters state that all human beings return to the Law of Requital according to which the consequences of their deeds are established. At other places it is noted that all matters ultimately are referred back to Allah. This also means that every matter in this world is decided according to the Law of Requital. For example:

... but to Allah do all questions go back (for decision). (2:210)
See also (11:123, 22:76, 35:4)

In *Surah Al e Imran* this point is further elaborated:

Do they seek for other than the Deen of Allah - while all creatures in the heavens and on earth have, willingly or unwillingly, bowed to His Will (His Laws), and to Him shall they all be brought back. (3:82) See also (3:108)

In *Surah Shoora* it is declared:

The Way of Allah, to Whom belongs whatever is in the heavens and whatever is on earth. Behold (how) all affairs tend towards Allah. (42:53) See also (57:7, 8:44)

In *Surah Miriam* it is stated that the earth and whatever is on it belongs to Allah and that all matters are decided as per the Law of Requital i.e. everything in the outer world is gripped within the confines of the Law of cause and effect (19:40). In human life also, everyone's deeds bear results according to the Law of Requital and so also for the future of nations.

In *Surah Yaseen* it is stated:

See they not how many generations before them we destroyed (evidence from history)? Not to them will they return: But each one of them all - will be brought before Us (for judgment). (36:31-32)

The nation which believes in this reality, that the result of their every act will be dealt with according to the Law of Requital, and that they are accountable for what they do, will never resort to tyranny, cruelty and the subjugation of other human beings, because they will know that the results of such doings will ultimately lead to their own destruction. Only that nation which does not believe in the Law of Requital will resort to exploitation and injustice. In this regard, the Quran has referred to Pharaoh and his cohorts as:

And he was arrogant and insolent in the land, beyond reason, he and his hosts: they thought that they would not have to return to Us! (28:39)

Contrary to this, when the magicians of Pharaoh beheld the Truth unfold itself in front of them, they accepted it without any hesitation. At this, when Pharaoh in fury declared, I will tear you into pieces and hang you, they replied with extreme tranquillity in their hearts, you do whatever you like, your command is only applicable to this physical life, but it cannot go beyond this life. They said, we have understood this reality, that all matters are decided as per the Law of Requital:

They said: 'For us, We are but sent back unto our Sustainer'. (7:125)

This is that conviction in the working of the Law of Requital which gives peace and tranquillity to man:

'Come back you to your Cherisher, well pleased (yourself), and well-pleasing unto Him!'
Enter you then, among My devotees! (89:27-28) See also (43:14)

(Intentionally left blank)

(Intentionally left blank)

6 *'Tauba'* (Repentance) – *'Maghfirah'* (Protection)

A patient went to a doctor and had severe pain where his kidney is located. He told the doctor that he had been sleeping soundly, when at midnight he had a sudden severe pain and was half dead till the morning and did not know why this had happened so suddenly. The doctor arranged an x ray and informed him that you have three kidney stones which have not appeared suddenly, they have been forming for at least a year and if you had undergone a check-up earlier, then treatment could have taken place earlier. You did not take notice of it in time, and now you will need an operation on your kidney.

This example illustrates the reality that the result of man's every act starts to form immediately. However, for the results to become apparent takes some time. This time interval between the deed and the result is called the respite period.

Now look at another case. A patient who is suffering from fever for a while is taken to the doctor. His attendant says, this youthful son of mine is suffering from a fever for one year, he was previously very healthy and strong, and the disease has made him half dead, do something for him. The doctor replied, you are right, this young man had a strong immunity which has resisted this disease for a time, but now his resistance has decreased, and we will try to ensure that the disease does not reach such a stage that his immunity is unable to overcome it. If he does not have this level of immunity, he will not be able to overcome this disease, and he will die.

Or for example, a disease has spread as an epidemic within a community. Some people died immediately, and some died after a few days, but some did not seem to be affected by the disease and if they did get it, did not succumb. When the doctor was questioned regarding this, he said that in those who have weak defences, i.e. weaker immunity, they will succumb immediately to the attack of the disease. In those whose immunity was stronger, they were able to ward of the effects of the disease for a few days before succumbing. Those whose immune defences were very strong, when the disease did attack them, they were able to resist it and overcome it.

These examples illustrate that in the world both constructive and destructive forces are competing with each other continuously. While the constructive forces are able to overpower the destructive ones, this is apparent as good health, strength, and life. When the destructive forces overpower the constructive ones, this is called weakness, disease, and death. It is made evident that even in weakness and disease and even at the point of death, some degree of constructive forces are present in the body, but the destructive forces become so powerful that the constructive forces cannot compete with them.

6.1   Time of Respite

Laws similar to those which control our physical life, control our 'human life' as well. As far as an individual is concerned, the purpose of his life is to develop his self. Bad deeds are those which weaken the human self, while good deeds are those which help the human self to develop and strengthen it – and as a consequence the self becomes able to reach the next evolutionary stages of life. Bad deeds can be called destructive forces, and good deeds constructive forces. (About nations, this will be dealt with later). In this continuous conflict between these two forces, if the constructive forces remain superior and are able to keep control over the destructive forces, man remains protected –if the destructive forces overcome them, then man becomes weak and finally succumbs to destruction. This time period during which these destructive forces are so strong that they overwhelm the constructive forces which cannot recover, is called the time of respite. This time of respite is a mercy from Allah and a functioning of the Law of Requital. If it had been the case that the moment a man committed a wrong deed, he was destroyed forthwith, then no man would have survived destruction:

If Allah were to punish men for their wrong-doing, He would not leave, on the (earth), a single living creature: but He gives them respite for a stated Term: When their Term expires, they would not be able to delay (the punishment) for a single hour, just as they would not be able to anticipate it (for a single hour). (16:61)

In *Surah Kahf* this point is further elucidated, that Allah's intention is not to capture and punish man immediately, in reality he wishes his protection and further growth and development:

But your Sustainer is Most protecting, full of Mercy. If He were to call them (at once) to account for what they have earned, then surely He would have hastened their punishment, but they have their appointed time, beyond which they will find no refuge. (18:58)
See also (35:45)

6.2   'Ajal Musamma' - Determined Term

The time of respite between the time a deed is committed and the manifestation of its consequences is also called *'Ajal'* (time duration) in the Quran. In *Surah Ibraheem* it is stated:

… It is He Who invites you, in order that He may provide protection for your wrong deeds[19] and give you respite for a term appointed!... (14:10)

In another verse it is reiterated:

Had it not been for a Word that went forth before from your Cherisher, (their punishment) must necessarily have come; but there is a Term appointed (for respite). (20:129)

---

[19] The provision of this protection is not for an indefinite time – there are scales for every deed as per the Quran. If one does not take positive steps to counter the effects of wrong deeds, then the period of this protection expires and one has to face the consequences of one's deeds. (Ed)

See also (42:14)

6 3   Man Tries to Take Wrong Advantage of This Respite

The time of respite is allowed so that before the final destruction of man, he can take action to save himself from the consequences of his wrong deeds[20]. (As already stated, with regard to the Law of Justice, having a Law of Respite is a mercy from Allah). However, wrong thinking man becomes misguided, and instead of taking advantage of this, becomes further misguided, and says, that I did this tyranny and injustice, and you say the one who does wrong will be destroyed, but as you can see I am fine, in fact I am getting richer and richer by the day. If there is a Law of Requital somewhere, why does it not take action against me. In this way he misguides himself as well as others. You will see that in a wrong system, wrong deeds spread quickly in intensity, because the society does not hold people to account who do wrong and Allah's Law of Requital does not deal with them immediately. In *Surah Sabaa* it is stated:

They say: 'When will this promise (come to pass) if you are telling the truth?' (34:29)

These people say that if the Quran declares the functioning of the Law of Requital to be effective, then why has no punishment descended on them so far? The Quran replies:

Say: 'The appointment to you is for a Day, which you cannot put back for an hour nor put forward.' (34:30)

In *Surah Ibraheem* (14:10) those people who similarly ask for the hastening of the punishment in return for their wrong doings, are told by Allah that this is to provide respite for a stated term, so that one can take advantage of it and stop doing wrong. Instead these people fell into doubt whether this will happen or not. The people who resort to injustice and inequity should never doubt that they will be held accountable for what they do:

Think not that Allah does not heed the deeds of those who do wrong. He but gives them respite against a Day when the eyes will fixedly stare in horror. (14:42)

When the delayed punishment comes in due course, his eyes will be filled with terror. In Surah Ankabut it is noted:

They ask you to hasten on the Punishment (for them): had it not been for a term (of respite) appointed, the Punishment would certainly have come to them: and it will certainly reach them, of a sudden, while they perceive not! (29:53)

---

[20] As per the Quran, there are scales for various deeds e.g. simple stealing will have a smaller scale than robbery, and murder will have a much bigger scale. Again within murder, the scales will be different depending upon the circumstances. (Ed)

When this fixed time of respite is fulfilled, then the destruction will come upon them so unexpectedly that they could not in their wildest imaginations have predicted where it would come from. The messenger himself was told not to be troubled with these types of objections which the people raise, because the results will come according to the Law of Requital and these will come surely. They are gradually going towards their end which is destruction, without being aware, as they continue to persist in following the same path:

Then leave Me alone with such as reject this Message: by degrees shall We punish them from directions they perceive not. A (long) respite will I grant them: truly powerful is My Plan. (68:44-45) See also (71:4, 73:11, 86:17)

This time of respite is different for different crimes – a banana bears fruit in six months, while a date tree takes much longer. Regarding this respite, no-one knows its duration. Therefore, in reply to these questions by the opponents, the Quran addresses the messenger:

Say: 'I know not whether the (Punishment) which you are promised is near, or whether my Cherisher will appoint for it a distant term.' (72:25)

The opponents used to pose such questions merely to raise objections; but the *Momineen* (Believers) also used to think that we have been engaged in this struggle for so much time, and we still do not know how long it will continue, and when we will succeed and our opponents will be defeated. The Quran is a witness that the messenger himself used to have such thoughts as to whether he would in his lifetime see such a day when truth will prevail and evil will be subdued. The Quran replies:

Whether We shall show you (within your life-time) part of what we promised them or take to ourselves your self (before it is all accomplished), your duty is to make (the Message) reach them: it is our part to call them to account. (13:40)

Your duty is to make this message common knowledge to all and it is Our responsibility to ensure as to when the results will appear:

...For each respite there is a law. (13:38) See also (10:46, 23:95, 43:42)

For every respite there is a law in place. But only Allah and no-one else knows the time duration of this respite. It is obvious that for the *Momineen* this requires a lot of perseverance and courage. What is it that will throughout this long period, during this extremely challenging and persistent struggle, keep their courage boundless, and not let it diminish? Let us understand it with an example. A farmer prepares his field and sows seeds, and then toils in the blazing sun with his blood and sweat, and returns empty handed to his home in the evening. The next morning he again with the same determination and strength, goes to his farm. He does not do this for a day, two days, ten days, or a month. For months on end he keeps doing this, and at no time does he sit down and say, that I work all day and in the evening I come back empty handed, so what do I receive from this? Why should I waste my life in this unrewarding toil? He never does this. The question is, what is that incentive, what is that idea, which keeps him motivated to carry on toiling and to never give up - this motive and idea, this conviction that he has, that my efforts will not go wasted. Between the sowing of seeds and the harvest being ready, there is a prescribed interval. At the end of this time period, he says I will get the full reward of all my labours. In Quranic terminology, this kind of belief is called conviction in the unseen, or *'Eimaan bil ghaib'*. In other words, the result of my hard work has not yet come to fruition. For the *Momineen*, it is this same conviction in the unseen which empowers them not to give up in very trying circumstances, and makes them persevere with great patience and suffering:

What! Do they say, 'He has forged a falsehood against Allah?' But if Allah willed, He could seal up your heart. And Allah blots out Vanity, and proves the Truth by His Words. For He knows well the secrets of all hearts. (42:24)

It is Allah's Law that truth ultimately prevails over falsehood, though it takes time for this to happen. The group of such *Momineen* who make the initial effort and are in the vanguard as pioneers, their status is higher than those who subsequently come to sustain the system. The Quran has called them *'Al sabi-qunal awwalun'*, those who were foremost from the rest and it has mentioned them at various places.

Going back to the issue of the time of respite between a deed and its results, this time interval varies depending on the circumstances. In the life of nations, this time duration can be very long, unlike the life of individuals which is in days, months and years. It can be spread over centuries. In Surah Hajj this point is referred to:

Yet they ask you to hasten on the Punishment! But Allah will not fail in His Promise. Verily a Day in the sight of your Cherisher is like a thousand years of your reckoning. (22:47)

So if the destruction seems to be delayed, it is not that the Law of Requital is not working, it is only that there is an interval between a deed and its result. It is just that it may take centuries before the effects of the deeds of a nation materialise and lead to its downfall. If you want proof of the truth of this Law, then go and look at the pages of history. How many nations were such that committed evil upon evil, but their seizure was not immediate. They were given respite and when this time was complete, then they were held to account:

And to how many populations did I give respite, which were given to wrong-doing? In the end I punished them[21]. To me is the destination (as per the Law of Requital). (22:48)

---

[21] The consequences of their own deeds were the cause of their downfall – the Quran relates it to Allah. One should keep this aspect in mind when studying the Quran. (Ed)

6.4 *'Tauba'* - Repentance

If you wish to travel to some village and take a wrong turning at a bifurcation of the road which is not sign posted, and after this from subsequent signs or from inquiring of someone, you become aware that you have taken a wrong turn, what do you do having realised your mistake? You retrace your steps and return to that same junction and after that turn in the direction of the right path. Have you pondered on what you had to do in order to reach the correct destination?

1. First of all, you realised your mistake in that you had headed in the wrong direction. If you had not become aware of this or not known about this, then you would have continued in this direction, and as a consequence you would never have reached the desired destination. Your time and energy which you would have expended on this journey would have been squandered.

2. If, after realising your mistake you had stopped going further, but stayed at the very place where you were, even then you would never have reached your destination.

3. After realising your mistake, you returned to the junction from where you could take the right direction. This return to the correct place after realising your mistake is called in Arabic and in Quranic terminology *'Tauba'*.

4. If having returned to the junction, you had not subsequently taken the correct direction, and had instead remained there, even then you would never have reached your desired destination. So going in the right direction is called *'Islah'* as per the Quran i.e. realising and accepting your mistake, then taking steps to compensate for your loss.

The Quran has called both parts of this programme *'Taub o Islah'* (realising your mistake and then taking the right direction). This is the way the effects of any mistakes are removed. We have seen that *Tauba* does not mean to just recite something and pray for forgiveness. It means to take some kind of action to counter the loss. The place at which you realised that you had taken the wrong direction, if you had sat there for a hundred years and prayed, 'O Allah forgive me, O Allah forgive me!', you would have never reached your desired destination. The way to compensate for the loss resulting from wrong decisions in life, is to do so many righteous deeds that their constructive results can compensate for the destructive results of your wrong actions. The Quran has declared this to be a Permanent Value:

> *...For those things that are good, remove those that are evil: ...* (11:114)

In relation to the example cited above, the Quran has directed us:

> *... to those who repent (Taba), believe (Amana), and do right (Amala Sale-ah), who, in fine, are ready to receive true guidance (Ahtada). (20:82)*

Analysing the above verse – 'Taba' means turning back from the wrong direction and determining the correct direction, 'Amana' means the desire and conviction to tread on the right path, and to do righteous deeds is known as 'Amala Sale-ah', and being on the right path is called 'Ahtada'. This is what the Quran declares:

Unless he repents, believes, and works righteous deeds, for Allah will change the evil of such persons into good... (25:70)

This verse covers all the steps discussed earlier[22]. In *Surah Al-Qasas* this is elaborated further:

But any that (in this life) had repented, believed, and worked righteousness, will have hopes to be among those who achieve success. (28:67) See also (40:7, 27:11)

In the functioning of the Law of Requital, the inclusion of this procedure to eliminate the effects of wrong deeds, is called 'Rehmat' or mercy[23] from Allah. This is why Allah calls Himself 'Tawwa-bur-Raheem', the One who helps someone to reach his destination – that is whichever person turns away from the wrong direction and opts instead to turn towards the right direction. This is called His Mercy and is only for the person who adopts the right path after abandoning the wrong path.

In *Surah Baqra* this is summed up:

Except those who repent and make amends and openly declare (the Truth): To them I turn; for I am Oft-returning (Tawwab), Most Merciful (Raheem). (2:160)

Only that individual can take the right path who first accepts his mistake. The one who does not accept his mistake can never take the right path. This fundamental reality has been referred to in the Quran in a metaphorical and very beautiful way in the story of Adam. Adam made a mistake and when he realised it he said:

...'Our Sustainer! We have wronged our own self. If You forgive us not and bestow not upon us Your Mercy, we shall certainly be lost.' (7:23)

In reply to this Allah said, when you realised your mistake and accepted your responsibility then there arose a chance for you to rectify your mistake. A mistake was

---

[22] These steps are not other wordly – they are simple steps which anyone can follow in their daily life and see tangible results. The Quran declares that following its Permanent Values will bring results in this life for all to see. (Ed)

[23] The common religious concept of mercy is not the same as noted in the Quran. Quranic mercy is based on taking the necessary steps to eradicate the negative effects of the wrong deeds done, and this places sole control in human hands. (Ed)

also made by *'Iblees'* (Satan). When it was said to him, why have you done this, he replied, how can I have done this[24]:

> *(Iblees) said: 'O my Cherisher! because You have put me in the wrong,'... (15:39)*

In reply to this, when you do not accept responsibility for choosing the wrong path, then how will you able to reform yourself. Therefore the doors of *Tauba* closed on *Iblees*[25].

Let us look at another example. If a person takes poison by mistake, when he realises this and after going to the doctor takes the antidote according to instructions, then he has a hope of saving himself and getting better. Contrary to this, if another person takes poison deliberately with a view to committing suicide, when the effects of the poison become apparent, he becomes satisfied that the poison is doing its job, and that in a short while he will achieve his objective, i.e. he will be dead. For this person the question of rectifying his mistake does not arise. He does not consider taking the poison as a mistake, therefore why should he worry about rectifying his mistake. In *Surah Nissa* this aspect is noted:

> *Allah accepts the repentance of those who do evil in ignorance and repent soon afterwards; to them will Allah turn in mercy: For Allah is full of knowledge (Aleem) and wisdom (Hakeem). (4:17)*

The opportunity of repentance and remedy to counter any mistakes made, is in reality a mercy (*Rehmat*) from Allah. Otherwise, if the situation is such that if a mistake is made and a person is condemned for ever for it, and there is no possibility of removing the effects of the mistake and all paths of repentance are closed to him, then this perpetual state of hopelessness on a human psyche can be clearly imagined.[26] In *Surah Zumr* it is stated:

> *Say: O my Servants who have transgressed against their self! Despair not of the Mercy of Allah, for Allah provides protection from all sin (as per His Laws): for He is Oft-Forgiving[27] (Ghafoor), Most Merciful (Raheem). (39:53)*

In His Law of Requital all this is included, but only for those who, after realising their mistakes, make efforts and take practical steps to rectify these.

> *And those who, having done something to be ashamed of, or wronged their own self, earnestly bring Allah to mind, and ask for protection (from the effects) for their sins... (3:134)*

---

[24] There are wrong religious beliefs (against Quranic teaching), according to which Allah 'misguides' as well. (Ed)

[25] The possibility of his being reformed was removed from his choice through his own volition. (Ed)

[26] According to religious beliefs, salvation is only obtained through God's mercy, as human beings are born sinful – this is not the Quranic teaching however. (Ed)

[27] Allah's 'forgiveness' is through repentance and seeking protection by following the Quran. (Ed)

It is not the case that they should be stuck in their wrong paths and then expect that Allah will forgive them through His Mercy (*Rehmat*).

6.5 *'Maghfirat'* – Protection

According to the concept and functioning of the Law of Requital, the belief in *'Bakhshish'* (blanket pardon) is erroneous. Let us illustrate it with an example. You do a wrong to someone and following this ask for his forgiveness, and he forgives you. The meaning of this forgiveness is that he will not retaliate for your crime towards him. If he does not forgive you and the case goes to court and the court subsequently forgives you, then you do not receive any punishment for your crime.

In both these cases you escaped physical punishment; however, by committing this crime, the effects that have taken place on your self cannot be rectified. None other can remove these effects. Only you yourself can remove these that is through *Tauba* - in other words, if you feel guilty about your mistakes and repent for these and then go on to perform such righteous deeds whose constructive results outweigh the negative effects of this crime. This is called *Maghfirat* or means of protection.

Maghfirat means to provide resources for protection – there are two aspects of these resources. According to the first, you take care to avoid wrongdoing and thus protect yourself from the consequences of wrongdoing. This is a very admirable and protective vision of life and is called *'Taqwa'* (righteousness). The second view is if a wrong deed has been committed by you, then through the power of the congenial outcomes from your righteous deeds, you can save yourself from the loss to your self – this is called *Tauba*. In medical terms, the first concept comes under preventive measures while the second will be curative. In both these cases, you can only receive protective cover through your own actions. As stated earlier, the Quran calls this *Maghfirat*. In Arabic, *'Maghfir'* means a helmet which is used for protection by soldiers in a battlefield. *'Istighfar'* means to seek resources for protection, taking precautionary measures in the beginning, and if a wrong step has been taken then to take curative measures. This makes it clear that according to the Quran there is no question of 'forgiveness of sins' without taking remedial measures as above.

Let us be aware that when we commit a crime (i.e. go against the Divine Laws), we do not commit a crime against Allah, so that He can forgive us. We actually commit excess against our own self which none can forgive, and the only way to address this is by doing righteous deeds ourselves as already explained. Wherever in the Quran, the term *'yaghfir ul zanoob'* (forgiving of sins) is used, or Allah has called Himself *'Ghafoor'*, it does not mean that Allah 'forgives' crimes or sins – it means that there is a provision made for removing the consequences of our wrong deeds within the working of the Law of Requital. The meaning of the term *'yaghfiru lae manyunshaw wa yuazibu manyunshaw'* is the same i.e. protection and punishment in human life is according to Allah's Laws. After taking a wrong step if a person wishes that he should get protection from his wrongdoing, then through his righteous deeds he can get this protection, but if someone does not want this, then he cannot protect himself from the negative consequences. Allah neither causes a person harm, nor does He forgive anyone's crimes.

6.6 'Light' and 'Heavy' Balancing Of Deeds

From the example of health and disease as noted earlier, we have seen that there is a continuous onslaught of destructive elements on our bodies. As long as we have immunity, then our bodily defences can overcome the destructive forces and we remain healthy. However, if our immunity is diminished for some reason, we can be overwhelmed by the destructive elements and fall ill. A doctor takes steps to halt these destructive elements and then tries to increase the immunity of the patient. When the immunity strengthens, the patient recovers. However, if our immunity does not increase proportionately in relation to the destructive elements then a time comes when these elements overcome the body and man dies. This conflict between the constructive and destructive forces is continuous in human lives, and the outcome depends on which is heavier in the scales of balance. If our constructive elements are heavier then we save ourselves from destruction, but if the destructive elements become heavier then we suffer loss and ultimately are destroyed. The Quran has stated this as a principle of protection and destruction:

The balance that day will be true (Haqq): those whose scale (of good) will be heavy, will prosper: Those whose scale will be light, will be their self in perdition, for that they wrongfully treated Our signs. (7:8-9) See also (23:102-103)

In another verse:

Then he whose balance (of good deeds) will be (found) heavy, Will be in a life of good pleasure and satisfaction. But he whose balance (of good deeds) will be (found) light, Will have his home in a (bottomless) Pit. (101:6-9)

This principle of '*saqqal wa khiffat mowazeen*'[28] i.e. the heavy and light balancing of deeds, comprises a great reality within it. The possibility of making mistakes is with every human being during this life. If with one mistake human beings are consigned to eternal hell, then no one can succeed and benefit and grow in this life.

The Christians created this doctrine that the first two human beings i.e. Adam and Eve, due to their one 'mistake' were thrown out of paradise. Now, because of this sin of theirs, every child is said to come to this life with this sin in tow which can never be washed away except by believing in the crucifixion of Jesus and as a result that he died for their sins. This one doctrine has pushed mankind into the caves of destruction, which the pages of history are a witness to. That sin for which this human child is not responsible, and which is so immutable that his thousands of righteous deeds can never rectify it! But the belief in the crucifixion of Jesus and his being the son of God, is a

---

[28] *Saqqal* = heavy, *khiffat* = light, *mowazeen* = balance

blank cheque for men that you can do whatever your hearts wish but will not be held accountable for it as long you believe in the above doctrine[29].

As specified earlier, the Quran in this life gives man a detailed programme for the nurture and development of the human self to such a degree that he becomes capable of entering into the evolutionary phase of the next life[30]. This is similar to any system of education in which there are examinations to assess which students have achieved a certain degree of competence and are capable of being promoted to the next class. For this a standard is set, for example, if the pass mark is 60%, a student securing this has exceeded the requirement and his balance is heavy on the side of his abilities. In other words the 40% of marks he did not achieve, are compensated for by the 60% he did manage to achieve. Contrary to this, a student who gets 40%, is not promoted to the next class. In other words, his marks go wasted. In Quranic terms, this is called '*Haabit ammal*' or deeds going wasted. At the time of death, there is some energy left in the human body, but because it is insufficient to support life it goes wasted, and death prevails. This is also an example of *Haabit ammal*. The Quran states:

They are those whose works will bear no fruit in this world and in the Hereafter ... (3:22)
See also (5:5, 9:69)

In *Surah Noor* these wasted deeds are compared to mirages, which have no reality and are fruitless (24:39). Also see (25:23), where these deeds are compared with the weight of a particle of dust. The state of the deeds of the hypocrites is the same, they may appear impressive, but their authenticity and reality are non-existent (33:19). These hypocrites are those people who do not believe in the truth of the Divine Laws. They themselves do not follow Allah's defined programme, and serve as a stumbling block trying to prevent others as well from following this righteous path (47:9, 47:1).

However precise a formula may be, for its success it is important that no impurities are added to it. It should be acted on in its pure form. If a person mixes the ingredients of one formula with some ingredients of another formula, then no matter how hard he works he will not get the results of the original formula. If a patient does not follow the instructions of a doctor, and takes some medicines from the doctor and some from a

---

[29] This doctrine essentially makes life very easy and totally removes one's own accountability for anything in life. The rich and powerful can do anything in their lives without any guilt and remorse, and then if they have belief in this doctrine their worldly life will be great and a certificate will be issued by the clergy for their next life as well. (Ed)

[30] The Quran provides details about human thought process and states that by virtue of having free will, there is no inbuilt guidance within human thinking. In order to have a challenging environment in this life, man is endowed with emotions, rational thinking and a body. In the absence of inner guidance, man requires the guidance of revelation in the form of Permanent Values as an external standard. These Permanent Values do not change and will remain the same for all time, therefore this will help to develop the human self. The Quran also explains the way human beings think and invites us to think like the Quran as this is the way we can solve human problems on a global basis and remove all conflicts and mutual rivalry. Since we do not think like the Quran, we are unable to produce anything like it; however, we can understand the Quran through the use of our intellect and reason and by relating it to the solutions of human problems. (Ed)

quack, and starts to treat himself by mixing both, then he is inviting death instead of recovery. In Quranic terminology this is called '*Shirk*' i.e. mixing the Quranic values with non-Quranic values. It is obvious that the result of this can be nothing but failure. It is not going to produce the intended results which are noted in the Quran [31] and such efforts are wasted:

If they were to join other gods with Him[32], all that they did would be vain for them. (6:89)
See also (9:17)

In *Surah Zumr*:

But it has already been revealed to you, as it was to those before you, 'If you were to join gods with Allah, truly fruitless will be your work (in life), and you will surely be in the ranks of those who lose (as per Allah's Laws). (39:65)

If, in order to pass a certain exam, some subjects are designated as being essential while others are optional, and a student has failed or not even sat the exam of an essential subject, then there is no need for him to even look at the optional exam papers. In Allah's syllabus there are some subjects which are essential. If someone fails in these subjects, he has no need to look at the other papers. The Quran has referred to this reality as follows:

Say: 'Shall we tell you of those who lose most in respect of their deeds?' Those whose efforts have been wasted in this life, while they thought that they were acquiring good by their works? They are those who deny the Signs of their Cherisher and the fact of their having to meet Him (in the Hereafter): vain will be their works, nor shall We, on the Day of Judgment, give them any weight. (18:103-105)

Bear in mind that these people will obtain the benefits of this life in accordance with their endeavours, because the benefits of this life are achieved through physical laws. Whoever works according to these laws will obtain the benefit of his labours. In this there is no distinction between Muslim and non-Muslim. For this there is no need to have belief or conviction in the life of the hereafter. But as far as self-development is concerned, they will have no share in it. The one who does not even believe in the development of the self, his self cannot take part in this process of development.

---

[31] Allah's Laws and Values have been clearly specified in the Quran and also the effects which will manifest themselves if these are followed as directed. The Quran deals with human thought processes which need to be willingly changed through the creation of an inner need to perceive life through the lens of guidance provided by the Quran. The Quran is a complete book of guidance and does not require any outside source to interpret it or to follow it. (Ed)

[32] To 'join gods' (Shirk) means to mix the Quranic guidance with other values - e.g. the Quran says that as per the Law of Requital there is no exception and all are accountable; however, if we start making exceptions to this then we start accepting human intervention and the impact of this law will be dissipated in terms of its implementation in the system of *Deen*. (Ed)

In *Surah Hud* this aspect is explained:

> *Those who desire the life of the present and its glitter, to them we shall pay (the price of) their deeds therein, without diminution. They are those for whom there is nothing in the Hereafter but the Fire: vain are the designs they frame therein, and of no effect are the deeds that they do! (11:15-16) See also (17:21)*

Having belief in life in the hereafter[33] is a compulsory subject in the educational syllabus of Allah, and it will be in the light of this that man's other 'exam papers' will be viewed (17:147). If one fails in this exam of life, then his other deeds will not be able to benefit him:

> *In front of them is Hell: and of no profit to them is anything they may have earned, nor any protectors they may have taken to themselves besides Allah, for them is a tremendous Penalty. (45:10)*

6.7 Taking Advantage of The Respite

This is the standard of success and failure which is defined through the Law of Requital. The time between an action and before its results become visible, means that if for some reason the balance of a man's deeds is tilted towards destructive results, then before that the destruction comes on him, this interval or respite gives him an opportunity to redress the balance with constructive deeds. He is given the opportunity to add constructive deeds to tilt the balance in his favour. If he does not do this, and his destruction reaches him and confronts him, then nothing can save him from this[34]. This is the reason that the Quran has declared that when death finally confronts a man, then his doing *Tauba* (repentance) at that stage is of no use to him. When death is facing man, it means he does not have any time left to do constructive deeds. And since *Tauba* means to take advantage of the period of respite, and add constructive deeds in the balance, therefore when there is no time left then what will one gain by merely uttering '*Tauba, Tauba*' at those final moments of life? In *Surah Nissa* it is stated:

---

[33] It is important to reflect on this point, as to why conviction *(Eimaan)* based on reasoning and intellect is important for the next life. All our deeds are preceded by our thinking – therefore a change in thinking affects our outlook i.e. our self. We have a mind which has the ability to think about one's thinking (metacognition) and we use our mind to make decisions and these decisions and our experiences develop our self which resides in our memory. If we have conviction that there is accountability in whatever we do and that this will affect our self, then we will regulate our behaviour differently from the one who does not believe in such accountability. This is the inner change in thinking to which the Quran refers, when it says that each self is accountable for what it does. Those who accept this value later in life, can easily differentiate between the two states if the self i.e. the one which was present before developing this conviction and the one after. (Ed)

[34] According to the Quran there are scales for everything we do e.g. helping someone on a regular basis is higher in scale than helping someone on request. (Ed)

Of no effect is the repentance of those who continue to do evil, until death faces one of them, and he says, 'Now have I repented indeed'; nor of those who die rejecting Faith: for them have We prepared a punishment most grievous. (4:18)

When facing imminent death or danger, if a man then prostrates himself and fervently prays, this does not mean that he is repenting about what he has done in his life. It actually means that he does not have the courage or resolution to face the calamity confronting him, and is searching for an escape from it. This is a vast character failing. From this point of view, when facing imminent death, resorting to protestations of *Tauba* is meaningless. This is why when Pharaoh was drowning and he said:

…At length, when overwhelmed with the flood, he said: 'I believe that there is no god except Him Whom the Children of Israel believe in: I am of those who submit (to Allah in Islam).' (It was said to him): 'Ah now! But a little while before, you were in rebellion! and you did mischief (and violence)!' (10:90-91)

Now, seeing death in front of you, you are declaring your *Eimaan*, though all your life you have gone against the Divine Laws and created tyranny in the land. And you were arrogant and boastful. And now your character is such that with the fear of death you are declaring that you accept *Eimaan*. In the Divine Balance what is the significance of such a declaration of *Eimaan*? When confronted by death, *Tauba* gives no benefit. When the time of respite has passed by, then any apologies mean nothing:

So on that Day no excuse of theirs will avail the transgressors, nor will they be invited (then) to seek grace (by repentance). (30:57) See also (40:52, 77:36)

They will say: 'Our Lord! twice hast Thou made us without life, and twice hast Thou given us Life! Now have we recognised our sins: Is there any way out (of this)?' (40:11)

They will be told:

'This, because you used to take the Signs of Allah in jest, and the life of the world deceived you': (From) that Day, therefore, they shall not be taken out thence, nor shall they be received into Grace. (45:35)

6.8   There is No Return to This World

At this time they will also say, 'Allah, My Sustainer, let me return to the world once more and see then how many righteous deeds I do':

Until, when death comes to one of them, he says: 'O my Lord! send me back (to life),- In order that I may work righteousness in the things I neglected.' 'By no means! It is but a word he says.'... (23:99-100)

According to the law of evolution, the caravan of life cannot go backwards. Those of mankind who wish to go forward, will move on, and those who wish to remain stuck in one place, will remain there. No-one can go back and compensate for any deficiencies they have. Life is not cyclic. It advances forwards and gains loftiness as it does so, therefore the concept of return and transmigration is against this reality and this concept is a creation of the human mind only. Therefore, despite their thousands of futile prayers, there is no question of coming back to this physical life. They will express excessive regret and say:

'Now if we only had a chance of return we shall truly be of those who believe!' (26:102)

In *Surah Sajda* it is noted that the criminals will say, that at that time I did not consider it to be truthful; now, having seen the reality with our own eyes and heard it with our own ears, we would like to have another chance:

If only you could see when the guilty ones will bend low their heads before their Cherisher, (saying:) 'Our Rabb[35]! We have seen and we have heard: Now then send us back (to the world): we will work righteousness: for we do indeed (now) believe.' (32:12)

The reply will be that the question of return does not even arise. You received the Divine Laws, and regarding them arrogantly, you rejected them and rebelled against them and persisted onwards in your wrongdoing. Now the time has passed when you could develop yourself and turn your wrongs into right:

Or (lest) it should say when it (actually) sees the penalty: 'If only I had another chance, I should certainly be among those who do good!' (The reply will be:) 'Nay, but there came to you My Signs, and you did reject them: you were Haughty, and became one of those who reject Truth!' (39:58-59)

In *Surah Al-Hadeed* it is stated that on the Day of Judgement the *Momineen* will be walking, and the light of their foreheads will illuminate their paths. Seeing them, the hypocrites will say, stop for a moment, can we get some of your light, so that the dark paths of our lives can be illuminated as well. The *Momineen* will reply, this light is the

---

[35] *Rabb* – a Divine attribute translated as 'Cherisher'. (Ed)

result of an individual's own righteous deeds, this light is lit by the oil of righteous deeds, you can neither get this light from someone nor can it be passed on to you. The only way to achieve it was in the worldly life through your own deeds. If you can go back to the world, then you can get the lights of your own life. Since no-one can go back to the world, therefore how can your dark paths be illuminated now?

> *One Day you will see the believing men and the believing women- how their Light runs forward before them and by their right hands: (their greeting will be): 'Good News for you this Day! Gardens beneath which flow rivers! to dwell therein for aye! This is indeed the highest Achievement!' (57:12)*

> *One Day will the Hypocrites- men and women - say to the Believers: 'Wait for us! Let us borrow (a Light) from your Light!' It will be said: 'Turn ye back to your rear! then seek a Light (where ye can)!' So a wall will be put up betwixt them, with a gate therein. Within it will be Mercy throughout, and without it, all alongside, will be (Wrath and) Punishment! (57:13)*

Do not pass this point without adequate reflection. This is a very important place and requires profound reflection - life after evolving and progressing over a very long period of time has ended in the creation of man[36]. Now man has been given an opportunity to live his life within the Divine Laws, and thus make his self capable of being able to live in the next evolutionary stage of life. Now think of the man who wastes this opportunity and does such a loss to his self of which there is no chance of salvage. If life were to end with death, then man could live it as he wished and all his affairs would have been ended with death.

But when life has to evolve and progress further, and man is going to be alive there, and possess self-consciousness and intellect, and then witness with his own eyes what a great destruction he has purchased for himself, neither will the destruction disappear, nor will there be an opportunity of salvage! Just think of this type of life – and of this life being very long. How is this life going to be lived!

From this you will also see why the Quran gives so much significance to *Eimaan* (conviction) in the next life and why the stage of this world is so important. The one who wastes this life, he will be destroyed forever.

---

[36] As far as is known, we are the only creation in the visible universe which has free will and the freedom to choose. With our intellect and reasoning, we make sense of this universe and this points to a great reality – that the universe is for us as we give it meaning. (Ed).

(Intentionally left blank)

(Intentionally left blank)

7 'Yaum Al-Deen' - The Day of Judgement

As we have seen in the previous chapter, during the period of respite, we have an opportunity to protect ourselves from the consequences of our wrong deeds through good deeds. But once this time of respite ends, then the decision is made according to the Divine Scales. This result will manifest itself in this life and most definitely will manifest in the next life. This time of manifestation of deeds is called 'Yaum Al-Deen' in the Quran. 'Al-Deen' is a very comprehensive term which has the meaning of 'Book of Laws'; obedience to these Laws and the subsequent results of deeds are all included in this meaning. In the first chapter of the Quran, Allah has called Himself the Master of 'Yaum Al-Deen' (1:3). That is He through Whose Law of Requital the results of deeds become manifest. He has full control and sovereignty over this Law and no other power can intervene and none can escape its grip.

In *Surah Infitar, Yaum Al-Deen* is defined as follows:

(It will be) the Day when no self shall have power (to do) aught for another: For the command, that Day, will be (wholly) with Allah. (82:19)

In reality this *Yaum Al-Deen* is a natural result of Allah's sovereignty. The sovereignty of Allah means that everything in the universe is decided through the Divine Laws and every matter is decided through the Law of Requital. In *Surah Al-Teen* it is stated:

Then after this, what other argument can there be for the one who lies about the Day of Judgment ('Yaum Al-Deen')? (95:7)

What, is it not true, that Allah is the ultimate Sovereign, whose Laws decide every matter:

Is not Allah the ultimate Sovereign? (95:8)

This is why it was said to the messenger regarding those who reject the Law of Requital, to proclaim to them with full conviction:

Verily that which you are promised is true; and verily Judgment and Justice must indeed come to pass. (51:5-6)

And further clarified it:

Then, by the Sustainer of the heavens and earth (these provide evidence), this is the very Truth, as much as the fact that you can speak intelligently to each other. (51:23)

The point to note is that this accountability process is as real as two people recognising and talking to each other. They ask when will this happen. In reply it is said its time cannot be disclosed, however at this time it is enough to understand:

They ask, 'When will be the Day of Judgment and Justice (Yaum Al-Deen)?' (It will be) a Day when they will be tried (and tested) over the Fire! (51:12-13)

In *Surah Infitar* this fact is put forth in a very refined and visionary way. It is stated:

Which they will enter, on the Day of Judgment. (82:15)

From this we might imagine that people will be collected in hell suddenly i.e. as if there is no link between deeds and their results and one will suddenly find oneself in the new state after death. The Quran says it is not like this – the consequences of everyone's deeds are with them continuously and it is only that they cannot be seen yet. They will see hell based on these consequences when these build up to the level where this hell will manifest itself:

…and they will not be able to keep away therefrom. (82:16)

At this time they are not feeling the presence of hell, and will see it in front of them when that time comes, whereas hell 'sees' man all the time. Because of this surety, this Day is also called '*Yaum Al-Haqq*' – the day the truth comes out and the day the balance for accountability will be raised:

That Day will be the sure Reality… (78:39) See also (14:41, 38:53)

At another place, referring to the evil consequences it is stated:

Such will be their entertainment on the Day of Judgement! (56:56)

In Surah *Al-Saffat*, those people who deny the hereafter, when they will be brought to the 'court of Allah' will say:

They will say, 'Ah! Woe to us! This is the Day of Judgment!' (A voice will say,) 'This is the Day of Sorting Out, whose truth ye (once) denied!' (37:20-21)

This is the day of decision which you used to deny:

Verily the Day of sorting out is the time appointed for all of them, the Day when no protector can avail his client in aught, and no help can they receive. (44:40-41) See also (77:14-15, 77:38)

In *Surah Naba*, it is declared that there is a time fixed for '*Yaum Al-Fasal*' – the day of final decision:

Verily the Day of Sorting out is a thing appointed. (78:17)

In some places *Yaum Al-Deen* has also been called '*Yaum Al-Baath*' (15:35-36, 38:78-79).

As already discussed, the criteria for success and failure according to the Law of Requital, is based on the balance between the righteous and wrong deeds. Students study all year and then there is an exam, and on the day of the result, those who have failed learn how much deficiency remained due to which they could not pass.

From this aspect, this day of decision is termed in the Quran as '*Yaum Al-Taghabun*' – this means to judge a deficiency by comparing with others. Those who 'fail' will be told:

> '*O you assembly of men (both nomads and from townships)! came there not unto you messengers from amongst you, setting forth unto you My signs, and warning you of the meeting of this Day of yours?' They will say: 'We bear witness against ourselves.' It was the life of this world that deceived them. So against themselves will they bear witness that they rejected Eimaan. (6:130)*

People who deny *Yaum Al-Deen* are mentioned in several places in the Quran. In *Surah Mudather* it is stated that when the criminals will be entering hell, they will be asked:

> '*What led you into Hell Fire?' They will say: 'We were not of those who prayed (salat)*[37]*; Nor were we of those who fed the indigent; But we used to talk vanities with vain talkers; And (thus) we used to deny the Day of Judgment, until there came to us (the Hour) that is certain.' (74:42-47)*

In *Surah Infitar*, people are told that you deny *Yaum Al-Deen*, though all your deeds are being recorded and on the day these deeds are disclosed, destruction will be awaiting you (82:9-10, 83:10-11).

In *Surah Al-Maoon*, this is again made very clear:

> *Do you see the one who denies the Judgment (to come)? Then such is the (man) who repulses the orphan (with harshness), and encourages not the feeding of the indigent. So woe to the 'worshippers'*[38] *who are neglectful of their prayers (salat)*[39]*; those who (want but) to be seen (of men); and refuse to keep open the means of sustenance which meet others' needs. (107:1-7)*

---

[37] The term used is '*Salat*' which is in reference to establishing a system. For a detailed meaning of this term, please refer to the book, 'Lughat ul Quran', compiled by the author. (Ed)

[38] The Quran invites us to follow the Permanent Values and not to worship in the religious context. (Ed)

[39] As per footnote 37, the term used is '*Salat*'. (Ed)

7.1   Results of Deeds

These are briefly the methods by which human deeds bear results:

1) Commission of a deed
2) Time of respite between a deed and its result
3) Opportunity to repent during the time of respite
4) Balancing of deeds between righteous deeds and wrong deeds
5) Manifestation of the results of these deeds

In the Quran these stages are not all mentioned together at every place nor was this required. In the Quran, generally reference is usually to the deed and its result e.g. in *Surah Baqra*:

Nay, whoever submits His whole self to Allah and is a doer of good, He will get his reward with his Sustainer; on such shall be no fear, nor shall they grieve. (2:112)

In *Surah Al-Zumr* it is stated:

They shall have all that they wish for, in the presence of their Sustainer: such is the reward of those who do righteous deeds. (39:34)

This is the reward to the people for their own good hard work. The end of human success is that whatever they wish for they should get, but the Quran goes a step further:

There will be for them therein all that they wish, and more besides in Our Presence. (50:35)

There, they will get everything they desire, in fact even more than this. This is a great reality which is referred to in a few words. The scales of human desires and wishes are according to this life. In this life he will acquire according to the scales of this life and this is viewed as the pinnacle of success. But after this when life moves to a higher stage, its requirements will change, which we cannot understand at our present level of consciousness. A child cannot imagine what will be the requirements of his life when he reaches adulthood. So the Quran says that as a result of their balanced deeds they will get all that they wish for according to the requirements of this life, but this is not the end of it. When the requirements of their life change, then they will have those things which will be as per the new requirements.

…that He may give glad tidings to the Believers who work righteous deeds, that they shall have a goodly Reward. (18:2)

In *Surah Hud* the purpose of human life is stated as:

...that He provides you opportunities to check, which of you is best in conduct... (11:7)

And regarding evil deeds it is stated:

Nay, those who seek gain in evil, and are girt round by their crimes, they are companions of the Fire: Therein shall they abide. (2:81). See also (41:27, 30:10)

Such destruction, that after seeing it they will experience regret and shock as to why they performed such deeds:

And those who followed would say: 'If only We had one more chance, We would clear ourselves of them, as they have cleared themselves of us.' Thus will Allah show them (the fruits of) their deeds as (nothing but) regrets... (2:167)

...but from people in crime never will His wrath be turned back. (6:147)
See also (7:41, 7:40)

Then the Quran says that you will see what the end was of those who created disharmony, conflicts and injustice in this world:

...And hold in your mind's eye what was the end of those who did mischief. (7:86)
See also (7:84, 7:103)

(Intentionally left blank)

8 'Azaab' - Destruction and Annihilation

As discussed in the previous chapter, according to the Quran the results of human deeds manifest themselves in this life and will of a certainty manifest in the next life. As far as worldly life is concerned, man happens to be an animal, which means he considers himself secure within a collective life called society. Though society is a collection of individuals, the sum is unlike a mathematical addition, it is more than this. Society has a defined system and individuals have to live life within this system. If a society is based or shaped on Divine Laws, which are established for the development of human life, then the life of the people will be according to these Permanent Values. This society will thus enjoy success, prosperity and a pleasant life in both this world and the life of the hereafter. It is possible that there will be individuals within this society who go against the Permanent Values. Because such deeds will go against the Laws of the society i.e. the Permanent Values, society will punish them for their deeds. As far as the next life of these individuals is concerned, it will be settled according to the balance of their deeds. The individuals of such a society will have a life of paradise in this world and their life in the hereafter will also be in paradise. It is possible that due to some unexpected events e.g. a natural disaster, they may have some trouble, but this loss or difficulty will not be termed as 'hell'. The Quran has referred to such a state as:

So lose not heart, nor fall into despair: For you must gain mastery if you are Momineen.
(3:139)

Contrary to this, the other society which is not established based on the Permanent Values, will be of two types:

1. Such a society which does not harness the resources and forces of nature will live in the hell of humiliation and disgrace, and the individuals of that society will live in hell in the next life also.

2. Such a society which harnesses these natural resources and forces of nature will have benefit and prosperity for a certain period of time. But as the people do not organise the society according to the Permanent Values, they also will ultimately suffer destruction and annihilation in this life. The forms of this destruction can have different aspects but as a collective definition can be termed as hell. As far as the next life of the individuals is concerned, that will undoubtedly be hell.

In each of these two types of societies, there will be individuals who are against those societal values which are against the Quran and would wish (and make efforts) to establish a system within the domain of the Permanent Values. Obviously if destruction comes to this society, these individuals will also suffer the consequences of this destruction regardless.

Regarding them, the Quran has stated:

And fear, tumult or oppression, which affects not in particular (only) those of you who do wrong: and know that Allah is strict in punishment. (8:25)

Therefore, these kind of people have to share in the destruction which comes to the society as a whole, but their future life will be of paradise, due to their righteous deeds tilting their overall balance of deeds.

The Quran has used the term *'Azaab'* for this destruction, whether it is in this life or in the hereafter - *'Azaab e Aleem'* (extremely painful destruction); *'Azaab e Maheen'* (humiliating destruction); and *'Azaab Al-Hareeq'* (destruction which burns everything connected to human life). The terms *'Azaab Al-Naar'* or *'Azaab Al-Saeer'* also have the same meaning as *'Azaab Al-Hareeq'*. Other terms are *'Azaab e Azeem'* (great destruction), *'Azaab Shadeed'* (intense destruction).

In some places the Quran has clearly stated that these destructions are in this life and in other places that these destructions are for the hereafter. In other places are mentioned destructions both in this life and in the hereafter. In some places there is no distinction and it is simply called destruction. We will first examine those verses in which destruction is mentioned without any distinction.

8.1 *'Azaab'* – Punishment without any Distinction.

1. Just *Azaab*: In some verses it is mentioned as simply *Azaab*. In Surah *Inaam*:

But those who reject our signs, them shall punishment touch, for that they ceased not from transgressing. (6:49) See also (5:80, 7:156, 19:79, 30:16, 34:8)

2. At another place it has been called *'Su Al-Azaab'* (6:158) i.e. the worst form of a punishment. In *Surah Maida* it is stated that the followers of the messenger Isa (Jesus) were warned that if they decided to go against the Divine System of Sustenance, then they would receive such punishment as no other nation had previously suffered (5:118). In *Surah Mariam* this punishment is described as being from *Al-Rehman*, from Allah (19:45) (*Rehman* being an attribute of Allah). At other places this is called *Azaab* from *Rabb* (Sustainer, an attribute of Allah) (25:19, 70:27-28). In *Surah Al Furqan* it is called *'Azaab Kabeer'* (great destruction) (25:19), and in *Surah Ghathia* it is called *'Azaab Akbar'* (greatest destruction) (88:24). In order to express the intensity of a destruction it has also been called *'Azaab'en Fauqa Al-Azaab'* (16:88) i.e. destruction upon destruction.

3. *'Azaab'un Shadeed'un'* – very severe destruction which expresses the intensity and severity of the punishment (3:4, 14:2, 2:165, 41:27, 58:15). To express the same intensity, in some places it is called *'Azaab'un Ghaleez'* (31:24, 41:50).

4. *'Azaab'un Azeem'* – Great Punishment: in *Surah Baqra* it is stated that those people who adopt such a mentality whereby they refuse to see, hear or understand, and without any reason wish to defy truth and reality, for them is a great punishment (2:7). In *Surah Al e Imran,* the people who even after receiving the clear message of the Revelation persist in creating sects and causing division among themselves, will receive great punishment (3:104, 3:175). The people who after having accepted *Eimaan* then turn against it, for them too is a great punishment (16:106).

5. *'Azaab'un Muheen'un'* – humiliating and degrading punishment. In *Surah Baqra* this type of punishment is specified for those who do not accept Allah's guidance (2:90). For those who refuse to accept the Divine Laws and oppose them, the consequence of their way of life is this type of punishment (3:177, 4:102, 4:151, 22:57). Those people who ridicule the signs of Allah and do not take them seriously, for them is the same punishment (31:6, 45:9). In *Surah Mujadila* a warning is given against those people who start a war against the Islamic System or Government that for them is a humiliating destruction (58:5).

6. *'Azaab Al-Hareeq and Azaab Al Saeer'* - 'destruction' of human life affecting the inner self. In *Surah Al e Imran* this is called punishment related to the human self (3:180). At other places this is also called *'Azaab Al Saeer'* (22:4, 67:5). The term *'Azaab Al-Naar'* has been mentioned so many times that this will require far more detailed explanation e.g. (2:126). This term has a similar meaning to *Azaab Al-Hareeq and Azaab Al Saeer.*

7. *'Azaab'un Aleem'* – extremely painful punishment. This term also appears many times in the Quran. In the beginning of *Sura Baqra* the hypocrites are mentioned, and this punishment[40] is predicted for them due to their behaviour:

In their hearts is a disease; and Allah has increased their disease: and grievous is the penalty they (incur), because they are false (to themselves). (2:10)

The trait of a hypocrite is that while a man remains in this state then the intensity of this malady keeps increasing and the life of such a person is lived in great agony and fear.

In *Surah Saba* it is noted that people who run about trying to oppose the Divine Laws in order to defeat them, their end is this type of punishment which will dissipate their power and there is a similar punishment for those who rebel against these Laws:

---

[40] This term for punishment has been used in many other places in the Quran e.g. 3:176, 9:61, 42:21, 3:187, 16:63, 16:104, 16:117, 58:4, 2:104, 5:73, 3:20, 9:34, 84:23, 31:7, 45:8, 22:25, 67:28, 61:10, 46:31, 43:65, 15:50, 37:38, 8:138, 4:173, 17:10, 33:8, 76:31, 73:12-13. From these verses one can also find the context in which these are used and which provides information about the types of people who earn this punishment.

But those who strive against Our Signs, to frustrate them, for such will be a Penalty, a Punishment most painful. (34:5). See also (45:11).

In the Quran, while discussing these different types of punishments, it is also stated, remember that it is a truth that this destruction from your Sustainer will definitely take place – it is not an empty threat:

Verily, the Doom of your Sustainer will indeed come to pass. (52:7)

In *Surah Al-Muaraj*:

A questioner asked about a Penalty to befall. (70:1)

The unbelievers, the which there is none to ward off. (70:2)

In *Surah Shoora*:

For any whom Allah leaves astray, there is no protector thereafter. And you will see the Wrong-doers, when in sight of the Penalty, Say: 'Is there any way (to effect) a return?' (42:44)

Since the punishment only comes when the time for respite has passed, therefore there is no question of going back or escaping from it.

These are the punishments mentioned in the Quran which do not differentiate between this life or the hereafter. In the next chapter, the consequences of the deeds which relate to this life are explained.

(Intentionally left blank)

(Intentionally left blank)

9   Reward and Punishment for the Deeds in This Life

What has been discussed previously is summarised below:

1. In the world individuals live as part of a society, which means their standard of living is proportional to the standard of living within that society. If the society is prosperous, the people will also be prosperous. If the society is in hardship then individuals will accordingly live a life of hardship.

2. Worldly gains are obtained by the subjugation and utilisation of the natural resources. In this regard there is no difference between a Muslim or a non-Muslim. Whichever nation works hard and exploits these natural resources within the remit of the physical laws, will see the fruits of its efforts.

3. But the nation which utilises the natural resources within the domain of the Permanent Values will live in harmony both within and with the rest of the world[41]. Contrary to this, if a nation goes against the Permanent Values, despite having material prosperity, it will live a life of hell and as a consequence of this other nations also will not have peace or contentment. Ultimately the prosperity of such a nation will turn into ruin and destruction.

The Quran has expounded these realities very comprehensively and in this chapter these realities will be explained relatively briefly with examples. In this regard it is important to keep this reality in mind, that the Quran presents two types of doctrines which oppose each other. According to one doctrine, the only purpose of life is to obtain all worldly materials and means. In this, there is no question of taking account of any Permanent Value. This is declared by the Quran as '*Ajila or Hayat Al-Dunya*', that is physical existence is the only life. The second doctrine of life is to obtain the material benefits of life while keeping in mind the Divine Values. This is declared by the Quran to be '*Hayat e Akhirat*' or life in the hereafter. The term 'life in the hereafter' does not mean that man should give up worldly benefits and only worry about the hereafter – this is the doctrine of monasticism which the Quran strongly opposes. The life in the hereafter means to utilise the natural resources within the remit of the Divine Values. Keep these two terms of the Quran in mind as we proceed.

---

[41] The people of this nation will also have a successful life after death. This point will be discussed later.

9.1 Obtaining Worldly Benefits

In the Quran there are verses in which it is stated:

And He has subjected to you, as from Him, all that is in the heavens and on earth: Behold, in that are Signs indeed for those who reflect. (45:13)

In these verses not only the *Momineen* but the whole of mankind is addressed, and the intention is that whichever nations use intellect, reason and effort, will be able to bring these natural resources under control to their advantage. In *Surah Bani Israel* this reality is put forward succinctly:

If any do wish for the transitory things (of this life), We readily grant them - such things as We will, to such person as We will: in the end have We provided hell for them: they will burn therein, disgraced and rejected. (17:18)

This verse explains the principle that whichever nation wants immediate benefits in this world, We will give it to them according to Our Laws. But because they do not utilise these within the Permanent Values, therefore the result is not beneficial in the long run. Contrary to this:

Those who do wish for the (things of) the Hereafter, and strive therefor with all due striving, and have Faith (Eimaan), they are the ones whose striving is acceptable. (17:19).

The above verse states that a nation which desires and works for worldly gains together with the benefits of the hereafter, i.e. they believe in the Permanent Values of the Quran, their lives both in the physical sphere and in the hereafter are enhanced, and they are rewarded accordingly. As far as the worldly gains of this life are concerned, Allah gives opportunity for both categories of people to benefit from the material resources distributed throughout the earth. In this respect, Allah does not restrict or put barriers in front of one group and let the other group prosper. Allah does not do this:

Of the bounties of your Sustainer We bestow freely on all - these as well as those: The bounties of your Sustainer are not closed (to anyone). See how We have bestowed more on some than on others (as per laws); but verily the Hereafter is more in rank and gradation and more in excellence. (17:20-21)

But the nation which keeps the Permanent Values in view, and utilises material gains accordingly, their status is far higher and real ascendency belongs to them.

In *Surah Baqra*:

... There are men who say: 'Our Cherisher! Give us (Thy bounties) in this world!' but they will have no portion in the Hereafter. (2:200)

Such people have only one aim i.e. to gain everything in this life. They gain these benefits, but their future is dark. Contrary to this, there are other people who wish for the prosperity of this life and the next life:

And there are men who say: 'Our Sustainer! Give us good in this world and good in the Hereafter, and defend us from the torment of the Fire!' To these will be allotted what they have earned; and Allah is quick in account. (2:201-202)

In *Surah Al e Imran* it is made clear that the nation which wishes worldly benefits attains these, and the nation which along with this desires the benefits of the hereafter, they also attain this:

...If any do desire a reward in this life, We shall give it to him; and if any do desire a reward in the Hereafter, We shall give it to him. And swiftly shall We reward those that (serve us with) gratitude. (3:145)

Allah says that He recompenses the efforts of everyone. The former group only gets the immediate benefits of this life and has nothing for the hereafter. But for the latter group, their state is as noted in the following verse:

And Allah gave them a reward in this world, and the excellent reward of the Hereafter. For Allah Loves (as per His Laws) those who do good. (3:148)

9.2   *Momineen* in This Life

Bearing this view in mind, do not think that success in the hereafter means that the life of believers (*Momineen*) in this world will be according to the doctrine of monasticism i.e. of deprivation and poverty. The Quran has made it clear in many places that the consequence of *Eimaan* and righteous deeds is of power and rule with peace and prosperity in life:

Whoever works righteousness, man or woman, and has Eimaan, verily, to him will We give a new Life, a life that is good and pure and We will bestow on such their reward according to the best of their actions. (16:97) See also (39:10)

In *Surah Noor* this is an assured consequence of *Eimaan* and righteous deeds:

Allah has promised, to those among you who believe and work righteous deeds, that He will, of a surety, grant them in the land, inheritance (of power), as He granted it to those before them; that He will establish in authority their Deen - the one which He has chosen for them; and that He will change (their state), after the fear in which they (lived), to one of security and peace... (24:55)

In *Surah Anbiya* this principle is reiterated that Allah had stated in the '*Zaboor*' (Psalms) also:

> *Before this We wrote in the Zaboor (Psalms), after the Message (given to Moses): My servants the righteous, shall inherit the earth. (21:105)*

In *Surah Zumr* there is a verse which narrates that those entering paradise say:

> *They will say: 'Praise be to Allah, Who has truly fulfilled His Promise to us, and has given us (this) land in heritage: We can dwell in the Garden as we will: how excellent a reward for those who work (righteousness)!' (39:74)*

At another place it is stated:

> *Allah has decreed: 'It is I and My messengers who must prevail': For Allah is One full of strength, able to enforce His Will (as per His laws). (58:21)*

In the next verse this party of *Momineen* is declared as being Allah's party *(Hizb-Ullah)*:

> *…They are the Party of Allah. Truly it is the Party of Allah that will achieve success. (58:22)*

In *Surah Ibraheem* the Quran explains in very clear terms that when Our messengers came with the Divine guidance, the opponents strongly rejected this invitation to the truth and threatened them with severe consequences. But Allah sent a revelation to the messengers not to worry, as ultimately this message will prevail:

> *And the Unbelievers said to their messengers: 'Be sure we shall drive you out of our land, or you will return to our ways.' But their Sustainer inspired (this Message) to them: 'Verily We shall cause the wrong-doers to perish! And verily We shall cause you to abide in the land, and succeed them. This for such as fear the Time when they shall stand before Me, for those who are apprehensive of the consequences of going against Allah's Laws'. (14:13-14)*

In another verse, the Quran provides an example from the history of *Bani Israel*. That We turned out Pharaoh and his cohorts from their orchards and lands and established the *Bani Israel* in their place (26:59). Another example is that of the last messenger and the *Momineen*, in that after a long struggle the opponents were eventually overcome:

> *And He made you heirs of their lands, their houses, and their goods, and of a land which you had not frequented (before). And Allah has power over all things. (33:27)*

9.3   You Continue with Your Efforts and I Will with Mine

In the initial period of conflict between truth and evil, the believers *(Momineen)* were fewer in number and had limited material resources. But due to their strong conviction in the mission and the truth of their guidance, and in their own ultimate success, they announced to their opponents:

Say: 'O my people! Do whatever you can: I will do (my part): soon will you know who it is whose end will be (best) in the Hereafter: certain it is that the wrong- doers will not prosper.' (6:136) See also (11:121, 39:39)

In another verse, they tell the opponents to wait for the results of your deeds to appear and we too are waiting:

…Say: 'Wait you: we too are waiting.' (6:158) See also (7:71, 10:20, 11:166, 32:29, 44:59)

In *Surah Hud*, the messenger announced to the opponents that you continue following your programme, and I will follow mine, and soon the results of both will be manifest:

'And O my people! Do whatever you can: I will do (my part): Soon will you know who it is on whom descends the penalty of ignominy; and who is a liar! and watch you! for I too am watching with you!' (11:93)

Regarding what has just been discussed, you will see who will soon be humiliated. Obviously, this humiliation will be visible in the present life and not in the hereafter, because humiliation after death cannot be seen in this life and so cannot be presented as evidence. These results are the ones that are going to become manifest during this life. In *Surah Yunus* this point is clarified by stating:

Do they then expect (any thing) but (what happened in) the days of the men who passed away before them? Say: 'Wait you then: for I, too, will wait with you.' (10:102)

This is obvious that the reference to the destruction of previous nations is in relation to this life and not after death. Therefore, the consequences of the programmes of both the *Momineen* and their opponents were going to show up in this life. And what is this result:

Of the wrong-doers the last remnant was cut off. Praise be to Allah, the Cherisher of the worlds. (6:45) See also (7:72)

Whatever happens, Allah's destruction only comes on those who are unjust and create inequities and are ultimately destroyed:

… will any be destroyed except those who do wrong? (6:47)

There is nothing in this world which happens by chance; everything is according to the Law of Requital:

> *... that those who died might die after a clear Sign (had been given), and those who lived might live after a Clear Sign (had been given) ... (8:42)*

This is the principle of the rise and fall of nations and this is how one nation is replaced by another (9:39, 47:38).

9.4   Forms of Destruction of Nations

In this world the destruction of nations takes place through physical causes. In this regard the Quran draws our attention to a great fundamental truth. As noted before, the Quran says that the laws which are given to mankind for guidance have two parts: one part is based on the natural laws which lead to physical effects; the second part is related to the Permanent Values which are related to the 'human life'. Both these sets of laws are called '*Al-Kitab*' (The Book) or Divine Laws. Whichever nation follows these Divine Laws wholly, their lives will be prosperous and blissful, whereas the nation which follows one part of the book only, their share will be of humiliation and ruin. Following one part of the book means:

1. The nation which follows moral values in practice but ignores the physical laws, lives a life of monasticism, due to which it is not capable of standing in the ranks of the nations which are alive.

2. Contrary to this, the nation which only follows the physical laws and avoids the moral laws (Permanent Values), its society is subject to immoral and social imbalances. This is why this nation also becomes destroyed.

The Quran has thrown light on these states in the following verse:

> *...Then is it only a part of the Book that you believe in, and do you reject the rest? But what is the reward for those among you who behave like this but disgrace in this life? and on the Day of Judgment they shall be consigned to the most grievous penalty. For Allah is not unmindful of what you do. (2:85)*

In the nation which creates social and moral imbalances and inequities in society, corruption gradually becomes widespread and as a consequence the administrative machinery becomes faulty and malfunctioning. This leads to ignoring those matters which provide the strength and capacity required by the society to face natural events and calamites e.g. floods, earthquakes, fires, volcanos, etc. (Further details will be covered later).

Another form of destruction which can face this nation is internal strife and civil war[42]. In *Surah Inam* it is said:

Say: 'He hath power to send calamities on you[43], from above and below, or to cover you with confusion in party strife, giving you a taste of mutual vengeance - each from the other.' See how We explain the signs by various (symbols); that they may understand. (6:65)

In this state, another nation can take advantage of this internal situation and attack and occupy the nation, thereby becoming the instrument of its destruction. If the attacking nation does not follow the Permanent Values then this conflict is between the two physical forces of the two nations. And with the defeat of one and the success of another, mankind does not gain any benefit, because in place of one tyrannical and oppressive nation, another similar nation arrives and replaces it. However, if the replacing nation follows the Divine Values of the Quran, then its success brings glad tidings for mankind because its supremacy is based on restoring justice and balance. These are various ways in which the wrongdoing of nations becomes the means of their destruction in this world. The Quran has discussed many forms of destruction and we will refer to these as examples.

9.5 Destruction of Previous Nations

The Quran has referred to the pattern of historical conduct of previous nations in order to focus attention on the gravest crime among many others committed by the people of these nations. This biggest crime was the cause of other evils and imbalances in these societies. At this time a messenger from Allah comes to this nation from among themselves, who warns them about the destructive consequences of their crimes and invites them to the right path. They ignore his invitation and continue following the same destructive path till some natural event destroys them. Apparently it looks as if there is no link between their crime and this natural event. This is why it is commonly viewed that Allah destroyed this nation through a supernatural way as a kind of miracle.

In reality this is not correct. There is a strong correlation between the criminal path which this nation followed and its destruction through natural events. In these nations the social and moral inequities and imbalances were so rampant and common, that they used to ignore taking any steps in time which were necessary to protect them from the effects of any natural disasters or events. The messengers of Allah not only communicated Divine guidance but also warned them of the consequences of their social inequities which were leading to dissatisfaction spreading through their societies, and all the while they were ignoring taking preventative measures. Even today, in

---

[42] This aspect is evident in various parts of the world – many nations face situations of civil war due to external interference by more powerful nations which take advantage of the internal imbalances within these nations which the ruling juntas have failed to address. (Ed)

[43] The Quran refers to these events which take place through human hands, as being to Allah. When studying these verses, we should bear in mind that wherever a reference is made to Allah, it means as per Allah's Laws. (Ed)

nations in which social inequities are common, they also do not take adequate measures to protect themselves from natural events. Contrary to this, those nations which take adequate measures against these natural events remain safer[44]. This is the correlation between social evils and natural events in many nations. The individuals in these societies who recognised and understood what the messenger of Allah was saying, but did not have the strength to bring about any change in the society, would migrate to a safer place and organise a new society. This is called 'migration' in the Quran.

9.6   Nation of *Noah*

The Quran begins from the nation of Noah to illustrate this manner of destruction of a nation. It tells us that in this nation the social stratification was so severe that the rich and wealthy looked down upon the poor and the working class and considered it a humiliation to interact with them. Along with this, the society was geographically located in a low valley, where the water from the hills around their dwellings passed close by[45]. Since the wealthy and powerful at the top were intoxicated with their own activities, no one thought about the wellbeing of all members of the society, and they ignored providing adequate defences against any flooding occurring in the future. The messenger Noah was born among them and drew their attention to all these evils and weaknesses in the society. But the rich and powerful strata opposed him strongly, ignoring his warnings. He also warned them about the risk of flooding, but was ignored. Noah, under the direction provided through revelation, started constructing a boat for a potential flood in the near future. The people ridiculed him for this. Then a time came when there was a heavy rainfall which flooded the valley and destroyed everyone except those who took refuge in the boat with Noah. For further details see (7:59, 11:26, 11:39, 25:37, 71:1)[46].

9.7   Nation of *Ad*

About the nation of *Ad*, the Quran has stated that these people were powerful, prosperous, wealthy, and had strong political influence in their time. They had plenty for their sustenance; their prosperity was displayed through their mansions, castles and economic power. However, they were extremely cruel towards weak and poor human beings and the Quran uses the following expression to illustrate this crime:

And when you exert your strong hand, do you do it like men of absolute power? (26:130)

It is apparent that excessive wealth and power and exceeding the limits in tyranny and cruelty, produce evils in a society which knows no bounds. The messenger Hud tried

---

[44] Sometimes it is observed that some of these big natural events may not directly destroy these powerful immoral nations, but have an indirect effect on their ability to wield power. Some of these extreme natural events have an economic effect which in the long term leaves an impact on the conduct of a nation. (Ed)

[45] Even today most human habitations are close to a source of water e.g. river, sea, lake, canal, etc. (Ed)

[46] Further details are provided in other books by the author. The issues which are dealt with in this book are confined to those aspects which relate to the working of the Law of Requital. (Ed)

his utmost that the people should leave the wrong path and follow the Divine Laws, but they ignored all his warnings. The evil kept spreading and they kept disregarding the measures to be taken against natural events. One time a wind storm blew through the area which lasted for a week and destroyed this nation. The wealth and power had intoxicated them to such an extent that they became blind and deaf and their intellect and reason was of no use to them. The Quran, after referring to their destruction, then addresses the opponents of the last messenger:

And We had firmly established them in a (prosperity and) power which We have not given to you (you Quresh!) and We had endowed them with (faculties of) hearing, sight, heart and intellect: but of no profit to them were their (faculties of) hearing, sight, and heart and intellect, when they went on rejecting the Signs of Allah, and they were (completely) encircled by that which they used to mock at! (42:26) See also (11:58, 46:24, 26:135-138, 54:21, 69:7)

9.8   Nation of *Samud*

After the nation of *Ad*, the nation of *Samud* comes before us. At that time most of the economy was based on animal husbandry. These animals used to graze in pastures and drink from springs. But the rich and powerful of the nation had assumed control of these pastures and sources of drinking water. This resulted in depriving the animals belonging to the poor and weak, of fodder and water. At this time, the messenger Saleh drew the attention of the rich to this issue and told them:

'And remember how He made you inheritors after the Ad people and gave you habitations in the land: you build for yourselves palaces and castles in (open) plains, and carve out homes in the mountains; so bring to remembrance the benefits (you have received) from Allah, and refrain from evil and mischief on the earth.' (7:74)

Allah's land should be open for the use of Allah's creation, and do not create those inequities one of the consequences of which is that the rich people without doing any work are becoming richer, and the accumulation of wealth in their hands has intoxicated them to such an extent that they are not taking preventative measures. The poor and needy are so lost in their own difficulties and worries, that they also cannot pay any attention. Earthquakes are common in this area and if you do not take adequate measures you will be destroyed. They completely ignored him, and finally a big earthquake overtook their dwellings and they were destroyed. The messenger Saleh and his companions just like Hud, left the area before the earthquake. Also see (7:73, 11:64, 26:156, 41:17)

9.9   Nation of *Lut*

This nation was located near the Dead Sea which was close to a volcano. Robbery and looting was common and they indulged in sexual perversions which were widespread (29:29). Homosexuality was accepted in the society. It is obvious that such a savage and ignorant nation is not going to think of any preventative measures. The messenger Lut tried very hard to bring them to the straight path, but they did not listen to any of his warnings and continued to increase in their criminal and immoral activities. They ignored all the warnings and finally were destroyed by the volcanic eruption. The messenger and his companions migrated to another safe place before the disaster. For further details see (11:76, 29:29, 51:37, 54:38).

9.10   Nation of *Shoaib*

This nation lived in Madian and had well developed businesses. However, these businesses were based on the capitalist system[47]. Their greatest exertions were to extract maximum advantage from others and in return give the minimum with which they could get away with. The messenger Shoaib made efforts to prevent them from practicing these wrong economic practices and used to say to them:

> *'And O my people! give just measure and weight, nor withhold from the people the things that are their due: commit not evil in the land with intent to do mischief.' (11:85)*

The capitalist class of people at the top ridiculed him and told him, 'You keep your preaching to your religious worship practices and don't interfere in our business. This is our business and we will run it as we please. How has all the pain of the poor and deprived become your responsibility. We know what sort of treatment they deserve and how much we should pay them. Talk such as yours is spoiling them' (11:87). A system based on such exploitation ultimately leads to destruction which finally came to this nation as well (11:84, 26:189).

9.11   Nation of *Saba*

These people lived in Yemen in a mountainous region, and initially their economy was based on agriculture. In order to support their agriculture, they constructed a dam to irrigate their fertile lands and this brought prosperity to the people. After a while the people developed a taste for business and like every capitalist, their lust for money increased day by day. In this race to accumulate wealth, they became so busy that the administration and management of their national affairs was neglected. One year, cracks began to develop in the dam to which they paid no heed and as a consequence the dam burst and the flood destroyed their villages and settlements. The Quran states:

---

[47] In the Capitalist System reward is for the capital and not the work, which makes it inherently exploitive. The Quran advises us to establish a system based on its Values – where the reward is for the work and not the capital. For further details see the book titled 'The Quranic System of Sustenance' by the author. (Ed)

But they turned away (from the guidance) and We sent against them the Flood (released) from the dams, and We converted their two garden (rows) into 'gardens' producing bitter fruit, and tamarisks, and some few (stunted) Lote-trees. That was the Requital We gave them because they ungratefully rejected Faith: and never do We give (such) requital except to such as are ungrateful rejecters. Between them and the Cities on which We had poured our blessings, We had placed Cities in prominent positions, and between them We had appointed stages of journey in due proportion[48]: 'Travel therein, secure, by night and by day'. But they said: 'Our Sustainer! Place longer distances between our journey-stages': but they wronged themselves. At length We made them as a tale (that is told), and We dispersed them all in scattered fragments. Verily in this are Signs for every (self that is) patiently constant and grateful. (34:16-19)

These are examples of the destruction which comes to nations due to their mismanagement and poor administration and thus not taking adequate preventive measures against natural events, which then result in destroying these nations.

9.12 Second Form of Destruction

The second form of destruction is when a nation becomes weak internally and another more powerful nation seizes it, invades and occupies its land, and colonises its inhabitants. To illustrate this, the Quran refers to *Bani Israel* as a lesson for us.

First of all, the Quran refers to the way *Bani Israel* lived as a nation under the subjugation of the Pharaohs of Egypt. The Quran calls this living under subjugation as a life of humiliation and slavery which is a form of *Azaab* as previously mentioned. When Moses went to confront Pharaoh, he began to remind Moses of his early life, and the kindness and blessings he had enjoyed during the time he was brought up in Pharaoh's household. On hearing this, Moses replied:

'And this is the favour with which you are reminding me, (while the fact is) you have enslaved Bani Israel!' (26:22)

Contrary to this, Allah was going to bestow a favour on this nation, which was going to be freed from the bondage of Pharaoh, and established on earth:

And We wished to be Gracious to those who were being depressed in the land, to make them leaders (in Faith) and make them heirs. To establish a firm place for them in the land, and to show Pharaoh, Haman[49], and their hosts, at their hands, the very things against which they were taking precautions. (28:5-6)

---

[48] Note how Allah in the Quran relates human activity to Himself (to His Laws). Whatever human beings do in their lives the results manifest as per His Laws which are explained in the Quran. (Ed)

[49] Haman – this figure represented the clergy of the time. In general terms the Quran refers to three pillars of the capitalist system – Pharaoh, who represents the political class, Qaroon, who represents the capitalist (28:76-82) and Haman, who represents the religious clergy. This is as much applicable today as it was then. (Ed)

Under the leadership of the messengers Moses and Aaron, after many years of struggle this nation became free from the clutches of Pharaoh. Then they were elevated in position and established in their own state, which was a bright period in history. This was a consequence of their own righteous deeds and labours. When they abandoned this path, they suffered a destruction unparalleled in the history of the time, at the hands of the King of Babylon. This is referred to in the Quran:

When the first of the warnings came to pass, We sent against you Our servants given to terrible warfare[50]*: They entered the very inmost parts of your homes; and it was a warning (completely) fulfilled. (17:5)*

The nation of *Bani Israel* learned a lesson from this destruction and repented for their previous conduct and made efforts to reform themselves. Because their destructive deeds were not heavily tilted, there was still potential to recover. The Persian King assisted them in getting rid of their invader, the King of Babylon, and helped to re-establish them in Jerusalem. After some time however, they again started rebelling against the Permanent Values and Divine guidance, and at this stage the time came for their final destruction. The Quran declares:

If you did well, you did well for yourselves; if you did evil, (you did it) against yourselves. So when the second of the warnings came to pass, (We permitted your enemies) to disfigure your faces, and to enter your Temple as they had entered it before, and to visit with destruction all that fell into their power. (17:7)

The destruction of *Bani Israel* commenced at the hands of the Romans. The Quran discusses in detail the crimes which led to their destruction, in order to serve as an example for others[51]. After this, their state was such that:

Shame is pitched over them (Like a tent) wherever they are found… (3:112)

From the history of these previous nations, there are many lessons to be learnt for those who ponder and remain on their guard against the consequences of flouting the Divine Laws:

Verily in this is an instructive warning for whosoever fears the consequences of going against the Divine laws. (79:26)

This is the second model of the destruction of nations, in which a more powerful nation destroys a weaker nation.

---

[50] Note that the Quran relates this destruction to Allah; as previously noted, everything in the world happens according to His Laws. If a nation becomes weak, then other nations which are stronger will take advantage of this. (Ed)

[51] For more details of the punishment of Bani Israel, see verses (2:49, 5:18, 7:141, 7:164-165, 14:6-7, 20:47). For the destruction of Pharaoh and his nation see verses (10:88, 20:47-48, 20:61, 40:45).

9.13 Third Form of Destruction

In the third type, a nation which is unjust and tyrannical is opposed by a nation which is righteous and follows the Permanent Values of the Quran. This nation establishes in this world a system based on justice and balance and this will be called the fight between *'Batil'* (Evil) and *'Haqq'* (Truth). It is possible that during this struggle the nation standing up for truth may have a temporary setback, but if it perseveres and remains steadfast then it can overpower opponents many times its strength (8:65). Remember, the nation fighting for truth will have to utilise its own full power (8:60) and its success will be brought about by its own exertions. This is called 'victory from Allah' or 'unseen help'. Remaining within the remit of the Permanent Values during these endeavours will compensate for any deficiencies of material resources. This belief and conviction in the continuity of life, (i.e. the belief that life does not end with death and that life after death will be far more prosperous, fulfilling and beautiful) will remove the fear of death. And it is obvious that if an individual is not fearful of death then who can defeat him? This fight is in reality the fight between the balancing of constructive and destructive deeds – because the nation standing for truth and justice has more constructive deeds in its balance compared to the opposing nation, therefore the former achieves success.

In *Surah Araf* this is noted comprehensively:

How many towns have We destroyed (for their crimes)? Our punishment took them on a sudden by night or while they slept for their afternoon rest. When (thus) Our punishment took them, no cry did they utter but this: 'Indeed we did wrong.' Then shall we question those to whom Our message was sent and those by whom We sent it. And verily, We shall recount their whole story with knowledge, for We were never absent (at any time or place).
(7:4-7)

And further clarifies it:

The balance that day will be true (Truth will come out): those whose scale (of good) will be heavy, will prosper: Those whose scale will be light, will be their self in perdition, for that they wrongfully treated Our signs. (7:8-9)

In relation to the destruction of a criminal nation, the Quran has made reference to Moses against Pharaoh and in even more detail the struggle of the last messenger against his opponents, the people of *Quresh*. A large section of the Quran is devoted to this struggle which is very illuminating and instructive. The repeated defeats of the opponents, and the ultimate end of their power is declared to be a natural consequence of adopting an immoral path in life and according to the Law of Requital. This is Allah's punishment, and this point has been repeatedly clarified as to why such punishment is visited upon the nations when they did this or that act (8:34-37).
In this connection the Quran declares:

We send the messengers only to give good news and to warn: so those who believe and mend (their lives), upon them shall be no fear, nor shall they grieve. But those who reject our signs, them shall punishment touch, for that they ceased not from transgressing. (6:48-49)

In this conflict, the evil nation is not eliminated in one go, instead they will suffer some loss which serves as a warning and as an opportunity for them to mend their ways and accept the righteous path. But as noted before, these people try to take advantage of this respite to develop further in the intensity of their opposition, and so they gradually move of their own accord closer to their own destruction. This was the pattern of the struggle between the last messenger and his opponents, e.g. see (9:101-102, 26:201-203, 25:41-42, 23:75-77, 9:126, 11:8)

Before the arrival of the last messenger, none of the nations residing around the Arabian Peninsula had their societies organised on the basis of the Divine Laws, therefore there was no chance of any conflict of ideology amongst them. The systems were purely based on 'worldly politics', according to which the Arabs had an arrangement in place that neighbouring nations will not harm them. With the advent of Islam, the struggle became now of ideologies. It was necessary now that people were informed as to which was the rightly guided path, and which was not. Then people needed to be provided with time and opportunity in order to leave the wrong path and adopt the right path. This time was provided for a long while. (The life of the *Momineen* in Makkah was devoted to delivering this message to people.) The Makkan period belonged to this spreading of the message, and organising training for those who accepted the Divine guidance. When, despite this, the opponents of the ideology did not mend their ways and instead resorted to violence which increased with time, then the process of their destruction commenced. The battle of '*Badr*' to the next stage of victory in Makkah was part of this programme of establishing the system. This is the purpose of these verses, which declare that no community is destroyed until they have been adequately warned through a messenger i.e. the third form of destruction is not imposed on them:

...nor would We visit with Our Wrath (based on the Law of Requital) until We had sent a messenger (to give warning). (17:15)

At another place it is said:

(The messengers were sent) thus, for your Sustainer would not destroy for their wrong-doing men's habitations whilst their occupants were un-warned. (6:131) See also (26:208)

As per this principle, the messenger is addressed:

And if We had inflicted on them a penalty before this, they would have said: 'Our Sustainer! If only You had sent us a messenger, we should certainly have followed Your Signs before we were humbled and put to shame.' Say: 'Each one (of us) is waiting: wait you, therefore, and soon shall you know who it is that is on the straight and even path, and who it is that has received Guidance.' (20:134-135)

In this way the messenger explains both paths and their consequences to the people. It is not something difficult to understand, but since by following the righteous path the interests of the rich and powerful cliques of a nation are attacked i.e. their living off the hard work of weaker human beings, therefore they are the ones who oppose this message. They have such confidence in their wealth and the number of their cronies at the top, that they feel they can ignore the warnings of this apparently weak group (34:34-25). They consider that this is merely a clash between two physical powers, and it never enters their heads that they could be defeated by this weaker group. Intoxicated by their wealth and power and bent upon protecting their vested interests, they do not even understand or we can say they do not wish to understand, that in this conflict the criteria for defeat and victory has changed. Now the state is:

It is not your wealth nor your sons, that will bring you nearer to Us in degree: but only those who believe and work righteousness - these are the ones for whom there is a multiplied Reward for their deeds, while secure they (reside) in the dwellings on high! Those who strive against Our Signs, to frustrate them, will be given over into Punishment. (34:37-38)

Victory and success is not based on accumulated wealth and numbers. Instead it is based on true conviction and acceptance of the Divine Laws, and whosoever according to this produces the ability within himself to live in life. Whoever does this will receive multiplied successes. Contrary to this, the people who oppose the Divine Laws and try to make them ineffective, their efforts will be wasted and they will face destruction.

Wherever in the Quran life and death are mentioned in relation to nations, it means that the decision is based on the Law of Requital (44:8).

This is the third form of the destruction of nations. For example, after defeat in the battle of *Badr*, it is stated:

This is because they contended against Allah and His Messenger. If any contend against Allah and His Messenger, Allah is strict in punishment. Thus (will it be said): 'Taste you then of the (punishment): for those who resist Allah, is the penalty of the Fire.' (8:13-14)

The common belief regarding hell is that it will happen in the next life, but according to the Quran, paradise and hell start in this world. Whichever society organises itself on the basis of the Permanent Values, its life is paradise - peace and tranquillity. Those who oppose such a system, their life is hell. This is the earthly hell into which incompetent leaders push their nations (14:28-29).

In *Surah Tauba* the *Momineen* are told:

> *Fight them, and Allah will punish them by your hands, cover them with shame, help you (to victory) over them... (9:14)*

And also:

> *...He punished the Unbelievers; thus does He reward those without Faith. (9:26)*

Whichever people oppose the system based on truth, their end is this - ignominy and defeat. At the time of the pact called '*Hudaibya*', the *Momineen* were prevented from fighting against the *Quresh* because there were still some Muslims living in Makkah, and in the event of a fight, they would have suffered:

> *...Had there not been believing men and believing women whom you did not know that you were trampling down and on whose account a crime would have accrued to you without (your) knowledge, (Allah) would have allowed you to force your way, but He held back your hands... (48:25) See also (59:15)*

From this it is made clear that the results of human deeds are not only made manifest in the hereafter, but show up in this life as well. It is not a correct concept that the jurisdiction of Allah's Law of Requital only works in the next life and that this life is outside the jurisdiction of Allah. The Divine Laws are equally applicable in this life as well as the next, though for the manifestation of the consequences of deeds there are established rules, according to which there are deeds whose results will manifest in this life. The rise and fall of nations for example comes into this category.

9.14 '*Ajal*[52] of Nations (Outcome)

As noted previously, regarding the life and death of nations, the Quran has based this on the scaling of their constructive and destructive deeds – if the constructive deeds are greater than the destructive deeds, the nation survives and prospers; however, if the evil deeds exceed the good deeds, then destruction follows. Sometimes this destruction or fall is temporary and a period of respite is allowed so that the nation can learn a lesson and do more constructive deeds to tilt the balance in its favour. But when this nation has no ability left to tilt the balance in its favour, it is destroyed. This time of respite is called the nation's *Ajal* - this means that both the time of respite and the onset of the

---

[52] '*Ajal*' is based on the conduct of a nation or people and will vary as per the scaling of their deeds. (Ed)

time of destruction are termed *Ajal*. The nation can neither be destroyed before this, nor can it survive after this. The Quran states:

To every people is a term appointed (Ajal): when their term is reached, not an hour can they cause delay, nor (an hour) can they advance (it in anticipation). (10:49) See also (7:34)

It does not mean that it has been decided in advance as to how long a nation will live before getting destroyed. Every nation defines its own *Ajal* i.e. its own term of respite, through its conduct and there is a law for this as the Quran defines:

...For each period (Ajal) is a Book (Law). (13:38)

In the next verse it is stated:

Allah does blot out or confirm as per His law: with Him is the source of all Laws (Mother of the Book). (13:39)

According to this law, everything in the universe including nations go through changes. The nation which follows this Law becomes established and makes progress - the nation which goes against it, is eliminated. This law is not man-made and its source is the Will of Allah. In Surah *Al-Hijr* it is called the '*Kitab e maloom*', 'Known Book':

Never did We destroy a population that had not a term decreed and assigned. (15:4)

This means that it is not such a law which cannot be understood. Historians and sociologists through the study of the philosophy of history can acquire knowledge of this law. This law can inform us as to which nation will progress and which will lag behind (15:24). It is a result of this law of respite (*Ajal*), that a nation is not destroyed at the commission of its first crime, but is provided opportunity with which to rectify the damage done as a consequence of their wrong. But when the balance tilts towards the destructive deeds, then the decision is not delayed for a single moment (16:61, 23:43). As noted before, the life of nations is not counted in days, weeks or a few years, but in centuries. Regarding this period of scaling, the Quran calls it '*Ayuaam-Allah*'[53] (Allah's Days):

Yet they ask you to hasten on the Punishment! But Allah will not fail in His Promise. Verily a Day in the sight of your Sustainer is like a thousand years of your reckoning. (22:47)

When people see that a nation has adopted the path of tyranny and oppression for itself, despite which it continues to prosper, they question that if Allah's Law of Requital is true, then why is this nation not destroyed?

---

[53] The literal meaning is 'the days of Allah' – it is a period during which respite is provided to nations to mend their ways and return to the right path. If they fail to do so, then the point of no return arrives and an evil nation suffers serious consequences as discussed. (Ed)

The Quran states:

> *Do they then ask for Our Penalty to be hastened on? (26:204)*

But this is only due to the given period of respite, after which, when its balance is tilted more heavily towards its destructive deeds:

> *It will profit them not that they enjoyed (this life)! (26:207)*

Then their physical power and material resources will not be able to save them (26:208-209).

In Surah Ankabut, this reality is further explained:

> *They ask you to hasten on the Punishment (for them): had it not been for a term (of respite) appointed, the Punishment would certainly have come to them: and it will certainly reach them, of a sudden, while they perceive not! They ask you to hasten on the Punishment: but, of a surety, Hell will encompass those who deny Our signs! On the Day that the Punishment shall cover them from above and from below, and (a Voice) shall say: 'Taste you (the fruits) of your deeds!' (29:53-55)*

The hell resulting from the consequences of their crimes is encompassing the evil doers; it is just they cannot see it for the present, but this hell keeps them in its sight all the time:

> *And Hell-Fire shall be placed in full view for (all) to see. (79:36)*

This hell that they could not see, will then become physically visible for all to see.

9.15 *'Al-Sa'at*[54]*' –* Time of Revolution

When the stage for such a time of revolution comes to a nation, i.e. its *Ajal* ends and destruction appears in some form or other, the Quran calls this *Al-Sa'at* i.e. the time for revolution. We generally consider *Al-Sa'at* as the Day of Judgment and its translation is commonly this. But in the Quran this term is used for the time when the consequences of deeds are made manifest whether in this world or in the hereafter. Since, at present, we are only dealing with those consequences of deeds which manifest in the physical life, we will therefore consider this aspect of *Al-Sa'at*.

In *Surah Jathia* the Quran states:

> *To Allah belongs the dominion of the heavens and the earth, and the Day that the Hour of Judgment is established that Day will the dealers in Falsehood perish! And you will see every*

---

[54] This term is commonly taken as the Day of Judgement.

sect bowing the knee: Every nation will be called to its Record: 'This Day you will be recompensed for all that you did!' (45:27-28)

Later the term *Al-Sa'at* is used (45:32), and the Quran then states:

Then will appear to them the evil (fruits) of what they did, and they will be completely encircled by that which they used to mock at! (45:33)

When the messenger Moses was initially directed by Allah to go to Pharaoh, and say that he had transgressed all bounds, the thought came to Moses as to what would be the outcome of this confrontation with Pharaoh. He received the following reply from Allah:

Verily the Hour (Al-Sa'at) is coming - My design is to keep it hidden - for every self to receive its reward by the measure of its Endeavour. (20:15)

A similar explanation was given to the last messenger at the end of the Makkan period, when it was said:

...And the Hour (Al-Sa'at) is surely coming (when this will be manifested). So dissociate yourself from these people gracefully and peacefully. (15:85)

After this dissociate yourself calmly from them because *Al-Sa'at* (the revolution) is about to come. In this connection, when after their initial defeats the opponents plotted and gathered together all their tribal forces against the messenger in order to try and defeat the Muslims, the Quran states:

People ask you concerning the Hour (Al-Sa'at): Say, 'The knowledge thereof is with Allah (alone)': and what will make you understand? perchance the Hour is nigh! (33:63)

In *Surah Shura* it is stated:

It is Allah Who has sent down the Book in Truth, and the Balance (by which to weigh conduct). And what will make you realise that perhaps the Hour is close at hand? Only those wish to hasten it who believe not in it: those who believe hold it in awe, and know that it is the Truth. Behold, verily those that dispute concerning the Hour are far astray. (42:17-18)

Those who believe in Allah's Law of Requital know that this is a reality which will take place. But they also know that in the struggle of revolution, there are very painful struggles and fights. So they also remain apprehensive. At another place it is noted that if they were to wait they would not know how long to wait, but when it does come it will come unexpectedly and the opponents will be caught by surprise (6:31). A verse in *Surah Yusuf* appears to point to the process which is applicable in the fall of nations – first, short shocks appear so that they may learn a lesson; if they do not mend their ways then finally *Al-Sa'at* (a big revolution) reaches them which turns over the last page of the story of their lives:

Do they then feel secure from the coming against them of the covering veil of the wrath of Allah, or of the coming against them of the (final) Hour all of a sudden while they perceive not? (12:107)

9.16 'Seero fil Arz' – Travel Through the World

This is the end of such nations:

Do they not travel through the earth and see what was the end of those before them? They were more numerous than these and superior in strength and in the traces (they have left) in the land: Yet all that they accomplished was of no profit to them. For when their messengers[55] came to them with Clear Signs, they exulted in such knowledge (and skill) as they had; but that very (Wrath) at which they were wont to scoff hemmed them in. (40:82-83)

After this, the Quran declares that these are not random events[56]:

… (Such has been) Allah's Way of dealing with people (for all times). And even thus did the Rejecters of Allah perish (utterly)! (40:85)

This is Allah's immutable Law which has been working from the beginning. In another verse it is stated:

Do they not travel through the land, so that their hearts (and minds) may thus learn wisdom and their ears may thus learn to hear? Truly it is not their eyes that are blind, but their hearts which are in their breasts. (22:46)

They should perceive the end of those before them and understand it well, that this is not related to any particular time or place. In the world, at whatever time period, people who deny the Permanent Values, their end will be the same (47:10).

Through these verses, this reality becomes as clear as a mirror that the consequences of a nation's deeds show up in this life. In this connection there are many more verses but we do not think we need mention them here. So we should proceed forward.

---

[55] Since messenger-hood has ended after the last messenger, giving this warning is the responsibility of those people who claim themselves to be the custodians of the Quran. The other way of warning is through one's own deeds and their results. (Ed)

[56] Nothing in the world or for that matter in the universe happens by chance. Human limitation is that we look at events over a short time period and do not take a very long term view. When we do not find any cause for an event in the immediate past, we consider it to be a random event which is not based on any Law. The Quran invites us to study it in detail and ponder a few facts – Allah is everywhere so He is aware of what is happening in the universe; there is the Law of Requital working in the universe which takes account of everything and no injustice is done to anyone since the accountability process is very precise. (Ed)

(Intentionally left blank)

(Intentionally left blank)

10 Punishment *(Azaab)* – In Both This Life and the Hereafter

After mentioning the consequences of the worldly life, we should have gone on next to discuss the life of the hereafter, but there are such verses in the Quran in which the consequences of deeds in both this life and in the life of the hereafter are cited. In this connection, this much explanation is necessary, that the Quran gives great significance to this life (as noted before) and says we must take full advantage of the natural resources and material goods in this world. Along with this, the Quran states that when there is a conflict between a worldly benefit and a Permanent Value, and between them only one can remain, then at that juncture the Permanent Value must take precedence. This is called the benefit of the hereafter, in other words, sacrificing the immediate benefits in order to achieve future benefits instead. This life of the future (hereafter) will be discussed in the chapters to follow. At this point, keep in mind the Quranic meaning of the two terms (*Dunya* and *Akhirat* – this world and the hereafter) and note the relevant verses.

10.1 Desiring *'Dunya'* And *'Akhirat'* – Wishing for the Benefits of Both Lives

As noted earlier in this regard, according to the Quran the true purpose of human life should be to attain the successes and pleasantries of this life (by being in harmony with the Permanent Values), and the life of the hereafter should also be lofty and pleasant. To re-emphasise this point, in *Surah Al e Imran* the Quran says regarding those groups who rise up in support of truth:

> *And Allah gave them a reward in this world, and the excellent reward of the Hereafter. For Allah loves[57] those who do righteous deeds. (3:148)*

In *Surah Araaf* the following prayer is noted in relation to Moses:

> *And ordain for us that which is good, in this life and in the Hereafter: for we have turned unto You ... (7:156)*

In *Surah Ibrahim*, the Quran declares that these righteous people have concrete results in this life as well as the next:

> *Allah will establish in strength those who believe, with the word that stands firm, in this world and in the Hereafter... (14:27)*

---

[57] One should not confuse this term 'love' used here with the emotive expression of love in human life. 'Love' here means that all those benefits which are associated with the righteous deeds will be made available to those who follow the Quran. The Quran has used this term in various places and linked it to righteous deeds. (Ed)

In *Surah Namal*, the opponents question the *Momineen*, what will you get by following this Quran given to you by your Allah? In response Allah states:

To the righteous (when) it is said, 'What is it that your Sustainer has revealed?' they say, 'All that is good.' To those who do good, there is good in this world, and the Home of the Hereafter is even better, and excellent indeed is the Home of the righteous. (16:30)

A little later the Quran says about the *Muhajireen*[58] (emigrants), that they will not only have a goodly life in this world but the reward of the hereafter will be multiplied for them (16:41).

Allah has called the *Momineen*, friends[59], and characterised them as follows:

For them are glad tidings, in the life of the present and in the Hereafter; no change can there be in the words of Allah. This is indeed the supreme felicity. (10:64)

Their life will be as follows:

...therein you will have all that your self shall desire; therein you will have all that you ask for. (41:31) See also (22:15)

Since the messengers of Allah were leaders of the *Momineen*, therefore this life of theirs was highly successful. For example, regarding Abraham, the Quran says:

Him We chose and rendered pure in this world: And he will be in the Hereafter in the ranks of the Righteous. (2:130)

What was this highly successful life in this world? To explain this, the Quran declares:

...but We had already given the followers of Abraham the Book and Wisdom, and conferred upon them a great kingdom. (4:54) See also (16:122, 29:27)

So much so that the Quran denies what is quoted in the Bible regarding the life of the messenger Isa (Jesus) that he (God forbid) lived a life of helplessness and humiliation. His followers with great pride present a picture of him to the world in which he is depicted as living the life of a beggar and in the last moments of his life, Jewish and Roman soldiers treated him with extreme humiliation. The Quran categorically refutes this and states:

...his name will be Isa (Jesus), the son of Mary, held in honour in this world and the Hereafter and of (the company of) those nearest to Allah. (3:45)

---

[58] *Muhajireen* were the people who left Makkah and went to Medina. (Ed)
[59] The term used in the Quran is 'Auliya Allah' – meaning friends of Allah, as they carry out those responsibilities which Allah has taken on Himself as per the Quran e.g. see (4:75) (Ed)

To benefit for the necessities of this life is very important according to the Quran. To those who have a capitalist mentality, and in pursuit of the accumulation of wealth, do not even spend on their own selves, it says you have ruined your hereafter you unfortunate people, at least you should live comfortably in the present life:

But seek, with the (wealth) which Allah has bestowed on you[60] the Home of the Hereafter, nor forget your portion in this world: but do you good, as Allah has been good to you, and seek not (occasions for) mischief in the land... (29:77)

10.2 To Desire Benefits Only of This Life

Then there are those people whose only aim in life is desiring the pleasures of this life and in the pursuit of this aim they completely disregard the Permanent Values. About them the Quran says:

These are the people who buy the life of this world at the price of the Hereafter: their penalty shall not be lightened nor shall they be helped. (2:86) See also (4:74)

In other verses the Quran states that these people prefer this life over the next life and as a consequence all their efforts in this life are wasted:

Those who love the life of this world more than the Hereafter[61], who hinder (men) from the Path of Allah[62] and seek therein something crooked: they are astray by a long distance. (14:3) See also (16:107, 79:38, 87:16-17)

In *Surah Kaaf*, it states that all their endeavours in the pursuit of worldly benefits are wasted (18:103-104), see also (10:7, 2:103, 3:76).

In *Surah Hud*:
Those who desire the life of the present and its glitter, to them we shall pay (the price of) their deeds therein, without diminution. They are those for whom there is nothing in the Hereafter but the Fire: vain are the designs they frame therein, and of no effect will be the deeds that they do! (11:15-16) See also (52:20)

In *Surah Ahqaaf* it is noted that these people will say in the hereafter, why don't we get a share in these benefits? In reply they will be told, it is because the aim of all your endeavours was declared to be for the gain of worldly benefits only, and you got them.

---

[60] This is in relation to *Qaroon*, who is mentioned as a representative of the capitalist system. Note that the Quran relates his acquisition of wealth to Allah as noted previously. (Ed)

[61] As already noted, our present life is extremely important, since the consequences of our actions here have a bearing on our next life. The point here is that whatever we do in this life, we should always bear in mind what impact this will have on our next life. (Ed)

[62] Hindering from the path of Allah - the righteous path as defined in the Quran – this is the consequence of not believing in the Law of Requital. (Ed)

This way the reward of your efforts ended there, and now there is nothing left from this, so what can you be given? You got all of your share there. What do you want now?

And on the Day that the Unbelievers will be placed before the Fire[63] (consequences of their deeds), (It will be said to them): 'You received your good things in the life of the world, and you took your pleasure out of them: but today shall you be recompensed with a Penalty of humiliation: for that you were arrogant on earth without just cause, and that you (ever) transgressed.' (46:20) See also (53:29)

The doors of worldly benefits were open for both the *Momineen* and non-Muslims.[64] In the worldly life, both groups obtained the benefits in proportion to their endeavours. For the life of the hereafter, benefits are only available to those who in the worldly life keep in mind the benefits of the hereafter (7:32, 18:46).

You used to be told there, why do you ask for the short term benefits of this life only? From Allah both the worldly benefits and those of the hereafter can be obtained. Why do you not labour for both these benefits? You used to be informed very plainly that there are great attractions in the glitter and glamour of the present life, and whereas you should certainly make an effort for these, do not forget this truth, that the life of the hereafter is far more valuable and you should desire and work for this also:

Fair in the eyes of men is the love of things they covet: Women and sons; Heaped-up hoards of gold and silver; horses branded (for blood and excellence); and (wealth of) cattle and well-tilled land. Such are the possessions of this world's life; but in nearness to Allah is the best of the goals[65] (To return to). (3:14)

While pursuing the necessities of this life along with desiring the hereafter, this means that if ever there is a clash between a worldly advantage and a Permanent Value, you should give up the former by saying that its advantage means nothing compared to the life of the hereafter. At this time you should state as per the Quran:

---

[63] It is important that wherever in the Quran punishment is mentioned, this should be related to human deeds and their consequences. Our thoughts precede our deeds, and this is how our inner self forms according to our thinking. Finite thinking confined only to the benefits of this life will result in a 'finite self'. (Ed)

[64] These opportunities are proportional to the condition of a society in this life. For example, the present world state (in 2015) is based on a capitalist system in which there is gross inequality in the distribution of wealth; therefore those born in an underdeveloped part of the world may not be able to get out of the circle of poverty despite their best efforts. It is important to relate this point to the environment of the society in a particular part of the world. (Ed)

[65] See how in this verse the Quran relates the benefits of the hereafter to Allah – it asks us to think profoundly on the consequences of our deeds and their effects on our whole life (this life and the next life in the hereafter combined together). (Ed)

What is the life of this world but amusement and play? but verily the Home in the Hereafter, that is life indeed, if they but knew. (29:64)[66]

The comparison of these two modes of life is like rain which gives life to a dry land for a short period and then the land becomes dead again (10:24, 57:20). To illustrate this same comparison, it is said in the battle of '*Uhad*', that the material left behind by the retreating party held great attraction, when duty demanded that the place of responsibility in the battle should not be given up. The former was a worldly advantage while the latter was the benefit of the hereafter. So among you some were attracted by the material gains and did not do their duty, ignoring it and their responsibility, and left their position (3:151). Otherwise, in normal circumstances, not only is there permission to obtain worldly benefits, but to make an effort for these is the responsibility of the *Momineen*:

And when the congregation for 'salat' is finished, then you disperse through the land, and seek of the Bounty of Allah... (62:10)

10.3 '*Azaab*'- Punishment both in This Life and the Hereafter

Now we look at the third group, about whom the Quran states that they live a life of ignominy both in this world as well as the next life. A group among these people is one which never even pays any heed to subjugating and utilising the forces of nature. As a result they live a life of misery, poverty, deprivation, helplessness, slavery, bondage and subjugation. This group generally belongs to deeply religious people, who are deluded into believing that one should shun all material benefits in this life, as staying away from these is what those who are closer to Allah do[67]. They believe this life is for non-believers and the next life is the one for believers.

Another group among these people consists of those nations which after attaining ascendency, fall into a state of humiliation and as a result live a life of subjugation and slavery. Both these groups live a life of *Azaab* or hell in this life and if they do not try to change their state, their life in the hereafter will also be hell. In *Surah Taha* it is stated:

'But whosoever turns away from My Message, verily for him is a life narrowed down, and We shall raise him up blind on the Day of Judgment.' (20:124)

In another verse:

But those who were blind in this world, will be blind in the hereafter, and most astray from the Path. (17:72)

---

[66] See also verses (4:77, 6:32, 7:169, 9:38, 10:70, 13:26, 20:131, 28:60, 30:7 and 42:36).
[67] Or their version of God – every religion in the world has its own version of God; all these characteristics associated with their God are different from the concept of Allah explained in the Quran. For more detailed discussion on this aspect please refer to the book 'Man and God' by the same author. (Ed)

The hereafter is only adorned for him who made an effort to put things right in this world. The one who did not try to improve his current life, how can his life in the hereafter be pleasant and prosperous.

The way in which punishments come in this life needs detailed explanation. However, the Quran has put it in a nutshell in two words i.e. fear and hunger:

... so Allah made it taste of hunger and fear[68] like a garment (from every side), because of the (evil) which (its people) wrought. (16:112)

You can see how the Quran has summed up *Azaab* in this life by these two words. The punishment in the life of the hereafter will be explained in more detail at a later point. At this stage it is enough to note that those people who will be in a state of punishment in this life, in the hereafter their lives will also be in hell, and this is according to the Law of Requital. In *Surah Baqra* it states about the people who transgress:

...but what is the reward for those among you who behave like this but disgrace in this life... (2:85) See also (2:114, 5:41, 22:9, 39:26)

In *Surah Qalm*, after narrating the destructive consequences of an erroneous economic system, the Quran declares:

Such is the Punishment (in this life); but greater is the Punishment in the Hereafter, if only they knew! (68:33)

In *Surah Maida* it is stated that the opponents of the Islamic System will be punished in this life as well as in the hereafter:

The punishment of those who wage war against Allah and His Messenger, and strive with might and main for mischief through the land is: execution, or crucifixion, or the cutting off of hands and feet from opposite sides, or exile from the land: that is their disgrace in this world, and a heavy punishment is theirs in the Hereafter. (5:33) See also (24:19, 24:23)

In the clash between truth and evil, when the opponents of *Haqq* (Truth) are defeated by the *Momineen*, the Quran calls this '*Azaab e Dunya*' or punishment in this life. After this, these opponents will also receive word of the punishment in the hereafter. For example, in *Surah Tauba*, in connection with the orders given to fight the opponents of Islam, these opponents (the non-believers and hypocrites of the Arab society of the time) are warned that they should desist from fighting against the *Momineen* as this will be better for them, otherwise:

...If they repent, it will be best for them; but if they turn back (to their evil ways), Allah will punish them with a grievous penalty in this life and in the Hereafter: They shall have none on earth to protect and help them. (9:74)

---

[68] Note that this state of hunger and fear is brought about by the people themselves i.e. through their own policies. For example, we can see that the politicians of today across the world have created this state themselves. As mentioned previously, the Quran relates it to Allah, as it all happens according to the Law of Requital. (Ed)

Regarding them it is said that they will be punished twice and then they will return for the severest punishment (9:101). In *Surah Ra'ad* it is noted that their plans will be worthless and they will be punished in this life and the punishment of the next life will be far worse still (13:34). In *Surah Kahf* it states that *Zulqarnan*[69] told the opposing nation that if they did not stop doing wrong to others, then he will punish them and when they will go to Allah they will be a severe punishment (18:87). In *Surah Ahzaab* there is a warning to those who create difficulties for the messenger and the *Momineen;* they will have a deprived life here as well as in the hereafter:

> *Those who create difficulties for Allah and His Messenger - Allah has condemned them in this life and in the Hereafter, and has prepared for them a humiliating Punishment. (33:57)*
> *See also (39:26)*

When the Jews[70] residing in Madina broke their covenant, a decision was made to extradite them. In this regard, the Quran has stated that if this decision to extradite them had not been made, they would have been subject to punishment:

> *And had it not been that Allah had decreed banishment for them, He would certainly have punished them in this world[71]: And in the Hereafter they shall (certainly) have the Punishment of the Fire. (59:3)*

In another verse it is stated as a principle that those people who oppose truth and do not believe in the Law of Requital:

> *Such are they for whom there is a grievous Penalty; and in the Hereafter theirs will be the greatest loss. (27:5)*

In *Surah Sajda:*
> *And indeed We will make them taste of the Penalty of this (life) prior to the supreme Penalty, in order that they may (repent and) return. (32:21)*

This approaching punishment either means that before the final destruction they will suffer minor shocks, so that they can learn their lesson and mend their ways, or that the supreme punishment is the punishment of the hereafter.

There can be two aspects of this punishment: minor punishments prior to an ultimate one, to provide warning or as translated here, punishment in this life and then the final one in the next life. This is also called punishment piled upon punishment (16:88).

---

[69] *Zulqarnan* was some *Momin* ruler from the past, who chose to follow the Divine Guidance - the Quran has not provided any further details as it is not required – the important aspect is that he followed the Guidance. (Ed)

[70] The name of the tribe is quoted as *Bani Naseer.*

[71] It is obvious that the punishment in this life would have been humiliation through defeat in battle.

Regarding the people who get punishment of their deeds in this life as well as in the next life, the Quran states:

They are those whose works will bear no fruit in this world and in the Hereafter nor will they have anyone to help. (3:21)

Contrary to this, the people who follow the righteous path will have a worldly life of paradise here as well as in the hereafter – this reality is noted in the following two verses of *Surah Fatah*. In this Surah, the last confrontations with the opponents from within the *Quresh* are referred to:

That He may admit the men and women who believe, to Gardens beneath which rivers flow, to dwell therein for aye, and remove their ills from them; and that is, in the sight of Allah, the highest achievement. (48:5)

It is apparent that this life of paradise had started during this worldly life. Contrary to this, regarding the non–believers it is said:

And that He may punish the Hypocrites, men and women, and the Polytheists men and women, who imagine an evil opinion of Allah. On them is a round of Evil: the Wrath of Allah is on them: He has condemned them and got Hell ready for them: and evil is it for a destination. (48:6)

10.4 Protection and Punishment According to His Will

Before ending this chapter, attention needs to be drawn to a very important point. In some of the verses of the Quran it is stated: '*Yaghfiro lemanyanshah wa yuazzibo manyanshah*'[72] – these verses are usually translated as, 'Allah punishes whoever He wishes and forgives whoever He wishes'. This interpretation means that with regard to Him, reward and punishment, hell and forgiveness, for these there is no procedure set, no law, principle or standard established. All these are dependent on His Will. He will punish whoever He wishes, and set free whoever He wishes.

This aspect is related to the doctrine of destiny[73] which is not included in the current topic covered in this book. However, suffice it to say that this interpretation of the verses is totally against the teaching of the Quran, which revolves around the Law of Requital. Therefore the term '*manyanshah*' used in these verses can by no means have the implications that hell and forgiveness are solely dependent on Allah's Will. The correct meaning of such verses is that Allah has established Laws and Principles for hell and forgiveness (protection from destruction), so that whoever wishes he can disregard these and purchase destruction for himself, and whoever wishes to gain protection, can safeguard himself by following them. However, if anyone insists that in these verses

---

[72] For example see verses (48:15, 2:284, 3:128).
[73] This subject is discussed in detail in 'The Book of Destiny' by the author.

'*manyanshah*' relates to Allah's Will, then even in that case we can say that these verses have the meaning that hell and forgiveness are related to Allah's 'Law of His Will' i.e. what we sow, so shall we reap.

The Quran has also made this aspect clear in some of its verses, that the Law of His Will is another name for the Law of Requital. For example, in *Surah Maida*, the Jews and Christians claim they are the preferred children of Allah. Regarding this, ask them if you are such favourite children of Allah:

(Both) the Jews and the Christians say: 'We are sons of Allah, and his beloved.' Say: 'Why then does He punish you for your crimes?'... (5:18)

After this the Quran using the same expression states:

...Nay, you are but men, of the men he has created: He forgives and punishes as per His will (His Law) ('Yaghfiro lemanyanshah wa yuazzibo manyanshah'):...(5:18)

Now it is obvious that if the meaning of this verse is that he gives punishment where He 'pleases', then why does the first part of the verse say, '*yo azibokum bay zanubekum*' meaning 'He gives you punishment in return for your crimes.' Both the verses will be contradictory, therefore this meaning of the verse is incorrect (i.e. that He gives punishment where He pleases).

In this regard the verse in *Surah Nisa* is very decisive:

What can Allah gain by your punishment, if you are grateful and you believe? Nay, it is Allah that recognises (all good), and knows all things. (4:147)

To date all that has been written so far has made clear that:

1. The state of individuals or nations is dependent on the results of their own deeds. Until a nation changes its own state, Allah will not help it change its state (8:53,13:11).

2. The results of human deeds manifest both in this life and that of the hereafter. The life of paradise and hell starts from this life itself and accompanies us till after we die.

We have seen the manifestation of results in the worldly life. Now we move on to the life in the hereafter.

(Intentionally left blank)

11 *'Sawaab'* (Reward) and *'Najaat'* (Salvation)

We commonly use the term *Sawaab* as being the opposite of *Azaab*. The meaning of the former is reward for doing good, while the latter is punishment for sins.

The term *Sawaab* in Arabic is taken from the root *S-W-B* and its basic meaning is to 'get something back'. For example, *'Sab Al Ma'* means whatever quantity of water is removed, the exact amount is replaced. Similarly, *'Saab Jismohu'* means that after illness the body recovers fully to its original healthy state. That is, that whatever energy was depleted has been replenished.

Whatever action you take in life you have to spend something, even if money is not spent, your time and energy will be expended. If the task is done according to a procedure, then whatever you have spent, you will get it back. This is called your action's *Sawaab*. In business language this is known as a 'return' and according to the Law of Requital its meaning is the natural consequence of human action. This is why this word has been used in the Quran in places as a term for describing 'recompense for deeds':

> *Will not the Unbelievers have been paid back for what they did? (83:36)*
> *See also (3:152, 5:60, 2:103)*

We have seen that the results of human deeds manifest in this life as well as in the life to come. In this life, righteous conduct leads to a life which is good and prosperous, successful, lofty, wealthy, with enhanced choices, provides government and power. The deeds which affect the human self, their consequences will appear in the next life. In this regard, two terms have been quoted in the Quran – *'Sawaab Al dunya'* (recompense in this life) and *'Sawaab Al akhirat'* (recompense in the hereafter). This means that if we wish to see whether whatever we are doing is bearing good results (work of *Sawaab*) or not, then for this we need to see if the good result of these deeds is manifesting in this life or not. This concept of *Sawaab* is not just an abstract idea or belief but should materialise into concrete results for all to see including us. For example, in *Surah Al e Imran* it is stated:

> *...If any do desire a reward (Sawaab) in this life, We shall give it to him; and if any do desire a reward (Sawaab) in the Hereafter, We shall give it to him... (3:145)*

It does not mean that those who desire *Sawaab* in the hereafter will not get any *Sawaab* in the worldly life - those desiring (and working for) *Sawaab* in the hereafter will get it in this life as well:

If anyone desires a reward (Sawaab) in this life, in Allah's (gift) is the reward (Sawaab in both) of this life and of the hereafter: for Allah is He that hears and sees (all things)[74].
(3:134)

This means that those people who strive in this life according to the physical laws but do not care about the Permanent Values, will obtain the benefits of this life[75]; but will have no share in the hereafter. But those who work according to both the physical laws and the Permanent Values, they will get *Sawaab* in this life as well as in the hereafter– this is the conduct of the *Momineen*:

Wealth and sons are allurements of the life of this world: But the things that endure, good deeds, are best in the sight of your Sustainer, as rewards, and best as (the foundation for) hopes. (18:46) See also (19:76, 28:80)

This is why it is said that the *Sawaab* gained from Allah is the best (28:80). All types of *Sawaab* are indeed from Allah only, i.e. it is the results of our deeds according to the Divine Laws. But according to Quranic teaching, obtaining *Sawaab* from Allah means such a *Sawaab* which adorns a man's life in this world as well as in the hereafter. This is why it is said that Allah gives the best *Sawaab* and He is the best to conclude matters (18:44). This type of *Sawaab* is obtained through migration, endeavours and striving to establish a system based on the Permanent Values (3:194). This means that in the clash between evil and truth, even if this leads to war, one has to remain firm (3:146-147). As a consequence of this, in this world a heavenly society is established and in the hereafter a never ending paradise. In *Surah Kahf* it is stated:

For them will be Gardens of Eternity; beneath them rivers will flow; they will be adorned therein with bracelets of gold, and they will wear green garments of fine silk and heavy brocade: They will recline therein on raised thrones. How good the recompense! How beautiful a couch to recline on! (18:31)

From this explanation it is clear that whatever material benefits you get in this life (*Sawaab Al dunya*), you can share these with others. But regarding the effects on your self of the results of your righteous deeds (*Sawaab Al akhirat*), there is no question of transferring these to another. Therefore, the prevalent belief (or tradition) in some religions, that by reciting something or by celebrating saints' days, the resulting perceived *Sawaab*[76] can be sent to the dead - this concept is against the Quran. With whatever state of his self the deceased exits this life – no-one can alter this in any way whatsoever, either in this life or after death. Whatever the deceased achieves will be entirely the results of his own deeds. Those remaining behind can do nothing for him.

---

[74] Important point to note is that Allah knows what we do and that none will be dealt with unjustly. (Ed)
[75] It is important to note that this will depend on the level of development of the nation in which individuals are living e.g. one who is born into a very poor family will struggle to make both ends meet even if he works very hard as compared to someone who is born in a rich country where he will have more opportunities. (Ed)
[76] There is no inherent *'Sawaab'* in these practices in any case. (Ed)

So much so that even a good prayer for him is only a manifestation of our own good desires for him (which every *Momin* should have for every other *Momin*) As a result of this, those who pray gain a psychological *Sawaab* but this *Sawaab* does not reach the deceased. Though if we express our good wishes, then by this we can gain psychological strength. In the case of the deceased, there is no question of any gain from this. The reality is that the deceased have no link with this world – this will be dealt with later.

11.1 *'Najaat'* - Salvation[77]

Another belief along with *Sawaab* is *Najaat* - salvation. If we ask any follower of religions as to why he observes religious beliefs, endures so many hardships, tolerates so many constraints and why he makes his life so trying with all these difficult meditations, his answer will be the same as all the others, that the point of it all is to somehow obtain *Najaat* (salvation). Terms like *Najaat*, *'Muktee'* or *'Nirvan'* are all synonyms for salvation. The common thread running through this is the assumption that man is caught in some kind of trouble in this life, and to get out of this trouble is the aim of his life. This is the reason he makes religious efforts to achieve salvation. In this regard:

1. The Christian doctrine is that every child is born with a burden of sin from their first parents (Adam and Eve) and the purpose of his life is to somehow get rid of the consequence of this 'original' sin and achieve salvation. He has no recourse to do this other than to believe in Jesus Christ as a 'saviour'.

2. As per the Hindu doctrine, every human being is born as a punishment resulting from the consequences of sins committed in the previous life. To get *Muktee* from the burdens of these sins is the purpose of his life, and he can only get it through the hardships prescribed by the religion.

3. The doctrine of Buddhism (and with this Jainism), is that man comes into this life riveted tightly in the chains of life's desires and wishes. Until the time that he gives up these desires to such a level that even the passing thought of a desire does not arise in his mind, he cannot attain *Nirvan* (complete peace). Till that time he cannot achieve *Nirvan* which will be achieved through complete obliteration of his self. This is the purpose of religious hardships.

4. According to *Vedant* (Hindu philosophy or mysticism), the view is that the human soul, *Atma*, is part of the soul of God, *Parmatma*. This soul has become separated from God's soul and as a consequence is caught up in the material quagmire of life. Getting out of this quagmire and re-uniting with its origin is the purpose of its life and this is not possible without undergoing the hardships of religion. This same concept of *Vedant* has been borrowed by Mysticism. All

---

[77] This can also mean liberation of the soul in some religious contexts. (Ed)

their religious hardships are aimed at getting the human soul back to join with the soul of God which is called 'Wasil bil Haqq'.

This is the purpose of human life according to the world religions i.e. that once man comes to earth, whichever trouble he is caught in, he needs to try and achieve freedom from this. The 'Ahle Tareeqat' (followers of mysticism) in religious Islam, believe exactly the same. But 'Ahle Shariat' (followers of Islam as a religion), say that man's self is stained by whatever sins he commits in this life. Therefore he will have to suffer the punishment of hell. To get salvation from this punishment is the purpose of their religion.

The Quran has totally rejected this fundamental view of religion by declaring that every human child is born with a clean slate. He is endowed with some potentials from nature and if he makes an effort to develop these potentials in a proper way, then he turns his worldly life into prosperity and success and as a consequence after death he attains the ability to reach a higher level of life from the present level. The one who does not do this, his potentials remain buried and he fails to attain further evolutionary stages of life. For the development of these potentials, it is necessary that man subjugates the forces of nature and utilises these according to the Divine Values.

From this you saw that according to the Quran, the purpose of human life is to achieve some things in order to make the present life more balanced and successful and then take this to a higher level. It is not to be rid of some suffering or misfortune in which man is imprisoned from birth. This is the reason that the Quran has called human efforts and endeavours as achievements and not salvation. Further details are covered later.

(Intentionally left blank)

(Intentionally left blank)

12 The Concept of the Hereafter

As you have seen in the previous chapters, *Deen* is based on the working of the Law of Requital, and the natural consequence of believing in the working of the Law of Requital is to have conviction of life in the hereafter[78]. Regarding this, it is important we understand fully the meaning of the term *Akhirat*.

Akhirun is such a thing which is the last stage in a series and the stage that comes next is unlike the previous stages. Therefore, *Akhirat* will be the start of a new series after the end of the previous series, with a proviso that the latter will be different from the former. In this regard, the word *Akharun* (note the difference in spelling i.e. '*i*' replaced with '*a*') will be the term used for everything which is different from other things.

'*Takhur*' is the opposite of '*Taqaddum*'. *Taqaddum* means something which happens before, whereas *Takhur* will mean something which happens later. This is the reason in the Quran the word '*Mustaqdimeen*' is used in opposition to the word '*Mustakhireen*' regarding the people who have gone before and those who came later, e.g. future generations:

To Us are known those of you who hasten forward, and those who lag behind. (15:24)

Also in the Quran '*Akhira*' is used as the opposite of '*Ajila*' - the latter means immediate benefits or advantages and the former means long term or future benefits (17:18-19, 76:27).

In opposition to the word *Dunya* the Quran frequently quotes the term *Akhirat*.

From this it is evident that according to the Quran:

1. In the life of an individual, when compared with today, his tomorrow is his future i.e. *Akhirat*.

2. In the life of nations, the generations coming after the present generation are included in their *Akhirat*.

3. For mankind, the humanity to come will be *Akhirat*.

4. For all of the above, the life after death is their *Akhirat*.

---

[78] The way human thinking works, if we are not looking for something, it may be around us but we may never notice it. The working of the Law of Requital becomes very obvious to us if in the light of this we observe events taking place around us in the world and in our own life as well. Without the awareness of this Law, we will look at events and these will seem to us to be random i.e. sometimes we get the results and sometimes we may escape the consequences of our actions. (Ed)

This is the reason that when it is said regarding the *Momineen* that they believe in the hereafter, it is apparent that they are the people:

1) Who prefer long term benefits over short term gains.
2) Each individual among them is concerned for his future.
3) As a collective nation, they not only care for their own interests, but they are also concerned about the interests of their future generations.
4) They not only have their own interests in mind, they wish to safeguard the interests of all mankind.
5) In front of them are not only the benefits of this life, but they also believe in the life of the hereafter. This is why they have firm conviction in the Law of Requital i.e. that human deeds and their effects are not restricted to this life only, but these effects will continue beyond death as well.
6) When the Quran refers to 'life after deaths'[79], it not only means an individual life after death, it declares the fall of nations to be a death also. Similarly, regarding nations which rise after their decline, the Quran also calls this 'life after deaths'. The Quran also calls those people 'dead' who do not make use of their intellect and reasoning.
7) In the same context there are a few more terms and expressions quoted in the Quran e.g. *'Qyamat'*, *'Ba'ath'*, *'Hashr'*[80] etc, which are not exclusively connected to the life of the hereafter. They are also applicable to this life as well. These will be discussed later.

I will add here that in the Quran when the word *Akhirat* is used, it will not only refer to the life in the hereafter. We will have to deduce from the above as to which meaning applies within the context of the verses.

12.1 Belief (*Eimaan*) in the Hereafter

At the beginning of *Surah Baqra*, the following is noted to be a characteristic of the *Momineen*:

> *…and (in their hearts) have the assurance of the Hereafter. (2:4) See also (27:3, 31:5)*

(1) According to the Quran there are five essentials of belief (*Eimaan*) i.e. by accepting these five conditions one enters into the category of the *Momineen*: belief in Allah, the messengers of Allah, the books of revelation, the angels, and the hereafter (2:177). Refusal to accept any one of these beliefs results in exclusion from the category of *Momineen* (4:136).

---

[79] Wherever in the Quran there is a reference to life after death, we need to think and reason as to which one category is referred in the verse.

[80] *'Qyamat'*, *'Ba'ath'* and *'Hashr'* mean the Day of Judgment.

(2) In some places only two constituents of this belief are mentioned i.e. Allah and the hereafter e.g. (2:232, 3:113, 4:39, 4:59, 5:69, 9:99) In other places there is mention of Allah, the hereafter and the Book (4:162)

(3) In some places only denial of the hereafter is mentioned e.g. (6:114, 6:151) and then it is declared that those people belong to hell (7:45) and whatever they earn, will go wasted (7:147, 16:22, 16:60, 17:10, 34:8).

(4) It is also stated categorically that only those can benefit from the Quranic guidance who believe in the hereafter[81] (17:45). The one who does not believe in the hereafter can never get guidance[82] (23:74, 27:4).

(5) The belief in Allah and the hereafter is only manifested by practical application by following the Permanent Values and getting others to do the same (24:2).

(6) Through acquisition of knowledge and the use of intellect and reasoning[83] life in the hereafter can be understood (27:66, 2:219).

(7) *Iblees*[84] (Satan) can only misguide those who do not have belief in the hereafter (34:21).

(8) Those who do not believe in the hereafter are declared as *Mushrik*[85] (41:6-7, 53:27).

(9) The messengers can only be models of conduct and a light on the paths of those who have belief in the hereafter (60:6).

(10) Those who do not believe in the hereafter, friendships cannot be maintained with them (60:13).

---

[81] As mentioned previously, the hereafter and the accountability process are interlinked concepts – not accepting one will not bring about the change in one's self which the Quran asks us to develop. (Ed)

[82] The important point to note is that this conviction in the hereafter which is reached through the use of intellect and reasoning, will impact on human behaviour which will then impact on the human self. This internal change will then affect all our choices in life which will be within the domain of the Permanent Values. (Ed)

[83] The Quran puts repeated emphasis on the use of intellect and reasoning and invites our attention to the signs in the physical world and also directs us to think about our mind and its ability to think. The creation of our mind and its ability to make sense out of the universe around us, makes us the most important creation in this known universe. The Quran draws our attention to this fact and then directs us to use our free will to create our own 'self' within the Permanent Values in order to be able to move on to the next stage of life successfully. (Ed)

[84] *Iblees* is the term used for '*Satan*' which essentially are human base desires. (Ed)

[85] The term *Mushrik* is used in the Quran for those who mix relative values with the Permanent Values of the Quran – thereby believing that the Quran is not a 'complete' book. It also means to associate other deities with Allah i.e. accepting human beings as a law giving authority (when their laws are not in accordance with the Permanent Values) in parallel with the Laws of the Quran. The Quran calls it '*Shirk*' and declares that those who do this can never get the benefits which one gets by following the Permanent Values and as a consequence they will be in loss both in this life and in the life to come. (Ed)

(1) The one who does not believe in the hereafter, his good deeds are superficial and shallow only to impress people (2:264). This is because if one does not believe in the Law of Requital then what can be the motive for doing these deeds other than to earn fame and admiration in this life?

(2) A hypocrite says verbally that he accepts the hereafter, but in his heart he denies it (2:8).

(3) The one who believes in the hereafter, he will be willing to go so far as to lay down his life for a higher purpose of life - in fact he awaits such a moment where he can give his life to uphold a Permanent Value. The Jews could not do this (2:94).

(4) The one who has awareness of possible destruction in the future will adopt the right guidance (11:103, 74:53).

(5) Those who prefer to have immediate profits and rewards are those who choose to ignore the hereafter (75:20-21, 76:27).

(6) The reward in the hereafter is more profitable and multiplied (12:57).

(7) By following the Permanent Values there are benefits to be had in this life as well as in the hereafter – meaning that both this life and the next life belong to Allah (53:25). All that is in the future belongs to Allah (34:1). Those who refuse to acknowledge the Permanent Values, lose in this life as well as in the hereafter (79:25).

(8) Those groups of people who claim to pursue a heavenly revolutionary system based on the Permanent Values will have to face very trying hardships and circumstances in the initial stages of their programme, but they will ultimately succeed (93:6).

12.2 'Qiyamat' - The Day of Judgment

'Qiyamun' means to stand up – if we add the word 'ta' at the end then this becomes 'Qiyamatun', which means something which stands up suddenly.

The common belief about Qiyamat is that once this world ends, then a Day of Judgment will be established. As far as this world and the universe is concerned, no matter how long it lasts, it is going to end at some time in the future. The Quran gives an indication that this universe has been created for a stated term:

... and He has subjected the sun and the moon (to His Law): each one runs its course for a term appointed...(35:13) See also (31:29, 39:5)

In another verse it is stated:

We created not the heavens, the earth, and all between them, but for just ends (bil Haqq)
(15:85)

The Quran declares that the universe has been created '*bil Haqq*' which is translated as for truth or just ends. The term *bil Haqq* is a very comprehensive term. Its meaning is also that this universe did not come about by chance, that its creation is according to a scheme with a particular aim. That is, its creation is purposeful. Further to this, it also means that it is not an illusion or a mirage as per Plutonic philosophy – it is real and exists. According to the philosophy of *Vedant* it is not '*Maya*' (deception). It is also neither a dream of '*Ishvar*' nor '*laila*' (sport) being played by *Parmatma* (God). Its existence is real and its creation is an established reality, but it has been created for a stated term (46:3). It is not infinite like Allah and there was a time when it did not exist. Allah created it for a specific term, and after this it will come to an end.

There are many verses in the Quran which, if their words were interpreted literally (not metaphorically), a picture is painted where celestial bodies will collide with each other and disintegrate. The sun and moon will lose their light and lustre. Mountains will blow away like cotton wool and the earth will become dust. The seas will boil up and the atmosphere will change drastically. So much so, that the whole system of the universe will appear to be in chaos. It will be as if all this never even existed. But this does not have any relation to the Law of Requital. The Law of Requital is related to this: that man will exist after death whether this universe remains or disappears. Therefore *Qiyamat* is not related to the disappearance of the universe, it is related to human resurrection.

This resurrection of man is both in this life and in the hereafter. In this world, the tyrannical and oppressive powers suppress the poor and weak to such an extent that their resurrection or rising up cannot even be conceived, never mind take place. But gradually conditions change, till suddenly some revolutionary change occurs, when this same oppressed and enslaved humanity suddenly rises up for their rights. This is called *Qiyamat* in this world.

If this revolution comes through the hands of those who follow the Permanent Values, then its characteristics will be:
- Instead of tyranny and exploitation, the society will have justice and equality.
- Everyone will be rewarded exactly according to their effort and work.
- None will be exploited by another.
- Every matter will be decided according to the Divine Laws[86].
- Truth will prevail over evil.

---

[86] No human being will be the slave of another human being, and the rule will be according to the values of the Quran in which all are equal. There will be no difference between people at the 'top' and the ordinary human beings. (Ed)

That type of revolution which succeeded under the leadership of the last messenger and his companions and whose example is unparalleled in history. The Quran has called this 'Al Qiyamat' and its characteristics are discussed next.

At the time of the last messenger of Allah, *Deen* was non-existent in the world and everywhere had converted into religion. A result of this was that the followers of all religions claimed that they each had divine revelation in its real form. But their teachings differed from each other and as a consequence they had mutual differences since they did not have any external standard or criteria which could differentiate between truth and evil and remove their differences. This led to their mutual conflicts and wars. The Quran declared that through this revolution a criteria will be revealed which will make it clear as to which teaching is from Allah and which is fabricated by human hands. This way differences will disappear among mankind. As a result, when followers of different religions (Judaism, Christianity, Zoroastrians, etc) accepted Islam as revealed in the Quran, their differences disappeared. Wherever in the Quran it is stated that on '*Yaum Al Qiyama*' their differences will disappear, this is what is referred to[87]. In the Arabic tongue, and in the Quran, '*Yaum*' does not mean a day only, it also means any time period, e.g. a term, a period, era etc. In this regard, *Yaum Al Qiyama* means that revolutionary era which was established according to the Quran. In this era, the differences between the followers of these religions disappeared once they accepted Islam. If, in these verses, we say, *Yaum Al Qiyama* is after death, then what will be gained by removing these differences?

In *Surah Baqra* it is quoted that the Jews say about the Christians that they don't have the true *Deen* and the same is claimed by the Christians against the Jews. Both claim to have books from Allah (and these books are different from each other). Under the circumstances, there is no possibility of the disappearance of these differences. The Quran states:

The Jews say: 'The Christians have naught (to stand) upon'; and the Christians say: 'The Jews have naught (To stand) upon.' Yet they (Profess to) study the (same) Book. Like unto their word is what those say who know not; but Allah will judge between them in their quarrel on the Day of Judgment. (2:113)

During this revolutionary era, Allah will decide regarding their differences i.e. the Quran will tell them regarding the correct teaching of Allah. In *Surah Al e Imran*, it is noted regarding the end of the messenger Isa (Jesus), there is a strong difference between the Jews and the Christians. During the revolutionary era (*Al Qiyama*), the Christians will dominate the Jews, but after that the Quran states:

---

[87] In Arabic '*yaum*' not only means a day, it also means a period, an age or a duration. In this respect '*Yaum Al Qiyama*' will mean a period during which the system of the Quran was established.

...I will make those who follow thee superior to those who reject faith, to the Day of Judgment (Yaum Al Qiyama). Then you will all return to Me and I will judge between you of the matters wherein you dispute. (3:55)

If these people turn towards Allah, then there will be a resolution of their differences. In *Surah Nisa*, regarding the hypocrites it says that in the war between the opponents and the *Momineen*, the mark of these hypocrites is that they keep waiting to see who is going to win. Then when the *Momineen* are victorious, the hypocrites rush forward and declare, we were with you all along. The Quran declares:

(These are) the ones who wait and watch about you: if you do gain a victory from Allah, they say: 'Were we not with you?' but if the unbelievers gain a success, they say (to them): 'Did we not gain an advantage over you, and did we not guard you from the believers?' but Allah will judge betwixt you on the Day of Judgment (Al Qiyama)... (4:141)

The Quran states, wait a while and let this revolution be established, then the hypocrites will be exposed and all matters will be decided. At this point, this reality will also be established that:

...And never will Allah grant to the unbelievers a way (to triumph) over the believers. (4:141)

Between the followers of the various religions, and among the followers of a religion, umpteen differences had arisen. Regarding these differences, the Quran declares:

...it was after knowledge had been granted to them, that they fell into schisms. Verily Allah will judge between them as to the schisms amongst them, on the Day of Judgment. (10:93) See also (16:124, 32:25, 39:3, 45:17)

Regarding various nations, their state is also that they invade others and yet each one claims to be on the true path. At that time there was no external criteria to decide what was the true path. But now with *Yaum Al Qiyama*, these matters will be made clear:

...Nor take your oaths to practise deception between yourselves, lest one party should be more numerous than another: for Allah will test you by this; and on the Day of Judgment He will certainly make clear to you (the truth of) that wherein you disagree. (16:93)

The nation which brings revolution has been made judicator of all nations, and will stop in its tracks the nation which exceeds the declared limits. This way no nation will oppress or enslave another nation:

Thus, have We made of you an Ummat justly balanced, that you might be witnesses over the nations... (2:143)

As previously noted, the Quran has stated that differences between the followers of different religions will be decided in *Yaum Al Qiyama*. In *Surah Hajj*, the Quran makes this point with particular reference to Jews, Christians, Sabians and Magians and polytheists:

Those who believe (in the Quran), those who follow the Jewish (scriptures), and the Sabians, Christians, Magians, and Polytheists, Allah will judge between them on the Day of Judgment... (22:17)

So much so that during this period this matter will also be decided as to whom man should have friendship with. The Quran has laid down fundamental criteria as to who should be considered to be friends and who should not. And that criteria is that those people who share the same *Eimaan* (ideology), they are of us, whether you have any other mutual relationship with them or not. And if there is no common ideology of *Eimaan*, then regardless of whether they are parents, brothers and sisters, or even husbands and wives, they are strangers. This revolution defined and established the boundary between man and man. Regarding this matter, the Quran gives detailed guidance and then states:

Of no profit to you will be your relatives and your children on the Day of Judgment (Al Qiyama): He will judge between you: for Allah sees well all that you do. (60:3)

Now in this period when the criteria for friendship has changed, it is of no benefit to be the father or son of someone. According to Allah's law, there will be a distance and differentiation between the two. This makes it clear that reference to *Yaum Al Qiyama* means that revolutionary period which was established according to the Quran.

In *Surah Baqra* in one place it is stated that in the eyes of the people who deny the Divine Laws, attraction for the material benefits of worldly life becomes many times multiplied and they resort to ridiculing the *Momineen*:

The life of this world is alluring to those who reject faith, and they scoff at those who believe. But the righteous will be above them on the Day of Judgement (Al Qiyama); for Allah bestows His abundance without measure as per His Law. (2:212)

People who observe the Divine Laws will be superior on *Yaum Al Qiyama*. Allah according to His Law bestows far more sustenance than human scales could anticipate. Undoubtedly after death however, the righteous will be loftier in the hereafter than those who deny the Divine Laws. But it appears in the above verse, that this superiority is related to this life. Therefore, this *Yaum Al Qiyama* refers to that period in which this revolution was about to happen. There are other verses in the Quran where it appears that *Yaum Al Qiyama* means that revolution when one group rises up all of a sudden to topple an unjust system. In *Surah Tatfeef*, this revolution is called '*Yaum e Azeem*'[88] and is explained as:

---

[88] Translated as 'a great day' – this can be a period during which major changes will take place in the world. (Ed)

The *Day when (all) mankind will stand for the Sustainer of the Worlds. (83:6)*

This is that day or period when mankind will rise up to establish Allah's universal system of sustenance.

Now we will come to those verses from which it is apparent that *Yaum Al Qiyama* refers to resurrection after death. In *Surah Baqra* there is reference to those people who believe in one part of the Quran and reject another part:

…Then is it only a part of the Book that you believe in, and do you reject the rest? but what is the reward for those among you who behave like this but disgrace in this life? And on the Day of Judgment (Al Qyiama) they shall be consigned to the most grievous penalty… (2:85)

Here the word '*Qiyama*' is used in contrast to *Hayat ul Dunya*, or *Dunya* (life of this world), see verses (7:32, 11:60, 11:98-99, 22:9, 28:61). In some verses *Qiyama* has been used without any specific reference but it is understood from the context to refer to the hereafter.

For example:

1) On the Day of *Qiyama* Allah will not speak to them, and neither will they get sustenance – for them is a severe penalty[89] (2:174, 3:76).

2) On the Day of Judgment, those who are dishonest, will have their dishonesty exposed and everyone will get full recompense for their deeds and none will be treated unjustly[90] (3:161).

3) The prayers of *Momineen* are – do not humiliate us on the Day of Judgment (3:193).

4) On the Day of Judgment, the messenger Isa (Jesus) will give evidence against his people that they invented beliefs which he did not give them (4:159).

5) It will not be possible to avoid the penalty on the Day of Judgment by giving wealth and riches in exchange (5:36).

6) Allah will gather you all up together on the Day of Judgment (details will be provided under *Hashr* in the next section) (6:12, 45:26).

---

[89] This is as a result of the consequences of their deeds – readers should keep this context in mind. (Ed)
[90] This can be the state of a society in this life if the system is established within the domain of the Permanent Values – this meaning can also be attributed to such verses.

7) The people who invent lies and then attribute these to Allah – what do they think regarding the Day of Judgment? (10:60). Here the Day of Judgment means the Law of Requital.

8) The people who misguide others will on the Day of Judgment carry not only the burden of their own crimes, but also the burdens of those whom they misguided (16:25, 29:13).

9) In *Surah Nehl*, after discussing the destruction of previous nations, it is said that on the Day of Judgment they will be humiliated and disgraced (16:26-27).

10) At this time, every individual is carrying the record of his deeds like a scroll wrapped up and hanging round his neck. On the Day of Judgment this will be opened up and shown to him (17:13-14). This could mean these results may manifest here in this life or later in the hereafter.

11) Those people whose deeds are wasted, for them on the Day of Judgment the scales of balance will not be raised (18:105). This can also mean the time when the deeds manifest themselves, wherever that is – in this life or in the hereafter.

12) In *Surah Mariam* it is noted:

And everyone of them will come to Him singly on the Day of Judgment. (19:95)

This verse points to a great reality and will be dealt with in more detail later. At this point it is enough to say that it can mean that on the Day of Judgment man will be alone, and none of his earthly relations i.e. his wife, children relatives, friends, even those who could give him security – none of them will be with him. He will be alone in the Divine court. It will also mean that those things which man called 'mine', will all remain in this world, and be left behind, e.g. my wealth, children, body, even life, and only the human personality or self, will go forward. The next life only deals with the human self – known as 'I', and not with 'mine'. 'Mine' includes all additional things. The personal thing which a human has, is only the 'I' and this is what is going to proceed to the next life.

13) On the Day of Judgment, criminals will be present with the burdens of their crimes (20:100-101) and to weigh their crimes the balances of justice will be raised up and none will be treated unjustly. Every iota of a human deed will manifest itself (21:47).

14) Though social crimes can be punished in this life according to the prevalent system of justice in a nation state, this however cannot avert the punishment of the hereafter to come for these crimes. This is because the commission of deeds which are against the law has effects on the human self which cannot be removed by worldly punishment. They will be faced with the outcome of this

on the Day of Judgment and that punishment will be far greater than the punishment in this life (25:69)

15) On the Day of Judgment man's friends will become his enemies (29:25).

16) The loss is theirs, who when the deeds manifest themselves on the Day of Judgment, will see what great damage they did both to themselves and to others that they dealt with. There can be no greater loss than this (39:15, 42:45).

17) Protection from the destructive consequences of wrong deeds can be availed through following the Divine Laws. Those people who try to seek protection by means other than this, their efforts will not be successful (39:24).

18) The humiliation of the Day of Judgment will 'darken' their faces (39:60).

19) Those who are in peace on the Day of Judgment – nothing can compare to this state (41:40).

20) On the Day of Judgment all of man's secrets will be exposed (58:7).

21) In *Surah Al-Qiyama*, the Day of Judgment is referred to as an evidence and in reply to the question as to when the Day of Judgment will come, the details given in the Quran may refer to some physical changes taking place in the universe. These references can also be with regard to the revolution which occurred after the emergence of Islam in Arabia and Persia. And could also be a reference to the Day of Judgment after death (75:1-15).

22) In *Surah Zumr* it is stated:

...On the Day of Judgment the whole of the earth will be but His handful, and the heavens will be rolled up in His right hand... (39:67)

If we take the literal meaning of this verse, then this could be a reference to some great change in the physical universe. However, if we take the metaphorical meaning, it will mean that in this heavenly revolution which will take place through the hands of *Momineen* – that politics of the world and religion will disappear and (earthly) affairs related to human economic life and Heavenly Values will become one, and be under the control of one centre.

23) In *Surah Bani-Israel* it is stated:

There is not a population but We shall destroy it before the Day of Judgment (Yaum Al Qiyama) or punish it with a dreadful Penalty: that is written in the Book of Laws. (17:58)

The common view of this verse as noted before, is that before the Day of Judgment the universe will come to an end. However, another view is that it means that it is Allah's immutable Law, that whichever nation adopts a wrong system, it is either destroyed completely or suffers such a decline that it cannot rise up again. In this verse, *Yaum Al Qiyama* means that revolution which has been referred to previously. It is also possible that the revolution referred to here is the one which took place through the *Momineen* in Arabia at the time of the last messenger in which the opposing nations were either destroyed or made ineffective, and subsequently replaced by the Islamic System[91].

We often use the phrase 'you cannot win till even the Day of Judgment' meaning it is either impossible to win or not likely for a long time. In the Quran this term *Qiyamat* has also been used in this context. For example, in *Surah Al e Imran* Allah has addressed the messenger Isa (Jesus):

> *...I will make those who follow you superior to those who reject faith, to the Day of Judgment... (3:54)*

Historically, Christian superiority and control over the Jews is an established fact; however, it cannot be said that this superiority will remain forever – so here the reference to the Day of Judgment could simply mean a very long time. In *Surah Maida* it is said about the various sects of Christianity that their mutual rivalry will continue till the Day of Judgment (5:14). The same is said about the Jews as well (5:64)[92].

In *Surah Qasas*, it is stated that if Allah turns day into night and keeps everything dark till the Day of Judgment, then who can remove this darkness and bring out the sunshine (28:71)? It is clear that the Day of Judgment here means forever. In *Surah Ahqaf* the Quran states that people who ask for help from false deities (the dead), they will not answer them till the Day of Judgment (46:51). In *Surah Qalm* it says regarding the evil doers – have these people got a written decree from Us that all their decisions will be accepted (68:39)? Here it also means forever.

In some verses the Quran has used '*Yaum Al Bath*' in place of '*Yaum Al Qiyama*'. This will be discussed later.

12.3 '*Hashr*' - Assembling People

This is also a comprehensive term of the Quran like *Akhirat, Sa'at, Qiyamat* and *Ba'ath*. Its basic meaning is to assemble people and lead them in some direction. In this context, this term is also applicable to armies in a battle or prisoners of war. '*Mahshr*' is the place where such an assembly takes place. *In Surah Naml* the army of Solomon is mentioned:

---

[91] This may also refer to some future changes in the world order as human beings may go on for many more millenniums. (Ed)

[92] It is not possible to remove this mutual rivalry as it is the consequence of not following the Permanent Values – relative values can change and thus lead to conflicts and the creation of divisions or parties. So this mutual rivalry will continue in every part of the world till mankind comes to accept the Permanent Values as an external standard of guidance. (Ed)

And before Solomon were marshalled his hosts....... (27:17)

During the first clash between Muslims and Jews, as a consequence of which the latter were forced to leave *Madina*, the Quran called this the first *Hashr* (59:2). In *Surah Al e Imran,* in relation to the battle of *Badr* it is declared:

Say to those who reject truth: Soon will you be vanquished and gathered together to Hell, an evil bed indeed (to lie on)! (3:11)

After this, the meeting in the battlefield between the two armies, that of the *Momineen* and their opponents, is mentioned. The word *Hashr* is used in reference to the opponents who were taken as prisoners of war and gathered together to be taken away after their defeat[93]. In the Quran this term is also used for the appearance of results in the hereafter as well. Two fundamental points need to be explained and understood here:

1. As has been discussed previously (Chapter 5) 'going to Allah' does not mean that He lives at some place and that after death man will go to that place to meet Him. Allah is free from the constraints of time and space and therefore the question of going to him does not arise. This actually means that the results of our deeds will show up as per the Law of Requital whether in this life or in the hereafter.

2. In order to help us understand, the Quran sometimes presents a court scene e.g. there is a court where a defendant, claimant, police, witnesses etc are present. The case and evidence is presented. The record is brought forward. The list of charges is read out and the defendant is given a chance to defend himself. Then a decision is reached by the court and the criminal is led towards hell. All this is to make us understand the working of the Law of Requital by relating it to the way decisions are made in a court of law in this life. It does not mean that after death, one day all human beings from the beginning to the end of time will be assembled and their verdict for reward and punishment will be announced. Wherever in the Quran the assembling of people is mentioned in front of Allah, it means the manifestation of the results of our deeds as per the Law of Requital.

Therefore this term *Hashr* refers either to the clash between evil and truth in this life or to the manifestation of results in the hereafter. It will become clear from the verses quoted in the next section.

---

[93] This also points to the fact that in this life the subjugation of a nation by a more powerful nation is a life of humiliation and enslavement.

12.4 The Day of Assembly

1) Allah will assemble them on this day about which there is no doubt and everyone will be recompensed for their deeds and none will be dealt with unjustly (3:24, 3:8, 6:22, 6:51, 10:28, 15;25, 34:40, 36:32).

2) This is called *Yaum Al-Qiyama* (6:12, 17:97) and also *Akhirat* (11:103) and '*Yaum Mashhood*' (11:103).

3) In *Surah Dukhan* it is called '*Yaum Al-Fasal*' i.e. the day of decision (44:40, 77:38) and in *Surah Taghabun* it is named '*Yaum Al-Taghabun*' (64:9) i.e. the day when by comparison everyone will find out how much is lacking or deficient from their self.

4) Whether you are murdered or die a normal death – you will all be gathered together towards Allah (3:157).

5) The day they will be assembled, they will feel as if they were only on earth for but an hour[94] and they will recognise each other (10:45).

6) In *Surah Ibrahim* it is stated that they will all be marshalled together before Allah (14:21). This will happen on the day when the earth and the heavens will change (14:48).

7) All these criminals (and their evil companions) will be gathered together and will be brought to hell on their knees (19:68). The colour of their eyes will change due to the terror of that day (20:102, 41:19). They and their false deities will be brought together (25:17). All people with the same beliefs will be grouped together (37:22, 46:6, 25:34).

8) From every nation a group which used to reject the signs of Allah will be gathered and they will be divided into different ranks (27:83).

9) The *Momineen* will be together as respected guests of Allah while criminals will be directed towards hell (19:85-86).

10) This type of assembling is not at all difficult for Allah (50:44).

11) In some places *Hashr* also means to 'just rise' e.g. in *Sura Taha* a man who goes against the Divine laws will have his sustenance restricted and will be raised up blind on the Day of Judgment (20:124-125).

12) In Surah *Mominoon* only this much is stated:

---

[94] This aspect will be discussed later.

And He has multiplied you through the earth, and to Him shall you be gathered back
(23:79) See also (67:23)

13) In *Surah Kahf* in relation to the wall erected by *Zulqarnain* to try and stop the attacks from Gog Magog, it is stated that there will be a time when this wall will fall and then these nations will attack each other wave upon wave. Then the Quran states that we will gather them together in one place (18:99). It appears that this gathering will happen in this life, when the armies of various nations will confront each other in a great war. After this, hell will be unveiled. This hell appears to be a metaphorical explanation for the ensuing large scale destruction in the world.

To conclude, *Hashr* means both the mutual clash of nations or parties in this life and after death it refers to the visible results under the Law of Requital.

12.5 *'Ba'ath'* – Removing Obstacles

This term is also part of the same series of terms noted previously. The basic meaning of *'Ba'athun'* is to remove something which prevents the free movement of something and thus facilitate its movement. In the Quran this is used in various contexts:

(1) When a party of *Haqq* (Truth) rises up in a society to bring revolution based on the Permanent Values, the opposing parties become a stumbling block in their path and thus try to stop the revolution. This term is used to describe removing these opposing parties and paving the path of revolution:

Do they not think that they will be called to account? On a Mighty Day, A Day when (all) mankind will stand before the Sustainer of the Worlds? (83:4-6)

These nations representing the capitalist system are obstructing the Quranic System of sustenance in the world. What, does it not occur to them that Our Law of Requital is so powerful and overwhelming that it will remove them from the path like a piece of straw. This will happen at that time when mankind rises to establish a universal system of sustenance (83:6).

(2) This term[95] is also used regarding nations which rise up and resurrect themselves and gain a new life – nations which are stagnant for some time and rise up again after removing their impediments and obstacles. In *Surah Baqra*, regarding *Bani Israel* (in Babylon), the Quran says that after

---

[95] This term is also used when someone is made responsible and sent on some mission e.g. a messenger of Allah.

remaining 'dead' for a hundred years they were resurrected and given a fresh life (2:259). This term is also used for giving someone responsibilities and then sending them off e.g. the messenger of Allah.

(3) Death is a stumbling block in the movement and action of man. By removing it this individual is given life again[96]. How one gets this new life, will be discussed later at its proper place. At this moment all I want to explain is that for this also the term *Ba'ath* is used. *Yaum Al Qiyama* is also called '*Yaum Al-Ba'ath*' or '*Yaum Yabathun*'. This is referred to in many places in the Quran and at every place it can be understood in the context in which it is used. Some examples are:

- In *Surah Inam* it is stated that Allah will definitely give life to the dead (6:36).

- *Kaffar* (people who do not believe in the Law of Requital) claim that there is no possibility of any resurrection after death (11:7). They swear over and over again that the one who has died can never be resurrected. Allah says this is wrong, He has promised that it is a reality and His promises are true. The promise of Allah is called Divine Law (16:38). So this will of a surety take place. They are told logically how it is possible (22:5). Allah will certainly give life to those who are in their graves (22:7). Their objection was that once our bodies decompose and are dust, how can we get a new life (17:98, 23:37). What! will we rise up as a new creation? In reply the Quran says that your creation and resurrection is like one individual creation and recreation (31:28).

- This process of getting another life is called *Yaum Al-Ba'ath* (30:56). It is also called *Yaum Al-Deen* i.e. the time for the manifestation of the results of human deeds (38:78-79, 15:36-38), and *Yaum Al-Qiyama* (17:62, 23:15) and '*Yaum Al-Kharoof*' (50:42). In other words the day when they will all rise and will be told about their deeds in this life (58:6, 58:18).

- No one has any knowledge as to when they will be raised (27:65). Neither do the dead have any connection with this life as there is a 'screen' behind them once they die and leave this life (23:100).

- The messenger Isa (Jesus) said that I have protection from the day I was born and the day I will die and the day I will be resurrected and get a new life (19:33). The messenger Ibrahim prayed that when I get a new life, I don't wish to be humiliated (26:87).

- In the Quran there is an event discussed in detail about the people of the cave. These were believers who in the initial days of their struggle when they saw

---

[96] How this new life is achieved – this aspect will be discussed later.

that they could not fight against the oppressive powers, escaped to a cave to hide and prepare themselves by building up their strength. When they saw that the conditions outside had become favourable, they emerged– the Quran has called this as a 'resurrection' as well (18:19). The word is also used in connection with awakening in the morning after sleeping during the night (6:60).

12.6 'Nofikha Soor' – Blowing the Trumpet or Getting New Life

This term has been referred to in the Quran in the context of the hereafter. The word 'Soor' has two meanings:

1. In olden times a bugle was blown to announce the commencement of battle and this was called *Soor*. When this term is used in relation to events in this world, then this means the start of conflict between the forces of 'Truth' and 'Evil'.

2. The word '*Soorat*' means a figure or the outline of a thing – its plural is '*Sooran*'. This means human figures or bodies. *Nofikha* means to blow and *Nofikha Soor* means to blow fresh life into human beings. Metaphorically, when applied to enslaved and deprived nations, this means giving them fresh life. When the dead are given life, this is termed as *Nofikha Soor*. By reading the verses in the Quran in which *Nofikha Soor* is mentioned, by reflection and reasoning one can understand the context. For example, in the case of Gog Magog as mentioned previously, this term *Nofikha Soor* is used (18:99). This will be the bugle blown at the start of a world war among the nations.

Further examples are as follows:

In *Surah Inam* it is stated:

> ...*His word is the truth. His will be the dominion the day the trumpet will be blown*...
> (6:74)

Control will revert to His authority i.e. decisions will be according to His laws.

In *Surah Taha*:

The Day when the Trumpet will be sounded: that Day, We shall gather the sinful, blear-eyed (with terror) (20:102)

- In *Surah Momin* it is noted that when the trumpet will be blown all relationships will come to an end and no one will care about each other anymore (23:101).

- In another verse it is stated that when the first trumpet will be blown then everyone in the universe will lose their senses due to fear (27:87) – then the second one will be blown and everyone will rise up and will be looking around (39:68).

- After the blowing of the trumpet, the dead will rise quickly and go towards Allah (36:51) as if there is someone with them (like a policeman) and there will be a witness or guardian with them – this is also called '*Yaum Al-Waeed*'[97] (50:20-21).

- At one place *Nofikha Soor* is mentioned and together with this a great upheaval in the heavens and the earth (mountains) is mentioned. This is called '*Al-Waqiah*' (69:13-17, 78:18-21).

- In *Surah Mudatthar* instead of *Soor* the word '*Naqoor*' is used with the same meaning (74:8).

In the Quran when the destruction of former nations is referred to, often this is preceded with a big 'shriek' or deafening 'blast' and then the nation lies in ruins. In the case of nations which were destroyed by physical events, e.g. an earthquake or volcanic eruption, this loud noise or blast could be related to the physical event, otherwise this can mean some sign, prior to the destruction, which indicates an imminent disaster.

In *Surah Yaseen* it is stated:

It was no more than a single mighty Blast, and behold! they were (like ashes) quenched and silent. (36:29) See also (36:49, 38:15).

The same thing is noted in the case of the nation of Samud (54:31). In another verse with *Nofikha Soor* there is the mention of one big blast and it is also stated that this will be a single one:

It will be no more than a single Blast, when lo! they will all be brought up before Us. (36:53) See also (50:42, 37:19, 79:13-14).

---

[97] This will be the Day of announcement of results or the Day of Judgment. (Ed)

(Intentionally left blank)

(Intentionally left blank)

13 *'Hayat e Nau'* - New Life

Now we come to the most important and delicate subject concerning the new life. In this regard it is important to bear in mind two fundamental points. The Quran declares:

1. Those people are also considered as being dead who are physically alive and are walking about like others, but their human potentials are defunct. They can get 'new' life from the Quran by using their intellect and reasoning.

2. Those nations are also declared as dead, which have declined and are lying dormant and in ruin. If among these nations there is any potential left to rise again, then they can do so by studying and living according to the Permanent Values of the Quran – this 'new' life is defined as life after their 'death'.

3. After the physical death of all human beings, their subsequent life in the hereafter is also called life after death. This is the most important part of this subject and merits special attention. However, the other two parts of this subject (1 and 2) are no less important.

13.1 Comparing With Agriculture (or Farming)

The Quran has explained the 'new' life by using the example of farm land. In reality this is a very comprehensive and pertinent metaphor which is used to compare with human life. Look at a landscape which is dry and barren, with no vestige of vegetation, freshness or bloom. This is called a 'dead' land. But with a single splash of rain, this land seems to awaken as if by rubbing its eyes, and in front of your very eyes the dead land becomes a scene of renewed life and freshness.[98] Similarly, look at a seed of wheat which appears to be dry and shows no signs of life or possibility of revival. When this seed is mixed in with the soil - that soil which appeared to have no sign of life - then following natural physical laws, from this seed fresh life as a seedling emerges and this one seed is turned into hundreds of seeds. If someone has not seen a seedling emerging from a seed or seen barren land turn into a lush field he will never accept that this can be possible.

But this fresh life will only be possible from a land which has the potential to support life and a seedling will only emerge from a seed which has the potential within it to grow. What do we mean by this 'potential to grow'? This, that there is the potential for growth in this seed but in a dormant form. It awakens and starts to grow i.e. it was initially hidden and then it became apparent. It did not come from outside but was present within – however, it was hidden from our eyes. We can say it was potent and

---

[98] Rain as a stimulus to revive a dead land – the same is true in the case of human beings. We need inner motivation and purpose to do something. The Quran helps us to provide this motive by drawing our attention to our inner thinking abilities and to the outer world and then provides incentive of another life to come based on our conduct and deeds in this life. (Ed)

then it actualised. If this seed has no potential to come to life and loses this ability, then no seedling will emerge from it. The Quran has used this simile in many verses:

...thus shall We bring life out of the dead... (7:57) See also (22:63, 2548, 30:24, 45:5)

In other words whatever life is present within it, We bring it out. This also means if there is no potential for life in it, then what can be brought out?

In *Surah Nehl* it states that when Allah sends down rain from clouds, then:

And Allah sends down rain from the skies, and gives therewith life to the earth after its death: verily in this is a Sign for those who listen. (16:65)

In *Surah Taha* after referring to the natural phenomenon of rain, the Quran states:

Verily, in this are Signs for men endued with understanding. (20:54)
See also (26:7-8), 36:33)

In *Surah Hajj*, it is stated that if you doubt the possibility of giving life to the dead, then reflect on the various stages of human creation - starting from inert clay, how this culminates in a human being with a physical self and a mind. Or observe the vegetation and bloom of life emerging from the land. Similarly, the dead can be given life (22:61). In *Surah Ankabut* it is noted that if you ask them, who gives new life to a dead land after producing rain from the clouds, they say only Allah does such a thing; but they do not use their thinking or reason beyond this:

And if indeed you ask them who it is that sends down rain from the sky, and gives life therewith to the earth after its death, they will certainly reply, '(Allah)!' Say, 'Praise[99] be to Allah.' But most of them understand not. (29:63)

In *Surah Rum* the same example of the hydrological cycle is used:

Then contemplate (O man!) the signs of Allah's Mercy[100] !- how He gives life to the earth after its death: verily the same will give life to the men who are dead: for He has scales[101] fixed for all things. (30:50) See also (41:39)

---

[99] In many places the word '*Hamd*' has been translated as praise, which does not do justice to this term. It is related to the acceptance of Allah's attributes after reflecting on the creation around us and within us – this should lead to the appreciation of the purpose of the universe and human life. (Ed)

[100] The word '*Rehmat*' which is translated as mercy deals with aspects of sustenance in life in this world. (Ed)

[101] This scaling is important to understand – everything in the universe works within the remit of the Divine Laws, and scales define the causes and effects. It is up to us to make efforts and discover these scales. (Ed)

In *Surah Qaf*, after a similar example, the Quran states:

*...and We give (new) life therewith to a land that is dead: Thus will be the Resurrection.
(50:11)*

This is the way dead men will rise again - their ability to live reveals itself.
In *Surah Fatir*, after the example of a dead land which receives new life, it is stated:

*It is Allah Who sends forth the Winds, so that they raise up the Clouds, and We drive them
to a land that is dead, and revive the earth therewith after its death: even so (will be) the
Resurrection! (Al-Nishoor) (35:9)*

The word *Nashoor*'s meaning includes the inherent ability to generate new life. The
basic meaning of this word is to open up and branch off into countless directions. Its
application is in the spring season when fresh leaves appear on trees. '*An-nashru*' is also
used to refer to the dry grass at the end of this summer season which revives after
rainfall. In *Surah Zakhrof* it is mentioned:

*That sends down (from time to time) rain from the sky in due measure; and We raise to life
therewith a land that is dead; even so will you be raised. (43:11)*

In this way, the autumn of your branches can also receive new spring and fresh life and
can blossom. We have said before that according to the Quran, dead nations can also
get a new lease of life. When the last messenger of Allah announced his revolutionary
invitation to the Arabs, there was strong opposition to the message. The *Momineen*
claimed that the opponents will be defeated and the new system would be established
despite their obstruction. The opponents had such pride in their power and ascendency
that they ridiculed the claims of the *Momineen*, and used to say, how can these 'dead
people' from this weak and helpless small group overcome us? The Quran has referred
to this ridicule in various places, and says they have no knowledge as to how Allah's
Law of life and death can give new life to the dead. They will soon witness this
happening. In *Surah Sajda* it is initially stated, have these people not seen how before
them many nations which opposed truth and justice were destroyed (32:26). After this
it says, what, do they not witness how the dead earth acquires new life. According to
this same Law, this party of Allah will also be re-energised (32:27). The opponents then
ask as to when this event will take place i.e. when they will be defeated (32:28). The
Quran replies, that day will definitely come and on that day their repentance will be
futile.

In these verses, the victory of this apparently weak and helpless group of the *Momineen*
is interpreted as a new life. This was the same new life to which the last messenger of
Allah used to invite the people. In *Surah Anfaal*, the *Momineen* are addressed:

*O you who believe! give your response to Allah and His Messenger, when He calls
you to that which will give you life; and know that Allah comes in between a man and his
heart, and that it is He to Whom you will (all) be gathered. (8:24)*

Regarding the Quran itself, it says that by using this, you can only give warning and divert from the dangerous paths those people who have a glimmer of life in them:

That it may give admonition to any (who are) alive… (36:70)

The people whose abilities to reason and reflect are extinguished or who do not even wish to utilise these potentials, the Quran has termed them as being 'dead'. The messenger of Allah is informed:

Truly you cannot cause the dead to listen, nor can you cause the deaf to hear the call, when they turn back in retreat. (27:80)

Then the Quran adds, you can only pass the message to those who accept the signs of Allah (30:52-53). Such 'dead' can only get life when they choose to follow the guidance.

When the messenger Ibrahim (Abraham) asked Allah to advise him regarding the technique by which the 'dead' can be made to come alive, he meant giving this type of new life to those who were 'dead' (2:260). Similarly, when the messenger Isa (Jesus) stated that he could give life to the 'dead' by the Divine Laws, then it too was in reference to the new life which was to be given to the nation of *Bani Israel*. This nation when it received new life after enslavement by the Babylonians, and was established in its place, was declared as gaining 'a life after death' by the Quran (2:259).

13.2 Emergence of Life from Death

This is mentioned in many verses of the Quran:

… He causes the living to issue from the dead, and He is the one to cause the dead to issue from the living… (6:96) See also (10:31)

In *Surah Rum*:

It is He Who brings out the living from the dead, and brings out the dead from the living, and Who gives life to the earth after it is dead: and thus you will be brought out (from the dead). (30:19)

This can have any of the following meanings:

a. Within every living being there is continuous death and regrowth of cells.

b. Regarding crops and vegetation, regrowth from apparently 'dead' seeds occurs and fresh crops materialise from which further similar dry seeds are produced.

c. The re-emergence and new life obtained following the decline and fall of nations including those that are overrun or colonised by other nations.

d. The death of human beings who were alive and then rise up again with new life.

13.3   The System of Death and Life

This issue of life and death is connected to the Divine Laws and there are many verses in the Quran which refer to this:

> …It is Allah that gives Life and Death, and Allah sees well all that you do. (3:155)[102]

In *Surah Rum* it is stated that Allah gives you life and provides you with sustenance and then He will:

> It is Allah Who has created you: further, He has provided for your sustenance; then He will cause you to die; and again He will give you life… (30:40)

Then the Quran says, 'Do you have anyone else among your false deities who can do this?'

In *Surah Jathia*, it is said that Allah gives you life and then as per the physical laws you will die and then:

> …It is Allah Who gives you life, then gives you death; then He will gather you together for the Day of Judgment about which there is no doubt… (45:26)

13.4   Death is Universal

The Quran declares that all human beings will taste death:

> Every self shall have a taste of death: And only on the Day of Judgment shall you be paid your full recompense… (3:184) See also (21:35, 29:50).

---

[102] See also verses (10:56, 22:6, 23:80, 36:12, 40:68, 42:9, 44:8, 50:43 and 57:2).

Death will come irrespective of where one is, even if one is hiding or living in an impregnable fortress:

Wherever you are, death will find you out, even if you are in towers built up strong and high... (4:78) See also (62:8).

Even the last messenger of Allah is told:

Truly you will die (one day), and truly they (too) will die (one day). (39:31)

In *Surah Baqra* it is asked, how can you deny the Divine Laws when you know - 'you were dead and He gave you life, you will die again and then you will be raised up' (2:28). In *Surah Momin* this is called the 'two deaths and two lives' (40:11).

Death takes place according to the physical laws. According to Quranic terminology, matters related to the physical laws or laws of nature are said to be carried out by 'angels' (forces of nature). This is why regarding death itself, the Quran has stated that it is carried out by angels. At the time of death, the state which passes through the mind of an individual is such that all his life, past events and memories (conscious and sub-conscious), come before him like a film. The Quran has referred to this state as a 'conversation with the angels':

Who is more unjust than one who invents a lie against Allah or rejects His Signs? For such, their portion appointed must reach them from the Book (of decrees): until, when our messengers (of death) arrive and take their souls, they say: 'Where are the things that ye used to invoke besides Allah'. They will reply, 'They have left us in the lurch,' And they will bear witness against themselves, that they had rejected Allah. (7:37)
See also (6:94, 16:28, 32:11, 50:19)

In some verses the Quran calls these bitter memories and the extreme sense of loss as punishment (8:50, 47:27). Contrary to this, the death of the *Momineen* is one in which they are given glad tidings of a life to come which will be far more satisfying and luxurious than the current one and they will welcome this news with tranquillity (16:32).

About the earth the Quran says that it is a place of temporary abode for a specified period only and is not for ever:

...On earth will be your dwelling-place and your means of livelihood - for a time. (2:36) See also (11:6).

Another verse states that the earth is your temporary residence and then it will hand you over to the next stage:

... here is a place of sojourn and a place of departure[103]*: We detail Our signs for people who understand. (6:98) See also (11:6)*

After death the human body disperses back into the earth whether through burial, cremation or just decomposition, and the Quran refers to this:

Therein you will live, and therein you will die; but from it you will be taken out. (7:25)

This point will be discussed later.

---

[103] The word used here is *'Mastaudaun'* and its meaning implies that earth will hand you over to the next stage.

(Intentionally left blank)

14   Giving Life to the Dead

Now we come to this important aspect of an individual's life which relates to his receiving life again after death. This is called life after death or life in the hereafter. This is the most sensitive and delicate subject in the whole discussion. For this we need to first understand some things about the present worldly life of man.

14.1   Human Birth

The Quran states:

Has there not been over Man a long period of Time, when he was nothing - (not even) mentioned? (76:1)

1. Human creation began from 'soil' (inert material) (32:7) – however, this inorganic matter does not have any signs of life in it. Life is dependent on water:

    ...We made from water every living thing... (21:30)

    Therefore life began with the mixing of clay and water:

    ...Them have We created out of a sticky clay. (37:11)

    This is the same clay which lies close to a body of water, is like dark coloured mud and when dried, becomes crumbly:

    We created man from sounding clay, from mud moulded into shape. (15:26)

2. This way, through the mixing of clay and water, the first life cell came into existence. From here, life passed through various stages of evolution and branched, progressing forwards and in the process changed to various forms. The Quran has called this first life cell a 'single cell' (uni-cellular), as there is no distinction between male and female at this stage. The Quran says:

    It is He Who hath produced you from a single 'cell', here is a place of sojourn and a place of departure: We detail Our signs for people who understand. (6:98)

3. This is how life emerged from this earth and its branches spread all around. In it was one branch which took the shape of sexual reproduction. The Quran points to this:

    And Allah has produced you from the earth growing (gradually). (71:17)

    Does not man see that it is We Who created him from sperm? (36:77)

Up to this point, the birth of men and animals is similar, so much so that the stages of a human embryo are not dissimilar from those of other mammals.

After this, a distinctive personality is produced in man that differentiates him from animals. This point requires deep reflection. This is that particular stage when a human child develops different characteristics which are not part of animal development. This is the point where the Quranic concept of human life differs from the materialistic concept. This is the trait which provides a basis for the foundation of *Deen* as a system and as explained in the Quran.

In *Surah Sajda* it is stated:

He rules (all) affairs from the heavens to the earth: in the end will (all affairs) go up to Him, on a Day, the space whereof will be (as) a thousand years of your reckoning. (32:5)

A scheme is conceived in Allah's universe of *'Amr'*[104]. Then to take shape, it begins on earth just as a seed grows. Then that scheme goes through many evolutionary stages before reaching its final intended destination. The time duration for this scheme could be very long, as one day by Allah's reckoning may be the equivalent of a thousand years by human calculation. This is how this scheme, through thousands of years from its starting point, reaches its final outcome. The creation of man is also one part of this scheme:

…He began the creation of man with clay. (32:7)

This is how life gradually reached an animal stage where:

And made his progeny from a quintessence of the nature of a fluid despised. (32:8)

Up to now there was no difference in the birth of a human child and an animal, both were passing through the same process up to this stage. But after this, the human creation diverged from the animal creation:

But He fashioned him in due proportion, and breathed into him Divine Energy. And He gave you (the faculties of) hearing and sight and feeling (and understanding)… (32:9)

After creating a special balance in man, Allah put a small part of Divine energy into him. This is what gives man his distinct status i.e. he was given a part of Divine energy, which is called human personality. And this is what converted him into a man with responsibility and possession of free will. He is given the ability to hear and see, the means by which to attain knowledge, and a mind which gives him the ability to make decisions (32:9). When he became capable of making decisions, he then became responsible for his actions. In the above verses (32:7-9), firstly man is referred to in the third person, but after mentioning the breathing in of Divine energy, man is addressed

---

[104] This may be another universe beyond this physical universe which we see around us. (Ed)

in the form of second person i.e. 'you'. Someone can only be addressed as 'you' if he can refer to himself as 'I'. This is man's 'I-am-ness' which gives him individuality[105].

In *Surah Mominoon*, after mentioning various stages of the development of a human child, the Quran states:

> ... *then we made out of that lump, bones, and clothed the bones with flesh; then we developed out of it another creature*[106] ... *(23:14)*

Then we turned him into such a creation, the human self, which was different from the previous stages. This human self is neither part of the human body nor is it subject to the physical laws - this is the reason that death comes to the body and not to the self, and why the self can survive beyond the physical disintegration of the body. The name of this survival is the life after death or the life in the hereafter.

This human self is given to every child; however, it is in an un-developed form. A man's righteous deeds, which the Quran calls '*Amal e Salhe*', help to develop this self and in the words of the Quran the self thus becomes crystallised. In *Surah Nuh* it is stated:

> *Seeing that it is He that has created you in diverse stages (71:14)*

Allah has put you through different stages gradually and made you in the form of man. Now you should desire from Allah that you can use this opportunity and work for your self-development:

> *Why don't you seek self-development from Allah? (71:13)*

Thus it will attain strength of character and this will lead to immortality. According to the Quran, man's present form is not the final stage of its evolutionary progression. At this latest stage of life, after going through all the previous evolutionary stages, a new stage has emerged. Now after physical death a new evolutionary stage will start which will be called the next life. The Quran states:

> *You will surely travel from stage to stage. (84:19)*

---

[105] Many modern thinkers and philosophers have acknowledged that man is not defined by his physical self alone and has something more than this which is called the self. I have discussed this issue in detail in another book titled 'What is Islam'.

[106] This is an important aspect of human creation. If the human mind is what was intended to be created, then the human body is of secondary importance – the mind now uses the human body to create and develop a 'self' by living within the domain of the Permanent Values and then this developed self becomes like a 'seed' with the potential to grow in the next life if the right type of environment becomes available. (Ed)

In another verse it is reiterated differently, that after making a beginning, and then taking it through subsequent stages:

It is He Who creates from the very beginning (from nothing), and He can restore life (and recreate). (85:13)

But these further stages of human life are not on this earth, because as the Quran states, man cannot return to this world[107]:

Until, when death comes to one of them, he says: 'O my Sustainer! send me back (to life), In order that I may work righteousness in the things I neglected.' - By no means! It is but a word he says. Before them is a Partition till the Day they are raised up. (23:99-100)

In *Surah Shu'araa*, the people who have earned hell will say:

Now if we only had a chance of return we shall truly be of those who believe. (26:102) See also (39:58, 7:53)

If only we could go back to this life just once, then we would certainly be of the righteous. The flow of time is only forward; either it stops at a place e.g. the death of the human body or it goes forward as the human self proceeds forward from the realm of this life to the next. The awakening of the human self is characterised by its self-consciousness, and it is this self-consciousness which continues forward after death. In *Surah Zumr* this is concisely stated:

It is Allah that takes the self (of men) at death; and those that die not (He takes) during their sleep: those on whom He has passed the decree of death, He keeps back (from returning to life), but the rest He sends (to their bodies) for a term appointed verily in this are Signs for those who reflect. (39:42)

In this for those people who use intellect and reason there are great signs to reach reality. The awakening of this self-consciousness is what makes us human. If it vanishes then man will live the life of an animal. This is a state of extreme degradation and for a thoughtful human being this is actually a state of great hell. The *Momineen* have been cautioned regarding this state:

And do not be like those who forgot Allah, and He made them forget their own self! (59:19)

The consequence for those who 'forgot' Allah, was that they ignored their own self. And as a result their sense of self disappeared, and they degraded themselves from the human level to the animal level. In *Surah Mohammed*:

...while those who reject Allah will enjoy (this world) and eat as cattle eat... (47:12)

---

[107] This refutes the doctrine of reincarnation which is prevalent among some religions e.g. Hinduism.

Those who deny the existence of the life of the hereafter, their common argument is that the body after death disintegrates, and reverts to different elements and in this way disappears into the soil, so there is no question of man getting another life[108]. The Quran answers this question:

We already know how much of them the earth takes away: With Us is a record guarding (the full account and is preserved). (50:4)

How will this 'preserved' self get a new life? What form will it take in the next life? What will be its state of perception? We cannot understand these aspects with our present level of consciousness. Our ability to perceive is confined to the physical environment of this worldly life, and the next life is not going to be a physical existence like the one in this life. Therefore we cannot grasp its concept. The Quran, (while declaring repeatedly that it will be of a totally different form), describes it using images from this life as examples. Apart from this we have no other method of understanding it. For example, we observe that dead bodies are buried in the ground, and the Quran has referred to the new life by saying that the dead will rise from their graves. Addressing the progeny of Adam, the Quran says:

He said: 'Therein you will live, and therein you will die; but from it you will be taken out (at last).' (7:25)

In *Surah Taha*:

From the (earth) did We create you, and into it shall We return you, and from it shall We bring you out once again. (20:55)

We know that a human being did not arise in its completed form from the earth. Being created from the earth is a reference to the beginning of life. So after death, being created from the earth does not mean that the human body will be raised up from the graves – it is a reference to the emergence of a new form of life. In another verse it is stated:

And Allah has produced you from the earth growing (gradually), and in the end He will return you into the (earth), and raise you forth. (71:18-19)

And in another verse:

…that Allah will raise up all who are in the graves. (22:7)

It is obvious that the dead will not be directly raised up from their graves, as many bodies are cremated, disposed of in a watery grave, electrocuted etc. The aim here is

---

[108] More details on this aspect will be covered later.

just to make us understand. In other verses different terms are used for graves, which mean the same e.g. see (36:51, 54:7, 70:43). In *Surah Yaseen* the term used is *'Marqad'* which means bedroom (36:52). In another verse, it is stated that He will call to you and you will rise up from the earth (30:25). In another verse it is stated that We have such power that We can recreate every bit of your body that is in pieces (75:4).

After explaining through illustrations from this life, the Quran makes it clear that in the next life man will not have his current form (body). It will be a new creation such that you cannot understand it now. The Quran says:

We have decreed Death for everyone and We are not to be frustrated from changing your Forms and creating you (again) in (forms) that you know not. (56:60-61)

In *Surah Luqman* there is a very delicate indication regarding the new form of life in the hereafter which will be different from this life. We have seen with regard to the initial human creation, that it started from a single cell i.e. through the mixing of clay and water. Obviously, this single cell came into being from mud, but possessing those characteristics which were neither in water nor in clay. This new creation was totally different. Presenting this reality, the Quran says:

And your creation and your resurrection is in no wise but as an individual self... (31:28)

As the first life cell came into being, leaving behind the inert matter from which it received a new form with different characteristics, in the same way the human self leaves its disposable physical body behind; and in the journey of life enters into such a valley which cannot be imagined by us.

This physical form will be changed, but every individual's self-consciousness will be retained, so that the self with this self-consciousness will leave the physical body and move forward to a different plane of existence. Man will go forward with his own individuality. In *Surah Inam* it is stated:

And behold! You will come to us bare and alone as We created you for the first time: you will leave behind you all (the favours) which We bestowed on you... (6:94)

At another place, it states that you will come to Us with your individuality (19:80, 19:95). The record of man's deeds which during his life was like a scroll wrapped up, will be unveiled like an open book and he will be told:

Read your (own) record: Sufficient is your own self this day to make out an account against you. (17:14) See also (7:37, 75:14).

In *Surah Nehl* it is noted:

One Day every self will come up quarrelling with itself, and every self will be recompensed (fully) for all its actions, and none will be unjustly dealt with. (16:111)

The actions which were made very attractive to man and lured him in this worldly life due to his vested interests, those deeds on that Day will scream out that they were evil. In *Surah Qaf*, he will be told:

You were heedless of this; now have We removed your veil, and sharp is your sight this Day.
(50:22)

At that time, you had drawn curtains over your sight, because of which you could not see the truth and reality. Today those veils have been lifted and your sight has now become sharp to such a degree that you can see through everything. Now there is nothing that can remain hidden from you (86:9, 10:45). Regarding those evil companions with whom he associated and who colluded with him in doing wrong, he will say:

Ah! woe is me! Would that I had never taken such a one for a friend. (25:28)

Those hypocrites, who in this life used to deceive their friends, will find them in front of them, and their real character will then become exposed. The hypocrites will be in hell, while the *Momineen* will be in paradise, and between them will be a wall which will have a gate (57:13). There will be a severe altercation between the religious leaders and their simple followers (37:21-22). There will also be a heated quarrel between the leaders and their followers whom they used for their interests. This has been referred to in the Quran at a number of places e.g. (14:21, 33:67-68, 34:32-33, 38:60, 40:47-49). Similarly, in hell various parties will curse each other and will say they misguided them (7:38-39). At that time those who will be in hell, through hopelessness and desperation will cry out:

Verily, We have warned you of a Penalty near, the Day when man will see (the deeds) which
his hands have sent forth, and the Unbeliever will say, 'Woe unto me! Would that I were
dust!' (78:40)

How this mutual recognition will work and what form this mutual argument will take place, we cannot understand at our present level of consciousness. According to the Quran this is an established reality in which there is no room for doubt. Conviction *(Eimaan)* in the next life is a required condition to be a Muslim and this is a natural consequence of the belief in the working of the Law of Requital.

14.2 The Moral View of Reality

As noted earlier, the whole discussion and argument about the human self and life after death are based on the functioning of the Law of Requital. It does not mean that without these concepts (the human self and life after death), belief in the Law of Requital would remain unrecognised and therefore these concepts are invented as a reason to accept the Law of Requital - this is not true.

Allah has created the universe and man himself in such a way that these three concepts - the Law of Requital, the human self and life after death - emerge as a reality. If this whole creation had come into existence accidentally then these concepts would have been irrelevant. But the Quran declares that the creation of the universe and man is part of a grand design and has a purpose, and is not for play and amusement. In *Surah Dukhan* it is stated:

> *We created not the heavens, the earth, and all between them, merely in sport: We created them not except for just ends: but most of them do not understand. (44:38-39)*

Regarding the purpose of creation, the Quran declares:

> *Allah created the heavens and the earth for just ends, and in order that each self may find the recompense of what it has earned, and none of them be wronged. (45:22)*

About man himself, the Quran states:

> *Did you then think that We had created you in jest, and that you would not be brought back to Us? (23:116)*

Allah, who evidently possesses all power and sovereignty, is far above this, that any such view should be held about Him, that He created without any purpose and He indulges in aimless play[109]:

> *Does man think that he will be left uncontrolled (without purpose)? (75:36)*

This type of belief is false. The caravan of life is not without a destination. Human creation is not aimless. Every breath of his life which a man takes, provides evidence that he is either going towards his objective or is turning far away from it. He has yet to traverse many more evolutionary stages, and the purpose of his life on this planet is to develop his self in such a way, that it is able to go forward after his physical death and become capable of rising higher. Death is in fact a test for him to see how successful he has been in achieving this objective:

---

[109] This means that those who wish to follow the Divine Attributes should ensure that their own life should have a clear purpose and be creative in their life. (Ed).

He Who created Death and Life, that you may get opportunities for righteous deeds...
(67:2)

This reality is stated in *Surah Yunus*:

... It is He Who begins the process of creation, and repeats it, that He may reward with justice those who believe and work righteousness... (10:4)

Life after death is another part of this process:

Verily, this is the Very Truth and Certainty. (56:95)

14.3 Those Who Deny the Next Life

Life after death is the basis of *Deen*. It is an inseparable part of the programme for the accomplishment of advancing the human self to its heights. The Quran has repeatedly referred to this. Before referring to these verses, it is important to mention that my purpose in writing this book is not to convince those people who do not accept the existence of Allah, the revelation, the human self, and life after death. The purpose of this book is to present Quranic explanations for these realities. This is the reason why the scope of this work is confined to these limits. Otherwise, in our time the issue of life in the hereafter outwith the Quran has had so much written about it, that if it had been brought under discussion, it would itself have become another book. Suffice it to say that in modern times according to research done on the human self, though they are not able to say anything with certainty regarding the possibility of immortality, survival after death has not been completely ruled out. Even this much research in this area is enough to counter the argument of the materialist concept of life.

The Quran brings out one aspect of the mentality of the opponents who reject this reality and who demand that in order for them to accept life after death, they want to be shown the dead being brought back to life. And this is their ignorance. That thing, (human self) which is what remains after death, and cannot be seen even in a living human being with the naked eyes; how can it be seen in a dead body? This can only be understood through the use of intellect and reasoning. The Quran addresses such people saying:

They know but the outer (things) in the life of this world: but of the End of things they are heedless. Do they not reflect in their own self? (30:7-8)

In another verse, the Quran says, that the way these people carry out their work on earth, using thinking and reasoning abilities, if they also used these to reflect on life after death, they would understand this reality as well:

...Thus does Allah Make clear to you His Signs: In order that you reflect and reason to understand these. (2:219)

The criticisers wanted to see life after death with their own eyes, while the Quran invites them to use their visionary 'eyes' of intellect and reasoning[110]:

...When we are (actually) dust, shall we indeed then be in a creation renewed? ... (13:5)

In *Surah Israel:*

They say: 'What! when we are reduced to bones and dust, should we really be raised up (to be) a new creation?' (17:49)

In reply the Quran says:

Say: '(Nay!) be you stones or iron, or created matter which, in your minds, is hardest (to be raised up), (Yet you will be raised up)'... (17:50-51)

In *Surah Hajj*, it states that if you have any doubt as to how you will get life after death, then you should reflect on your present existence. You were nothing. Then your life was begun from inert material (mud), and after going through various stages, you reached this present form. Then your body reaches old age, and you lose your physical abilities, and the machinery of your body wears out. Reflect that if life can begin from inert material, then why can a new life not be brought into existence in a similar way?

This is so, because Allah is the reality: it is He who gives life to the dead, and it is He Who has fixed scales for all things (power over all things). (22:6)

In this current life, because you see the birth of children in front of your eyes, you are not surprised by this. If this life was not in front of you and someone had mentioned this birth process to you, you would have been astonished at this, and would have rejected this as well. This is not intelligent or logical to accept one part of a law because it is visible with physical evidence, and to reject outright another part of the law just because it is not yet tangibly visible. In *Surah Yaseen* it is stated:

...he (man) says, 'Who can give life to (dry) bones and decomposed ones (at that)?' Say, 'He will give them life Who created them for the first time!' for He is Well-versed in every kind of creation!... (36:78-79)[111]

Now, as you say, at least his bones exist, but at the time of his first creation there was nothing present, not even bones, and even then it developed into a human being. Therefore based on this logic, what can be the reason for denying a new life?

---

[110] As noted earlier, the Quran repeatedly invites us to use our mind to understand its message and Values. It is the use of our mind and its ability to think about thinking which helps us to develop our self. (Ed)
[111] See also verses (17:98, 19:66, 23:35-37, 23:82, 32:1, 34:7, 37:16, 56:47-48, 64:7, 75:4, 75:36-40,79:11).

In *Surah Dukhan*, their demand is mentioned that we will only accept your claim that man can be brought back to life after death, if you bring our deceased forefathers back to life (44:35-36). In another verse it is stated:

And they say: 'What is there but our life in this world? We shall die and we live, and nothing but time can destroy us.' But of that they have no knowledge: they merely conjecture.[112]
(45:24)

A little later, the Quran says that if this life is confined to the physical human life and there is nothing more to a human being, then there is no difference between a human's life and an animal's life, it is the same. According to this dogma, how can they then differentiate themselves from animals?

...while those who reject Allah will enjoy (this world) and eat as cattle eat; and the Fire will be their abode. (48:12)

In *Surah Qaf*, in reply to their objection that after a 'body' disintegrates into the earth, how can man get another life, the Quran says that We know how much is taken away by the earth from the human body (50:4) and what thing is left behind which can be given a new life. Further on, it is stated that We did not get tired after their first creation nor will recreating them be any more effort:

Were We then weary with the first Creation, that they should be in confused doubt about a new Creation? (50:15)

Nay, we are able to put together in perfect order the very tips of his fingers. (75:4)

After dealing with these various objections, the Quran makes it clear that the real reason for their denial to accept this possibility is something else. And that is the thief hidden in their subconscious, that they do not wish to be take responsibility for the results of their deeds:

For that they used not to fear any account (for their deeds). (78:27)

They do not wish that they should be held accountable for the crimes that they used to be busy in. They do not wish that this peace and contentment, (which is not really peace but only a self-deception), be snatched away from them i.e. we should be able to do whatever we wish and there should be none to question us. Belief in the next life raises a sense of responsibility in man and they do not wish to give birth to this sense of responsibility. But what difference does their denial make to reality. What, by closing one's eyes will the sun stop shining? So tell them, that regarding the possibility of life

---

[112] The word used here is '*Zunn*' which is translated as conjecture. This is used in another verse (53:28) which says,' *But they have no knowledge therein. They follow nothing but conjecture; and conjecture avails nothing against Truth'*. (Ed)

after death, even if you try a million times to avoid thinking about it, this is going to take place:

(Then) shall each self know what it has sent forward and (what it has) kept back. (82:5)

Have you pondered on the fact that the basis of all these objections is based on the materialistic concept of life i.e. this belief that man is defined by his physical body alone. As long as the machinery of his body follows the physical laws, he remains alive. When death stops this machinery, man ends and nothing is left. The natural consequence of this concept of life is that if, for example, one makes such an arrangement whereby whatever he does, he is never caught by society, then there is no power in the world which can stop him from cruelty and oppression and deceit and deception. Then no concept of Permanent Values or of an external immutable law can remain other than the self-created constitution and laws. Its consequence is that hell in which today's world is ablaze and smouldering (from the materialistic concept of life).

From the above you will have realised why the Quran puts so much emphasis on conviction about life in the hereafter, and why *Eimaan* is essential for deeds to be righteous.

14.4 One Important Issue

It has been already noted that according to the Quran:

a) Every human being is given a self (or personality). This self is in an undeveloped form. On this earth, the purpose of human life is to develop this self to that extent from which it becomes capable of being able to move on to the next evolutionary stage of life in the journey of further development.

b) The natural consequence of the presence of the human self is the emergence of the ability to make choices and to be responsible for the choices. Due to this, man becomes different from all other animals.

c) Whatever man does by using his choice and intention, that effect is imprinted on his self. If these are good deeds, then the accumulated effect of these deeds will develop his self in due proportion. If the balance of these positive effects exceeds those of the negative effects, then this self is characterised as a developed self (and in the hereafter becomes eligible for a life in paradise)[113]. If this balance is light, then that self remains undeveloped (in the hereafter it is called hell)[114].

---

[113] This will be called the heavenly life in the hereafter.
[114] This will be called the life in hell in the hereafter.

d) The criteria for any deed to be declared good or bad is according to the Revelation of Allah which is now preserved in the folds of the Quran.

From these explanations it is clear that:

i. The human self is only affected by those deeds which an individual does through his own choice and intention. Regarding the decisions in which his choice is not involved, he cannot be held accountable for these, and therefore they do not affect his self.

ii. If someone has never heard about the standards for right and wrong which have been set by the revelation (the Quran), then all he can do is those deeds which he feels are right to him and avoid those which he thinks are wrong. However, this does not necessarily mean that what he considers to be good, is in actual fact good. In the world there are hundreds of wrong deeds which people do with a genuine and sincere belief that these are good. Obviously the results of such deeds cannot be good. Wrong deeds will always have wrong effects, irrespective of how sincere the intention behind it. How many wrong medicines are given to patients with good intentions, but which leave their adverse effects and ultimately may even lead to death.

iii. It is also possible that the criteria given by the revelation reaches a person, but he does not have the necessary intellect or mental ability to understand it or make decisions based on it e.g. children, those with mental health issues, or people who are very backward. (Those people who have the ability to reason and use their intellect, but do not wish to make use of it, and make their decisions based on emotive thinking, they will be responsible for what they do).

From the above it is evident that responsibility is imposed on that individual who has received the revelation and who also has the ability to think and make decisions. Those who are not in this category are outside the remit of this aspect of accountability for their deeds. They will be counted in the category of other things in the universe such as inanimate objects or animals. The Quran makes these two points clear in various verses. The first point is that these people should have received the revelation.

In *Surah Momin*, it is stated that the inmates of hell will ask the guardians of hell if the intensity of the punishment can be reduced and the reply will be:

Those in the Fire will say to the Keepers of Hell: 'Pray to your Sustainer to lighten us the Penalty for a day (at least)!' They will say: 'Did there not come to you your messengers with Clear Signs?' They will say, 'Yes'. They will reply, Then pray (as you like- nothing will happen)! (40:49-50) See also (67:8-9)

In *Surah Qaf* it is stated that on the Day of Judgment the criminals will accuse each other and there will be a reply from Allah:

He will say: Dispute not with each other in My Presence: I had already in advance sent you Warning. (50:28)

As already written, the same principle applies to the destruction of nation states as well i.e. until a nation has not been clearly shown both the right and the wrong path, it is not destroyed. See (17:15, 26:208-209, 30:9, 9:115, and 6:132). In *Surah Qasas*, it is noted to such an extent, that the messenger used to 'come' to the capital of a nation state (28:59).

It is obvious that after the ending of messenger-hood, this responsibility for passing on the message (the Quran) to other people and nation states, lies with the Muslim *Ummah* who read and understand the Revelation.[115]

As far as the second point is concerned, the responsibility lies with that individual who has the ability to understand and think about the message. In this regard the Quran is very clear:

Many are men (rural and city dwellers) we have made for Hell[116]: They have hearts wherewith they understand not, eyes wherewith they see not, and ears wherewith they hear not. They are like cattle - nay more misguided: for they are heedless. (7:179)

In *Surah Mulk*, the denizens of hell will say:

They will further say: 'Had we but listened or used our intelligence, we should not (now) be among the Companions of the Blazing Fire.' (67:10)

The same has been declared about the nations which are destroyed, that in spite of being able to think and reason they did not use their intellect (29:38, 46:26). About the Quranic truths themselves, it is stated that only those benefit from them who have a mind which they use to listen, think and reason with, or when they are told something, they listen to it attentively and then carefully pursue it (50:37). Therefore, the responsibility is his:

- To whom the message of Allah i.e. the Quran, has reached
- Who has the ability to understand, think and reason
- Who does a deed with deliberate intention and inclination (33:5, 16:106)

These are those deeds whose effects leave an imprint on the human self. Examples of these details will be covered under the subject of '*Jahannum*' i.e. hell.

---

[115] But the nation which has lost its way, how can it guide others? This is the reason that we (Muslims) are subjected to double punishment from Allah, firstly because we have departed from the true path of the Quran and secondly as a consequence of this, other nations of the world remained on the wrong path. But in this era when knowledge is common, at least the civilised nations of the world cannot say that Allah's message did not reach them.

[116] As noted previously, Allah refers this to Himself – the next part of the verse makes it clear as to why these people live a life of self-created hell. (Ed)

(Intentionally left blank)

(Intentionally left blank)

15 *Barzakh* – Partition

There is a belief held among some people in the Islamic world that there is an interval between the time of death and the resurrection, during which the dead body gets either *Azaab* or *Sawaab* i.e. punishment or reward. This is commonly known as '*Aazaab e Qabar*' or punishment in the grave. There is no support in the Quran for this view. According to the Quran there are two deaths and two lives:

They will say, our Sustainer, *twice have you made us without life, and twice have you given us Life! (40:11)*

In *Surah Baqra* it is stated:

How can you reject the belief in Allah - seeing that you were without life, and He gave you life; then will He cause you to die, and will again bring you to life; and again to Him will you return. (2:28)

In other words, the state before being born into this life was like 'death' and then a human being is born into this world and this is called 'life'. Then the life in this world will come to an end and this is called 'death'. After this another life will be given, and regarding when this second life will be given it is stated:

After that, at length you will die. Again, on the Day of Judgment, will you be raised up. (23:15-16)

It is clear from this verse that this second life will be on the 'Day of Judgment'. Therefore, the notion of another life between departure from this world and the day of resurrection on the Day of Judgment is a non-Quranic concept.

The reality is that if we do not understand what death is and what life is, we cannot understand the truths stated in the Quran. Let us try and understand this through an example. The sounds broadcast from a radio station disperse as waves in the atmosphere, but we are not aware of their presence. We only become aware of the sounds when they reach our ears from a radio set which can receive these transmissions. Even before we become aware of these sounds, these were present and had not disappeared[117].

Allah created this universe from nothing; before this there was no material universe and there was no existence of life. Then, as per His Laws, life emerged in the universe. We cannot say when and how this appeared. We only became aware of its existence when it appeared in a physical form. Then life passed through an unknown number of stages, to eventually reach its final form in the persona of a human being. We only become aware of human life at this stage. The Quran has called this stage as being 'life' and all

---

[117] Communication technology has now developed and the same is applicable to mobile phones etc. (Ed)

the stages which were before this (from our perspective) as 'death'[118]. After life ends in this world, it progresses forward from its present stage, but we cannot be aware of this with the means of perception available to us – it is not that life has disappeared. It is very much present, but it goes outside the grasp of our means of perception i.e. according to the above example, our radio set is out of order and the sound wrapped up in the waves does not reach us. The sound is still present, but we have no awareness of it. The Quran has called this state as 'death' again (death number two). After this our radio set is restored, and from our human point of view, life returns – this is called 'life after death'.

If we think that there is no continuation of life after a human being's physical death, and assume that we will get a totally new life on the Day of Judgment, which has no connection with this worldly life, this contradicts the concept of life after death presented by the Quran. The Quran clearly states that in the next life they will remember all of their lives which were lived in this world. They will recognise each other and will have knowledge and feelings of their mutual relations in this life. From this it is proved that there will be continuity of consciousness.

Those people who believe in the materialistic concept of life, and consider that the centre of consciousness (memory) is located in the brain, say that when the brain disintegrates after physical death, there can then be no question of any consciousness remaining. Contrary to this, the Quran says that consciousness is the human self, which remains even after the disintegration of the human body[119]. In reality this consciousness is the name given to those effects which are continuously imprinted on the human self throughout its life. The human self takes these effects with it, and goes forward to the next stage. What will be the form of these effects in the next life, we cannot say at our existing level of consciousness in our present life. But whatever the mode of their appearance in the next life, according to the Quran the emergence is a reality[120]. This is what is called 'Eimaan e bil Akhirat' – the conviction in the hereafter. This is the reason that the Quran calls the human self (Nafs) and consciousness as being synonymous. In Surah Zumr this reality is stated in a very eminent way:

It is Allah that takes the self at death; and those that die not (He takes) during their sleep: those on whom He has passed the decree of death, He keeps back (from returning to life), but the rest He sends (to their bodies) for a term appointed. Verily in this are Signs for those who think and reflect. (39:42)

---

[118] We should keep in mind that this is from our i.e. human point of view.
[119] The entity called the 'self' is the personality which each one of us creates through the use of our mind, body and interaction with other human beings as we live this life. In the later part of life, if our memory is affected then we may not remember our past and this aspect has been noted in the Quran (16:70). The Quran states that whatever happens to our body after death has no consequence on our resurrection and that whatever we have done in this life will appear before us in the hereafter. (Ed)
[120] This is termed as belief (Eimaan) in the hereafter.

It is obvious that during the state of sleep man is physically alive, but his consciousness is suspended. On awakening, this consciousness becomes active and this is called *Nafs* (human self) by the Quran. Therefore *Nafs* and consciousness are synonymous terms. After the death of man, this *Nafs* or consciousness is withheld but it does not disintegrate, nor is it destroyed or terminated. Therefore the belief that the consciousness will end and then another life will be given, is not a correct concept as noted earlier. According to the materialistic concept of life, the consciousness is totally destroyed or disappears after death. According to the Quranic concept of life, this does not happen. Life or consciousness is a continuously flowing stream which goes from the plains of this world, and enters into the gardens of the hereafter. Death is just a partition which is blocking our view across this stream of life and while standing on the plains of this life we cannot see the stream on the other side because of this barrier. Therefore this belief is not correct, that all those people who die after death are held back in their graves, and then one day they will all be resurrected together, which is usually known as *Hashr* or the Day of Judgment[121]. The reality is that the Day of Judgment of each one of us commences with death.

From the Quran we get indications in some places where it appears that the effects on the human self (self-consciousness) will take a period of time before it can transform into another form. Before we progress further, it is important that we throw some light on the concept of the time interval or time itself. According to philosophical thinking, the concept of time is one of the most difficult problems of life in the universe. But we will leave aside the most difficult aspects of time and will only look at the common understanding of time. Only he can have awareness of time whose consciousness is awake. He who is sleeping has no sense of time. This awareness is only available to those who are awake. Similarly, the one who is under the influence of an anaesthetic like chloroform, also has no awareness of time. In common terms we can say that time is a relative thing. This is why philosophers call that time about which we do not have any conscious awareness of its passing, as the 'duration-less time'.

15.1 *Barzakh*[122] - Partition

It is apparent from our discussion so far that in the so-called 'interval' in which the self-consciousness transforms into a new form, an individual will have no awareness of this. This is why the Quran states that at the time of regaining consciousness man will say in a surprised state:

They will say: 'Ah! Woe unto us! Who has raised us up from our beds of repose?' (36:52)

Note that this interval has been referred to as a state of sleep. In another verse regarding this interval it is stated:

---

[121] Consciousness is merely suspended for an indeterminate time and is not in the graves. (Ed)

[122] This term means a partition or a screen separating two things e.g. walls.

...Before (or after) them is a Partition (Barzakh) till the Day they are raised up... (23:100)

In this verse the word used in the Quran for 'before' can mean both before and after. If the meaning is taken as after (behind), then it will mean that during this period the dead will not know about the life left behind in this world, and if the meaning is taken to be before (in front), it will mean that their consciousness will not be awake yet for the future life to come. It will be as if they are in a state of slumber.

15.2 The Dead Cannot Hear Us

As far as this world is concerned, after death man has no contact with the life left behind. At that time in the hereafter, when he will gain consciousness, he will remember all the details of his previous life, but he will not know anything about what has been happening in the world after his death. This is why the Quran has clearly stated:

And those whom you invoke besides Him have not the least power. If you invoke them, they will not listen to your call, and if they were to listen, they cannot answer your (prayer). On the Day of Judgment they will reject your 'Partnership' and none, (O man!) can tell you (the Truth) like the One Who is acquainted with all things. (35:14)

An answer can only be given by one who can hear (6:36). And you can never make the dead to hear (30:52). You cannot make those who are in their graves hear (35:22). The dead and the living can never be equal (35:22). The ones to whom people call standing at their graves, do not even have an idea of who is calling to them and what he is saying – so much so that they do not even have any knowledge of when they will be resurrected (46:5, 16:21, 27:25). And in this there is no distinction between the great and the small. After death, all will have the same status and condition. And in addition the Quran addressed the last messenger, saying that death will come to you as well as to others (39:30).

15.3 The Life of Those Who Die in the Path of Allah

About those who die in the cause of Allah, the Quran has declared in one place:

And say not of those who are slain in the way of Allah. 'They are dead.' Nay, they are living, though you perceive (it) not. (2:154)

In another place:

Think not of those who are slain in Allah's path as dead. Nay, they live, finding their sustenance in the presence of their Sustainer. (3:169)

In these verses there are one or two points which require further attention:

- These people are alive, but their life is unlike the life of human beings living in this world, because we can understand the worldly life, whereas about the other life it is stated that we cannot understand its reality. Therefore that life is different from the life here in this world.

- They are alive with their Sustainer (*Rabb*) – therefore they have no remaining contact with this life. Further, it should be kept in mind that the Quran has clearly stated that death is for every living being (3:184), even as stated earlier, for the messengers of Allah and none is exempt (39:30). Therefore what we call death, comes to those who lay down their lives in the cause of Allah. So their 'living' as mentioned in the above verses relates to the next life and not the present life in this world.

A great deal has been discussed in the Quran about the people who sacrifice their lives for the cause of Allah. But in the light of what has been explained above, we understand that the interval we have discussed earlier in which there is a temporary suspension of consciousness after death, will not apply to those people who have sacrificed their lives for the cause of Allah, as they are exempted from it. The procedure for the development of the human self is that when a clash arises between a Permanent Value and a worldly benefit, then whichever person preserves the Permanent Value by sacrificing the worldly benefit, this deed of his will enhance his self-development. It is now obvious that in such clashes, the time which is most testing and demanding of courage is that in which a man lays down his life to stand up for the truth (because there is nothing dearer in this world than life). So whichever man in such a situation willingly and happily lays down his life for the defence of truth (*Haqq*), his self develops to such an extent that he does not have to pass through this interval of temporary suspension of his consciousness after death. In the continuity of their self-consciousness, there will not be an iota of interruption. This assumption of ours is supported by another verse:

They rejoice in the bounty provided by Allah. And with regard to those left behind, who have not yet joined them (in their bliss), they glory in the fact that on them is no fear, nor have they grief. (3:170)

This indicates that their consciousness will awake immediately with the time of death and there will be no temporary suspension between death and the next life.

Furthermore it should also be understood that if an individual participates in a fight or war for the sake of truth and justice against evil and is not killed but returns victorious, then he also will not be deprived of this greatest reward which comes to those who are slain (martyrs). Such people also have such a higher grade (3:156, 4:74, 9:111-112).

15.4 The State of Consciousness in the Next Life

From some verses of the Quran it appears that in the next life consciousness about time will be different when compared to this life. So the estimate of the amount of time spent in this life will be different by people in the next life. In *Surah Yunus* it is stated:

One day He will gather them together: (It will be) as if they had tarried but an hour of a day: they will recognise each other... (10:45) See also (46:35)

In *Surah Rum*:

On the Day that the Hour (of Reckoning) will be established, the transgressors will swear that they tarried not but an hour: thus were they used to being deluded! But those endued with knowledge and assurance will say: 'Indeed you did tarry, within Allah's Decree, to the Day of Resurrection, and this is the Day of Resurrection: but you were not aware!'
(30:55-56)

In other words, both categories of people, the good and the bad, will not be able to estimate the amount of time spent in the previous life, but will say that only Allah has knowledge of its correct duration. In *Surah Mominoon*, Allah will ask them regarding how long they stayed in this world:

He will say: 'What number of years did you stay on earth?' They will say: 'We stayed a day or part of a day: but ask those who keep account.' (23:112-113)

In *Surah Taha* it is noted:

In whispers will they consult each other: 'Ye tarried not longer than ten (Days)'; We know best what they will say, when their leader most eminent in conduct will say: 'You tarried not longer than a day!' (20:103-104)

From this it is clear that the state of consciousness at least about time will be different in the next life from this world. (More details about this will be covered later).

(Intentionally left blank)

(Intentionally left blank)

16 Details of the Great Revolution

It has been previously stated that there are three types of revolutions which are referred to in the Quran:

1. That revolution which occurs in the life of nations in this world. In this, powers which are at their height plummet to a low level. And nations which are lowly and humiliated rise and reach new heights. When this revolution takes place through a war, the Quran has covered the resulting destruction and ruin caused by such conflicts. Sometimes populations are destroyed through physical events e.g. storms, floods, earthquakes. This is also an aspect of destruction.

2. In the Quran such universal events are also mentioned from which it appears that these are about such a time when this whole universe will be in commotion. The heavenly bodies after colliding with each other will disintegrate. The earth will become dust and disperse into space. This will be the greatest revolution in the universe.

3. The third revolution is in the life in the hereafter, when the fate of human beings will be decided according to their deeds. Their future will be ascertained according to the state of their self-development. The Quran has described the grief stricken scene of this event.

The Quran while narrating the details of these revolutions has not specified which part is related to which revolution and has left it to our intellect and reasoning to work it out. And indeed we can through the use of our intellect and reasoning understand which scene is applicable to which revolution.

As with other languages of the world, in fact to an even greater extent, the Arabic language also uses literal and metaphorical meanings of words and phrases. For example, when we say that a lion in the jungle roars, then lion will be a literal meaning. But when we say he is a lion, then the metaphorical meaning of the word lion here is that he is very brave. From this point of view, the details noted under the revolution in category 2 noted above, refer to some physical events in the universe about which we do not know at present. But if its metaphorical meaning is taken then these will be related to those clashes which take place between various groups or nations in this world i.e. in this situation this will be covered under the revolution under category 1. As far as the revolution in category 3 is concerned, this will be taken metaphorically as we cannot understand its nature at our present state of consciousness. This is the reason that the Quran has referred to these metaphorically e.g. if fire is mentioned then it is not the fire which we know of which is lighted in cookers or ovens. This is a metaphorical explanation of inner human turmoil and disturbance.

In my book, the 'Exposition of the Quran', I have ascertained such metaphorical meanings in various verses and have explained these further. And I could have presented the same exposition here, but after deliberating on this question I reached the conclusion that in the current book the literal meanings of the verses should be left. And to leave it to the readers' own intellect as to which meanings they want to take of these words, e.g. literal or metaphorical, or refer to the book, 'Exposition of the Quran', for further explanations.

16.1 Great Upheavals

Regarding these upheavals, the literal translations of these verses are noted below – you can refer to these verses in any translation of the Quran:

1) Mankind! Fear your Lord! for the convulsion of the Hour (of Judgment) will be a thing terrible! The Day you will see it, every mother giving suck shall forget her suckling-babe, and every pregnant female shall drop her load (unformed): you will see mankind as in a drunken riot, yet not drunk: but dreadful will be the Wrath of Allah (22:1-2).

2) …And that Hour will be most grievous and most bitter (54:46). This will be heavy on the heavens and the earth (7:187).

3) Then, when one blast is sounded on the Trumpet, and the earth is moved, and its mountains, and they are crushed to powder at one stroke, on that Day shall the (Great) Event come to pass (15:13-15). See also (39:68-69).

4) When the sky is cleft asunder; and the stars are scattered (82:1-2).

5) When the sun (with its spacious light) is folded up; When the stars fall, losing their lustre; When the mountains vanish (like a mirage); When the she-camels, ten months with young, are left untended; When the wild beasts are herded together; When the oceans boil over with a swell (81:1-6), (77:8-10).

6) A Day whereon men will be like moths scattered about, and the mountains will be like carded wool (101:4-5).

7) They ask thee concerning the mountains: say, 'My Sustainer will uproot them and scatter them as dust; He will leave them as plains smooth and level. Nothing crooked or curved will you see in their place' (20:105-106).

8) The Day that We roll up the heavens like a scroll rolled up for books (completed) (21:104). On the Day of Judgment the whole of the earth will be but His handful, and the heavens will be rolled up in His right hand…(39:67)

9) One day the earth will be changed to a different earth, and so will be the heavens, and (men) will be marshalled forth, before Allah, the One, the Irresistible (14:48). The Day the heaven shall be rent asunder with clouds, and angels shall be sent down, descending (in ranks), that Day, the dominion as of right and truth, shall be (wholly) for Allah Most Merciful (25:25-26). And the sky will be rent asunder, for it will that Day be flimsy (69:17). The Day that the

Spirit and the angels will stand forth in ranks, none shall speak except any who is permitted by ((Allah)) Most Gracious, and He will say what is right (78:38). See also (11:105).

10) One Day We shall remove the mountains, and you will see the earth as a level stretch, and We shall gather them, all together, nor shall We leave out any one of them. And they will be marshalled before your Lord in ranks... (18:47-48)

11) You see the mountains and think them firmly fixed: but they shall pass away as the clouds pass away... (27:88)

12) On the Day when the firmament will be in dreadful commotion. And the mountains will fly hither and thither (52:9-10).

13) When the Event inevitable comes to pass, Then will no (self) entertain falsehood concerning its coming. (Many) will it bring low; (many) will it exalt; When the earth shall be shaken to its depths, And the mountains shall be crumbled to atoms, Becoming dust scattered abroad (56:1-6).

14) The Day that the sky will be like molten brass, and the mountains will be like wool (70:8-9).

15) One Day the earth and the mountains will be in violent commotion. And the mountains will be as a heap of sand poured out and flowing down (73:14).

16) Then watch you for the Day that the sky will bring forth a kind of smoke (or mist) plainly visible (44:10).

17) The Day when the Earth will be rent asunder, from (men) hurrying out: that will be a gathering together, quite easy for Us (50:44).

18) ...The Day that the Caller will call (them) to a terrible affair, they will come forth, their eyes humbled - from (their) graves, (torpid) like locusts scattered abroad, hastening, with eyes transfixed, towards the Caller! 'Hard is this Day!', the Unbelievers will say (54:6-8).

19) At length, when the sight is dazed, and the moon is buried in darkness and the sun and moon are joined together (75:7-9).

20) The Day that the Trumpet shall be sounded, and you will come forth in crowds; and the heavens shall be opened as if there were doors, and the mountains shall vanish, as if they were a mirage (78:18-20).

21) Concerning what are they disputing? Concerning the Great News, about which they cannot agree (78:1-3).

22) One Day everything that can be in commotion will be in violent commotion, followed by oft-repeated (commotions): hearts that Day will be in agitation; cast down will be their eyes (79:6-9).

23) Therefore, when there comes the great, overwhelming (Event) (79:34).

24) At length, when there comes the Deafening Noise (80:33).

25) Has the story reached you of the overwhelming (Event)? (88:1).

26) When the earth is shaken to her (utmost) convulsion, and the earth throws up her burdens (from within), and man cries (distressed): 'What is the matter with her?' On that Day will she declare her tidings: for that your Sustainer will have given her inspiration. On that Day will men proceed in companies sorted out, to be shown the deeds that they (had done) (99:1-6).

27) And Our Command is but a single (Act), like the twinkling of an eye (54:50).

These are the details of that revolution which is referred to in the Quran. As already written, these are the literal meanings of these verses. You can look these up and decide for yourself as to which meanings are the best i.e. literal or metaphorical. And also which of the revolutions each refers to. In this respect there are two or three further verses which require special attention:

A Day when (all) mankind will stand before the Sustainer of the Worlds. (83:6)
And your Sustainer will come, and His angels, rank upon rank. (89:22)

And the Earth will shine with the Glory of its Sustainer: the Record (of Deeds) will be placed (open); the messengers and the witnesses will be brought forward and a just decision pronounced between them; and they will not be wronged (in the least). (39:69)

From these and other similar verses, it seems that they are related to some revolution which is going to take place on earth. However, let us now proceed.

16.2 The State of People

The verses noted above are those which are related to the universe. We now come to those verses which mention the state of the people in this revolution. In these verses also it is important that you keep the differences in mind between the literal and the metaphorical meanings and decide to which revolution out of the three it refers:

(1) The day when some faces will be 'dark' and some 'bright' (3:105-106, 67:27). Some faces will be pleasant and fresh while others will be sad and depressed (75:22-24, 76:11, 80:38-42, 88:207).

(2) The criminals will come to Allah with their heads bent down (32:12). Their speech will be sluggish (20:108-111).

(3) People will give evidence against their own self (6:131, 7:37). Everyone will be at odds with his own self (16:111). His hands, feet and tongue will give evidence against him (24:24-25, 36:65, 41:20-21).

(4) Everyone will have his 'book' of deeds with him (17:71, 69:19-27).

(5) Everyone will come alone just the way they were born (or created) alone (6:95).

(6) Different groups will differ with each other. Their perceptions including seeing and hearing will be very sharp. The day all matters will be resolved and for the transgressors this will be a day full of regrets and disappointments (19:37-38).

(7) This day the balance of justice will be raised and a deed as small as an atom will be brought forward (21:47, 99:7-8). The ones whose righteous deeds exceed in balance will be successful, while those whose wrong deeds exceed in balance will be in loss (101:6-11).

(8) The day the full control will rest with Allah and He will decide all matters (22:56). Everyone will get full recompense of his deeds and none will be treated unjustly (40:16-17).

(9) Eyes and hearts will be transformed (24:37). When hearts will come right up to the throats (40:18). They will be looking with a stealthy glance (42:45).

(10) The punishment will cover them from the top and the bottom (29:55).

(11) The criminals will separate (36:59). They will be recognised from their appearance (55:41).

(12) And We have put a bar in front of them and a bar behind them, and further, We have covered them up; so that they cannot see (36:9).

(13) Their crimes will be manifested in front of them and the consequences will encompass them from all sides (39:47-48, 40:16, 45:33).

(14) The day the criminals will be brought to the court with a guard pushing them forward and a witness to accompany them (50:21). The witnesses will stand with them (40:15).

(15) The day all veils will be lifted from their eyes and their eyesight will be very sharp (50:22).

(16) Excepting the *Momineen*, all friends will become enemies (43:67).

(17) The day none will be able to speak due to fear and no apology will be accepted (77:35-36).

(18) Everyone will be questioned about the joys and indulgences of this life (102:8).

16.3   References to Various Nations

In some verses nations are mentioned instead of peoples e.g. in *Surah Araf* it is stated that when a nation enters hell, other nations will condemn them and they will quarrel among themselves. Every nation will accuse the others that it misguided them and will say to Allah that that nation should receive double punishment. The answer will be given that you will all get double punishment, because every nation's conduct and behaviour affects other nations (7:38-39). In *Surah Jathia*, it is stated that every nation will enter on bended knee and everyone will be invited to look at their record of deeds so that they can receive the full recompense of these (45:28 and 38:59).

16.4   Mutual Quarrels

In many verses of the Quran, it is mentioned that in hell various individuals and groups will fight amongst each other and will accuse each other of misguiding them onto the wrong path. Those quarrels will be the most revealing and illuminating which are between leaders and their followers. The Quran has presented their mutual accusations and condemnations in great detail:

(1) In *Surah Ibrahim* the followers will tell their leaders that we followed you faithfully and therefore can you now remove this punishment from us. You used to make many claims about your might and power. In response they will say that we ourselves are in punishment, what help can we possibly give to you. So howling and wailing is useless (14:21, 40:47-48).

(2) In *Surah Ahzab* the followers will say to Allah that we are not responsible for our crimes. We just obeyed these leaders and they misguided us so give them double punishment (32:67-68). Undoubtedly this excuse of theirs will not be accepted. Who told them not to use their intellect and reasoning and persist in blindly following these leaders.

(3) In *Surah Saba* is stated that the leaders will tell their peoples, that you yourself wished to follow the wrong path, since what power did we have over you to force you onto the wrong path. The followers will reply in return, that day and night you used to contrive such tricks to persuade and induce simple people like us and thus you used to put us onto the wrong path (34:31-33, 37:27-32).

(4) In *Surah Saad* is noted that when people of the same faith enter into their hell they will also squabble among themselves and try to apportion blame for their plight. Along with this they will also query, where are those people who used to warn us against wrongdoing in the world, and we were wont to call them the worst of creation (they will be in paradise) (38:59-63). After describing all of

this, the Quran proclaims that these mutual quarrels among the dwellers of hell is of a surety the truth[123] (38:64) See also (39:31).

(5) In *Surah Momin* after the quarrels between the leaders and their followers, it states that they will then address the guards of hell themselves, and ask them can they not do something to lighten this punishment on them. But the guards of hell will not have the authority to do so (40:47-50).

(6) In *Surah Qaf*, instead of the quarrels between leaders and their followers, there is mutual argument between those people who were friends in this world. There, every one of them will accuse each other for persistently misguiding them onto the wrong path (50:23-28). Contrary to this, in *Surah Safaat* there is mention of such a friend who used to misguide his close companions, but they did not listen to him, thus they were in paradise, while this friend of theirs was in hell (37:51-57).

16.5 Squabbles with the Religious Clergy

The previous quarrels were between the followers with their leaders. In other verses are also mentioned the mutual disputes occurring between the spiritual leaders and religious clergy with their devotees and followers. The same is said regarding them, that they will accuse each other, and the spiritual leaders and religious clergy will refuse to take responsibility for misguiding their supporters (26:62-66, 28:74-75, 30:13-14)[124].

16.6 The Mutual Conversation between the Occupiers of Hell and Heaven

In *Surah Hadeed* it is stated that the inhabitants of paradise will have the light of their foreheads going ahead and keeping their path illuminated in front of them. The hypocrites will say to them, that we also used to be with you, so stop a bit, so that we can borrow some light from your torches. In reply they will say, that these lights only glow due to the results of our deeds and cannot be received by merely requesting it and if you want to achieve the value of this light, you will need to go back to the previous life (where none can return). Then it is said that there will be a partition between these two groups in which there will be a door, within which will be blessings (opportunities for self-development), and outside of which will be hell (57:12-13).

In *Surah Mudathar*, the inhabitants of paradise will ask the inhabitants of hell as to what they did which has landed them in this punishment and they will reply, detailing what crimes they did (74:40-46). Since the inhabitants of paradise will live as a brotherly community, their lives will therefore be like a society. Their mutual conversations are

---

[123] We see these types of arguments daily in today's world, with a continuous flow of accusations and counter accusations in the media where politics is being discussed. (Ed)
[124] More details are covered in the chapter on '*Jahannum*'.

mentioned in great detail in various verses of the Quran e.g. (52:25-26). (Further details will be covered in Chapter 20).

16.7 Regrets of the Denizens of Hell

The inhabitants of hell seeing their deeds will be in a state of great regret[125]. In *Surah Al-Haqah*, it states that when the record of his deeds is handed over to such a one he will shriek on seeing the consequences and with hopelessness will cry:

Ah! Would that (Death) had made an end of me. (69:27)

Woe unto me! Would that I were dust. (78:40)

At that moment he will realise that he did not comprehend this reality in the worldly life:

He will say: 'Ah! Would that I had sent forth (good deeds) for (this) my (Future) Life!' (89:24)

16.8 No Return to This Life

But these regrets will be of no use, because the future of the human self was going to be established according to the deeds in this worldly life and this worldly life had ended. Over there, there will be no longer opportunity for him and there will be no return to this world. As noted before, the one who is dead will say:

O my Sustainer! send me back (to life), 'In order that I may work righteousness in the things I neglected.' By no means! It is but a word he says. (23:100)

In this same *Surah*, a little later it is stated that the inhabitant of hell will say to Allah, take me out of here and send me back and if I do the same again then I will truly be a criminal. The reply will be given that this cannot be done (23:107). In *Surah Sajda* the criminals will say that now we have seen the reality unveiled in front of us and have heard the judgment with our own ears:

...Our Sustainer! We have seen and we have heard: Now then send us back (to the world): we will work righteousness: for we do indeed (now) believe. (32:12)

But this will not be possible. Life only progresses forward in a straight path and its movement is not cyclic. In *Surah Fatir*, in reply to this request of the criminals to go back, it is said that now you say that if we get another opportunity then we will show you by following the right path this time. Tell Us, did you get insufficient time in the

---

[125] The Quran helps us to avoid the regrets and disappointments which are the consequences of our deeds and are the products of our interaction with other people. (Ed)

first life. You had time and there were people who told you which is the path of virtue and which is the path of evil. Why did you not take advantage of this (35:37) In *Surah Zumr* it is even stated that at that time you used to be told that now there is time so change your path, and do not say afterwards that if we get another chance then we will improve ourselves, as another opportunity will not be given (39:58 and 42:47).

16.9 There Will Not Even be Death There.

To rid oneself of this punishment, the second way could have been that death comes to man, but there will be no death there:

> *But those who reject ((Allah)) - for them will be the Fire of Hell: No term shall be determined for them, so they should die, nor shall its Penalty be lightened for them. Thus do We reward every ungrateful one. (35:36) See also (37:58-59, 44:56)*

The Quran makes it clear that man was not alive before he was born in this life and that state was akin to death. Then he was given life – this is called one death and then one life. After this will be another death at the end of this life and then he will get another life. Thus there are two deaths and two lives. The Quran has referred to these two deaths and two lives e.g. see (2:28, 40:11).

But the life of hell will be neither life nor death:

> *...for him is Hell: therein shall he neither die nor live. (20:74) See also (87:13)*

The condition will be such that:

> *...death will come to him from every quarter, yet will he not die... (14:17)*

These are those details about the Day of Judgment about which is said, that their occurrence is a true reality (69:51). Such a certainty as when you converse with each other and have no doubt about your mutual conversation (51:23).

Before we conclude this subject, there is one point which requires particular consideration. As written above, nations will enter hell. Regarding this hell, if it is related to the destruction in this life, then it is self-evident that the destruction of a nation comes to all people of that nation equally who are present at the time of its occurrence, regardless of whether they are good or bad. If we take it as being hell in the next life, then a nation or group will mean those people who have the same ideology. That is, that it happens in this life, that a wicked nation on the wrong path will have individuals who do not conform to their policies. These individuals admonish them from following the wrong path, and according to their capacity, try to change things as well. The Quran has spoken in detail about an individual *Momin* (believer) in the great court of Pharaoh, who in a full assembly, opposed Pharaoh's policy, and with great courage and logic supported the message of Moses. This speech was so illuminating that the Quran has secured it in its pages and given it immortality (40:28-44). Similarly, the Quran has referred to the *Eimaan* of the wife of Pharaoh and acknowledged it

(66:11). In the next life, these kinds of good people will be separate from this nation, and only the wrong-doers will go to hell. The wrong-doers are the groups of individuals with the same ideology and deeds that the Quran has referred to:

The Unbelievers will be led to Hell in crowd: until, when they arrive there, its gates will be opened... (39:71)

And about the righteous:

And those who were righteous will be led to the Garden in crowds: until behold, they arrive there; its gates will be opened... (39:73)

In the present life all live mixed up together amongst each other, but in the hereafter they will be separated into two groups. Those individuals whose self has developed to such an extent that after this life in the next life they will be capable of moving on to further evolutionary stages, will be in a separate group which will be called the group of paradise. During the whole year students remain in one class, but after the annual examination they are divided into two groups, i.e. those who pass and those who fail. According to the law of evolution, this is the same process. The individuals belonging to one species are counted as one group. But those who become fittest move on to the next stage of life. Those who do not attain this ability are stopped from progressing forward. This is called *Jahannum* or *Jaheem* (hell). The meaning of *Jaheem* is 'to be stopped'. More details will be given on these aspects under the topics of Paradise (*Jannat*) and Hell (*Jahannum*).

(Intentionally left blank)

(Intentionally left blank)

17 'Shifa'at' – Intercession

The subject which we have discussed so far could have been continued, but such a point is reached where a break is very necessary, and here that is related to the belief in intercession.

The Quranic concept of reward and punishment has already been presented to you. According to this concept you will have seen that:

(1) According to the Law of Requital an individual's every deed (even to the extent of every inner thought) gives birth to its own effect – this is Allah's firm and immutable Law.

(2) Some deeds produce positive (constructive) effects while others produce negative (destructive) effects and the result of every deed leaves its imprint as it is done.

(3) If the balance of the results of constructive deeds of an individual is heavier, he moves on a step further to the next stage of evolution - this is called his reward, or a life of paradise. The one whose balance of constructive deeds is lighter, will not go forward - this is called punishment, or the life of hell.

From this concept you can see that there is no question of any external intervention in the reward or punishment of an individual. However in prevalent Islam (like other religions), it is commonly believed that the 'devotees of Allah'[126] will intervene on the behalf of those people who are deemed to be eligible for punishment because of the results of their deeds, and that Allah will then 'forgive' them and they will go to paradise. This is called 'Shifa'at' (intercession), and the one who intercedes is called 'Shafee'[127]. It is obvious that this belief or doctrine is the creation of that mentality according to which Allah is like a dictator or king or president, who can forgive people according to his whim and does not follow any law or procedure. For no rhyme or reason, he bestows tracts of land to some when he is pleased with them, and when he is annoyed, he can incarcerate anyone. The one whom he incarcerates can have intercession in his favour by the king's cohorts and those close to him, and he can accept their intercession and thus forgive the criminal and set him free.

According to such a belief, the complete eminent structure of the Law of Requital as explained in the Quran - the most refined and pristine form of justice which has no parallel - comes tumbling down. Regarding the daily dealings of bureaucrats about whom it is known that they accept intercession in making decisions, society has a contemptuous view of them. Therefore this reality is explicitly clear, that such a

---

[126] For example, messengers of Allah, saints, members of the religious clergy, mystics etc. (Ed)
[127] Plural is 'Shifaa'.

concept of intercession is completely non-Quranic, and can never be part of its system of justice.

The Quran has mentioned the beliefs of those who follow falsehood and who used to say that their gods whom they worshipped, would intercede and save them:

They serve, besides Allah, things that hurt them not nor profit them, and they say: 'These are our intercessors with Allah.' Say: Do you indeed inform Allah of something He knows not, in the heavens or on earth? Glory to Him! and far is He above the partners they ascribe (to Him)!' (10:18)

In *Surah Baqra*, the Quran addresses the Jews who held belief in intercession:

Then guard yourselves against a day when one self shall not avail another nor shall intercession be accepted for him, nor shall compensation be taken from him, nor shall anyone be helped. (2:48)

In the same *Surah* a little later, these very same words are unambiguously reiterated:

Then guard yourselves against a Day when one self shall not avail another, nor shall compensation be accepted from him nor shall intercession profit him nor shall anyone be helped. (2:123)

And later, the Muslims are addressed with the same warning:

O you who believe! Spend out of (the bounties) We have provided for you, before the Day comes when no bargaining (Will avail), nor friendship nor intercession. Those who reject this Truth, do harm to themselves. (2:254)

In *Surah Saba*:

So on that Day no power shall they have over each other, for profit or harm...(34:42)

In *Surah Momin*:

That Day will every self be requited for what it earned; no injustice will there be that Day, for Allah is Swift in taking account. (40:17)

And also:

No intercessor will they have among their 'partners'... (30:13)

Then will no intercession of (any) intercessors profit them. (74:48)

'And behold! you come to us bare and alone as We created you for the first time: you have left behind you all (the favours) which We bestowed on you: We see not with you your intercessors whom you thought to be partners in your affairs: so now all relations between you have been cut off, and your (pet) fancies have left you in the lurch!' (6:95). See also (7:53, 26:100)

From the above, the position of the Quran regarding the concept of intercession is made very clear. But in the Quran there are some verses in which *Shifa'at* is mentioned and the question is, what does *Shifa'at* mean in these verses. So it is important that it should first be ascertained and established as to what this term means based on the Quran and the lexicon of Arabic. I think that because of the importance of the subject, it would be more appropriate that a part of the 'Lughat ul Quran'[128] related to this subject be incorporated here.

17.1 Meanings of *Shifaa* as per the Lughat Ul-Quran

'Shaf'un' basically means to join one thing with another, or to join two things together, or put two things together so that these become a pair. *'Shafa tun'* means while helping others or looking after them to join with them. *Shafa tun* means to try and acquire a desired thing and thereby enhance one's own things[129]. In terms of *fiqah* (shariat), this is a special right of ownership and whoever has it can pay for a property and become its owner. The payment is based on what a third party has valued for that property. *'Naqatun Shafeun'*[130] is that she-camel whose one offspring is walking after her and following her while she is also pregnant with her second one. After this, the word *Shafa tun* started to mean intercession, because in this one person stands with another with a view to support him, and intercedes in his favour. It has also come to mean to perform supplications. *Ibn-e-Faris*[131] has noted that *'Shafa fulanan le fulanen'* is said when an individual comes as a helper with someone else, and whatever his companion wants he also desires it for him.

The Quran teaches a collective life instead of an individual life because the self-development of an individual and its further progress is possible only within a collective system of living. In this respect, in a community of *Momineen* every individual is a *Shafi un* of another *Momin* i.e. always with him to support and offer help. The centre of this system is called *Shafi* (*Amir*[132]) – he does not allow anyone to feel isolated in his community. This mutual support is called *'Shifa'at'* and this is its basic gist.

---

[128] The 'Lughat ul Quran' is a dictionary of the Quranic terms with their prevalent meanings at the time of revelation. It is available in English free on the internet and in book form, and is based on the translation from the original work written and compiled by the author. (Ed)

[129] For further details please refer to the Lughat ul Quran, Volume I, under the root Sh-F-Ain. (Ed)

[130] *'Naqatun'* is a she-camel

[131] He compiled a Lughat (dictionary).

[132] *Amir* means leader.

Such a community of *Momineen* extends this *Shifa'at* (support) to others outwith its own group as their responsibility is to provide and cater for the sustenance of the whole of mankind. For this the Quran states:

> *…Help you one another in righteousness and piety, but help you not one another in sin and rancour… (5:2)*

In another verse:

> *Whoever recommends and helps a good cause becomes a partner therein: And whoever recommends and helps an evil cause, shares in its burden… (4:85)*

We should note that cooperation means to aim to help one another, while *Shifa'a'* means that one person goes specifically with another to provide help.

Now let us move forward. The prevalent belief generally among Muslims is that on the Day of Judgment when the verdict will be announced and the order will be given for hell for the criminals, then those individuals who are closest to Allah such as the messengers and especially the last messenger[133], will intercede on behalf of these criminals and have them forgiven so that they too will enter paradise. This belief is called *Shifa'at*. Obviously this belief extinguishes the whole basis of *Deen* as explained in the Quran, whose very foundation is the Law of Requital:

> *Then shall anyone who has done an atom's weight of good, see it and anyone who has done an atom's weight of evil, shall see it. (99:7-8)*

It can be seen that this belief of *Shifa'at* came into existence during the time of kingship (known as *Malukeat*), when the cohorts of these tyrannical and oppressive rulers used to intercede with them on behalf of criminals who would then be pardoned. In addition, this belief was reinforced by the prevalent belief among Christians who believed in salvation and atonement through belief in Jesus[134]. When the Christians said look at our messenger Jesus, whoever believes in him can be saved by him from hell through *Kuffara* (atonement) for his sins and contrary to this your messenger (Muhammed) can do nothing for the sinners, then to counter this allegation, similar claims were invented by Muslims, that on the Day of Judgement when the accountability is over and criminals have been consigned to hell, then the last messenger (Muhammad) will prostrate himself (*Sajda*) in front of Allah and until Allah forgives every individual in his *Ummah* (the Muslim community) and sends each and every one to paradise, the messenger will not raise his head or go to paradise himself till this process of intercession is complete. This may have countered the Christian claim, but this shook the very foundation of the whole basis of *Deen* (the Law of Requital) and the nation fell

---

[133] See *Surah (2:285)*. The Quran makes no distinction between the messengers. (Ed)
[134] See *Surah (5:116-120)*. In these verses the Quran makes it clear that Jesus will not be able to intercede. (Ed)

into the hell of destruction. There is nothing in the Quran which supports this false concept, nor is there any possibility of the existence of such a belief. It has been stated in very clear terms that according to the Law of Requital:

Then guard yourselves against a day when one self shall not avail another nor shall intercession be accepted for him, nor shall compensation be taken from him, nor shall anyone be helped. (2:48)

To support this belief of *Shifa'at*, verses such as the following are quoted out of context:

...Who is there who can intercede in His presence except as He permits?...(2:255)

The conclusion drawn from this verse is that intercession can be done with Allah's permission and the last messenger will intercede for his Ummah after obtaining Allah's permission. But to draw such a conclusion from these verses is wrong. Firstly, because such a belief of *Shifa'at* is totally against the Law of Requital, which is continuously referred to in the Quran from beginning to end. Therefore, if with the Law of Requital the belief of *Shifa'at* is also present in the Quran, then it will mean that contradictory beliefs are noted in the Quran (Allah forbid)[135]. For example, see the verse which is quoted above – the previous verse to this states:

O you who believe! Spend out of (the bounties) We have provided for you, before the Day comes when no bargaining (Will avail), nor friendship nor intercession. Those who reject Faith they are the wrong-doers. (2:254)

If this meaning is taken that intercession can be availed with Allah's permission, and this intercession will be successful, then there is a blatant contradiction between these two verses.

Now the question remains, what is the true meaning of the second verse (2:255)? According to the Law of Requital, the effect of every deed imprints itself continuously on the human self. But the Quran, in order to make us understand the truth of reward and punishment, has illustrated this by painting such pictures as prisoners attending court and the verdict being announced after the court proceedings. In a court, other than a ruler or judge, an accused, a plaintiff, witnesses, and police etc are present. The Quran has used such examples to make things clear. For example, in one verse the person who is being held accountable will be standing alone in the dock:

And behold! you come to us bare and alone as We created you for the first time: you have left behind you all (the favours) which We bestowed on you: We see not with you your intercessors whom you thought to be partners in your affairs: so now all relations between you have been cut off, and your (pet) fancies have left you in the lurch! (6:95)

---

[135] The Quran clearly states that there is no contradiction in its message e.g. see (4:82). (Ed)

In another verse:

And there will come forth every self: with each will have someone to drive, and someone to bear witness. (50:21)

These witnesses will not stand up of their own accord: whoever is called will come and will then be given permission to give evidence. These are those *Shafi un* (standing with) which are referred to in such verses where it is stated:

…Who is there who can intercede in His presence except as He permits?…(2:255)

These witnesses will be messengers as well, about whom the Quran has stated:

One day will Allah gather the messengers together, and ask: 'What was the response you received (from men to your teaching)?' They will say: 'We have no knowledge: it is You Who knows in full all that is hidden.' (5:109)

And apart from the messengers, the forces of the universe (angels) will also be similarly called:

The Day that the Spirit and the angels will stand forth in ranks, none shall speak except any who is permitted by (Allah) Most Gracious, and he will say what is right. (78:38)

It is clear that in these verses the term *Shifa'at* means giving evidence, because giving truthful evidence in support of someone is of great assistance to him. A further explanation of this is given by the Quran:

And those whom they invoke besides Allah have no power of intercession; only he who bears witness to the Truth, and they know (him). (43:86)

Those whom these people call on apart from Allah, they have no right to *Shifa'at*. Only he has a right to it, who gives evidence based on truth. In other words, the meaning of *Shifa'at* is evidence. To remove this confusion or doubt, the last messenger of Allah is called 'Shaheed un' (witness) (16:89). He has not been called *Shafee un* (intercessor). About the people of other religions who maintain this belief of intercession, the Quran states:

Then will no intercession of (any) intercessors profit them. (78:48)

This is why the Divine Law is as stated:

… no bearer of burdens can bear the burden of another… (6:164)

Paradise is only gained in exchange for righteous deeds (7:43). Birth is given to the belief of gaining paradise through intercession in a nation which becomes inactive and loses the desire to work. The Quran informs us that such a belief took birth among the Jews when they had reached their lowest ebb and used to say:

And they say: 'The Fire shall not touch us but for a few numbered days:' Say: Have you taken a promise from Allah, for He never breaks His promise? or is it that you say of Allah what you do not know? (2:80)

Regarding this, the Quran declares that these beliefs are wrong. Allah's Law is that he who follows the wrong path will be destroyed. And the one who has acquired *Eimaan* and does righteous deeds, he will inherit paradise:

But those who have faith (Eimaan) and work righteousness, they are companions of the Garden: Therein shall they abide. (2:82)

From the above discussion we can conclude:

1) In this life, *Shifa'at* will mean to be with someone in a task with a view to providing help. If it is a good work then the helper will also be rewarded; however, if the work is evil, then he will also partly share the consequences of doing wrong.

2) In the next life, the concept of *Shifa'at* is such that a witness stands up to give true evidence in support of someone. This is a metaphorical explanation.

3) Criminals escaping from punishment through the intercession of someone on their behalf, or anyone receiving something to which they have no right through another's intercession, is against the basic Quranic teaching. That is why this interpretation of *Shifa'at* is not correct. Wherever this word is mentioned in the Quran, it is important to see the context in which it is used.

So this is the correct Quranic interpretation of this word *Shifa'at*. From this it is clear that the Quran has strongly opposed the concept of intercession; however, the Quran has used this term to mean support or evidence. The Quran has permitted the word *Shafee* to be used with the meaning of a companion or helper. This point is also clarified by the fact that in various verses Allah has called Himself *Shafee*. It is obvious that if the word *Shafee* is taken to mean the one who intercedes this will not make sense, as Allah is Sovereign or the One who makes decisions. It is clear that someone who is Sovereign cannot be an intercessor at the same time. Therefore its meanings are a companion or helper. For example, in *Surah Inam* it is stated:

*Give this warning to those in whose (hearts) is the fear that they will be brought (to judgment) before their Sustainer: except for Him they will have no protector nor helper...
(6:51) See also (6:70, 32:4)*

In *Surah Zumr* it is initially stated:

What! Do they take for helpers others besides Allah. Say: Even if they have no power whatever and no intelligence? (39:43)

Then the Quran makes it clear:

Say: To Allah belongs all protection ... (39:44)

This verse means that man can receive support and favour only through being in line with the Divine Laws of Allah - none can help man if he goes against these Laws. This same meaning is in those verses where it is said that apart from '*Allah's Eza'an*[136]', no-one's *Shifa'at* can be of any use. This means that if an individual stands with another according to the Divine Laws, his standing thus with him will give benefit, otherwise it will not.

... No intercessor (can plead with Him) except as per His laws... (10:3)

In *Surah Miriam*:

None shall have the power of support, except those who have a Covenant with the Most Gracious (Rehman). (19:87)

In another verse:

On that Day shall no intercession avail except for those for whom permission has been granted by (Allah) Most Gracious and whose word is acceptable to Him. (20:109) See also (21:28, 34:23)

In a few places there is mention of *Shifa'at* by 'angels' – the angels are those forces of nature through which the system of the universe is functioning. These forces of nature can prostrate before Adam (man), i.e. man can subjugate them. If man utilises these forces of nature according to the Divine Laws, then these will support his endeavours and help him. If he goes against these Divine Laws, then these forces will not be of assistance to him. This is the aim of *Shifa'at* by angels, which if carried out after *Eza'an* of Allah:

How many-so-ever be the angels in the heavens, their intercession will avail nothing except after Allah has given leave for whom He pleases and that he is acceptable to Him. (53:26)

This is the correct concept of *Shifa'at* as per the Quran. It does not mean that a criminal can escape due to another's intercession. Whoever puts his finger into fire and burns it,

---

[136] The common meaning of '*Eza'an*' is giving permission or to order, but when this word is used in reference to Allah, it means the Divine Laws, because Allah has said there can be no change in his order. Therefore the order which cannot be changed becomes a Law.

no intercession, even that of a greatly influential person, can save him from pain. This is an immutable Law of Allah. He can only be helped by one who gives him treatment according to Allah's Laws.

(Intentionally left blank)

(Intentionally left blank)

18 An Introduction to Punishment in the Hereafter

In relation to the punishment in the Hereafter, we should have come to the subject of *Jahannum*. (So that its complete concept could be understood). But we think that the various words used in the Quran for this punishment should first be defined.

The root of the word '*Azaab*' is Ain-Z-B, which has basic meanings: (1) That pain or trouble which affects or interferes with the comforts of life. (2) An obstacle or obstruction lying in someone's path.

Punishment in this life includes all kinds of destruction and ruin which can include physical or mental or psychological suffering. But what the punishment in the hereafter will be, we cannot understand that at our existing level of consciousness, because at present we cannot visualise what type or form or state of life it will be. From the Quran it is clear that in the next life feelings will be very intense. This is why we can get some inkling of the severity of internal distress which will be experienced in the next life due to one's failures and disappointments.

The second meaning of the word *Azaab*, in other words the unassailable obstructions in the path of life, puts some light on this aspect. The purpose of the present life is to develop the human self. The person whose self has developed to such an extent that he is capable of going from this stage of life to the next stage of life, will progress forward – this is defined as the life of paradise. The one whose self is not developed to such an extent will not be able to go forward and he will be stopped. This is that intense sense of failure which is called *Azaab* in the hereafter. '*Azubun*' or '*Azebun*' refers to that man or horse or camel that stops eating or drinking due to the severe intensity of thirst.

From this, you will appreciate the delicate point that this condition is not imposed from the outside but is a natural consequence of the internal state of the individual or animal. It is apparent from this that though the words used in the Quran to describe the punishment in the hereafter are those used in reference to this current life, the aim is to expose the internal state of turmoil and unhappiness of an individual in the next life (because this is the only way to explain it).

As already stated, this state will be the consequence of the stoppage of further progress of the human self – this punishment of the hereafter is called '*Azaab Al-Jaheem*'.

18.1 'Azaab Al-Jaheem' – Stoppage of Further Development

Jaheem is another name of *Jahannum* or hell. *'Ajama Unha'* means 'he stopped from something'. The stoppage which is in the path of life's evolutionary progress is called *Azaab Al-Jaheem*. This punishment in life is referred to as the internal turmoil due to the stoppage or being prevented from going forward in the evolutionary progress of human life. Regarding the inhabitants of paradise, the Quran states that the light emanating from their 'foreheads' will brighten the path in front of them and this process of their going forward will be unimpeded and continuous. The Quran states:

> *Nor will they there taste Death, except the first death... (44:56) See also (40:7, 52:18)*

Then another death will not be imposed on them[137] and they will be protected from that punishment which causes internal turmoil due to the stoppage from being able to proceed on the paths going forward (40:7, 52:18). Contrary to this, regarding the denizens of hell:

> *With Us are Fetters (to bind them), and a Fire (to burn them). (73:12)*

These internal shackles which will not be externally imposed, are even now affecting human beings at every step, but at this stage they are not aware of it. At that time these will become visible[138]:

> *And Hell (Jaheem) shall be placed in full view for (all) to see. (79:36)*

The invisible will become visible for all to see.

18.2 'Azaab -un Maheen' – The Punishment of Inner Humiliation

In contrast to those who will move forward, for the ones who remain behind, the sense of inferiority they will feel is known as *Azaab-un Maheen* i.e. utterly humiliating punishment.

> *...And they shall have a humiliating punishment. (4:14) See also (6:94)*

The reason for this has been explained:

> *...You received your good things in the life of the world, and you took your pleasure out of them: but today shall you be recompensed with a Penalty of humiliation: for that you were arrogant on earth without just cause, and that you (ever) transgressed. (46:20)*

---

[137] The Quran recognises the fear of death in man and thus points to the finite status of this physical life. Death is a deadline in this life, and a reminder about the higher purpose of life. (Ed)

[138] Examples of these internal shackles which we wittingly and unwittingly put around our necks include wrong beliefs, both religious and non-religious, self-objectification, wrong attitudes, relative values, celebrity worship, thinking life will end with death, fatalism, prejudices, jealousies etc. (Ed)

In other words while in this world these people tried to become renowned without doing anything productive or constructive for mankind. Now the reality is made clear, that false pride once unveiled, becomes a source of *Azaab-un Maheen* - humiliation and ruin[139]. If we heat up the false coating on an ornament, the underlying reality or truth becomes clearly exposed. And the resultant sense of humiliation of being thus caught and exposed is their punishment (4:56).

18.3 'Azaaba Yaume Aqeem' - The Punishment of Failure

The meanings of *Aqeem* include not only sterility, but also failure in one's labours. It also means to close something or to stop or to cut off. So this term is applicable to man's utter failure and hopelessness in a situation (22:55).

18.4 Comparison

In *Surah Raad*:

> For them is a penalty in the life of this world, but harder, truly, is the penalty of the Hereafter: and defender have they none against Allah. (13:34)

From this it is obvious that no matter how much pain and distress there is in this life, it is far less when compared to the life in the hereafter[140]. In the hereafter, human consciousness will increase manifold as compared to this life.

18.5 'Azaab -un Azeem' - The Great Punishment

This is why the punishment in the next life is described as being *Azaab-un Azeem*, very severe. In *Surah Baqra* it is stated:

> ...For them there is nothing but disgrace in this world, and in the world to come, an exceeding torment. (2:114) See also (5:33, 5:41, 24:23)

Regarding this it is stated in *Surah Al e Imran*:

> Be not like those who are divided amongst themselves and fall into disputations after receiving Clear Signs: For them is a dreadful penalty. (3:105) See also (10:15, 39:13)

In some verses it is quoted that the last messenger also said that if I go against the Divine Laws then:

> Say: 'I would, if I disobeyed my Sustainer, indeed have fear of the penalty of a Mighty Day.'
> (6:15)

---

[139] We have seen how the gap between the rich and poor keeps increasing despite the rhetoric of the rich nation states about reducing poverty. (Ed)
[140] In this life those who commit suicide think that their death will end their predicament. (Ed)

In some verses this is also called '*Azaab Yaum Ul-Qyama*' (5:36, 39:24, 39:47).

18.6 'Azaab-un Muqeem' – The Sustained Punishment

In the life in the hereafter, punishment will not be temporary or short lived. (Its details will be covered in the next chapter on *Jahannum*). Those who go forward will continue to progress, and those who have stopped progressing will remain stuck. That is why their state will be permanent. This is called *Azaab-un Muqeem*. In *Surah Maida* it is stated:

> *Their wish will be to get out of the Fire, but never will they get out therefrom: their penalty will be one that endures. (5:37) See also (9:68, 42:45).*

This is also called *'Azaab e Khuld'*, the sustained and never ending punishment (32:14). (The word *'Khalud'* as related to hell and paradise will be discussed in the next two chapters). There will be no diminution in this punishment (40:49, 35:36). Instead, as the awareness about the state of punishment increases, the effects of the punishment itself will also increase (78:30).

18.7 'Azaab-un Naar' - The Punishment of Fire

For complete destruction, fire is an example commonly used, as it burns everything to leave nothing but a heap of ashes. Since those who follow the wrong path have their life destroyed (in the hereafter), the Quran has used fire to denote hell and all the details of hell are related to this metaphor. The fire of hell is not like the physical fire in this world. The Quran declares:

> *(It is) the Fire of (the Wrath of) Allah kindled (to a blaze), the which does mount to the Hearts. (104:6-7)*

This is that punishment which the *Momineen* wish to protect themselves from:

> *Our Sustainer! Give us good in this world and good in the Hereafter, and defend us from the torment of the Fire. (2:201) See also (3:15)*

> *Our Sustainer! any whom You do admit to the Fire, truly You cover with shame, and never will wrong-doers find any helpers. (3:192)*

From this it is made clear that it is not that fire which burns in ovens. It is that fire which leads to the deprivation of any humaneness from an individual – this is a state of the worst ruin (32:19-20, 46:35).

18.8 Heat and Grief

Using fire as an example, the various states of punishments in hell have been described in terms in which heat, grief and extreme temperatures are prominent. For example, in some verses it is likened to '*Azaab e Hareeq*' in which *Hareeq* means the fire which is produced when we rub a file on iron and sparks are produced – this is what is called the fire of the 'soul'. This is the correct meaning of this *Azaab*. In *Surah Anfaal* it is stated that the angels will slap the criminals and will say:

> ...taste the penalty of the blazing Fire (Hareeq)... (8:50)

In another verse:

> ...for him there is disgrace in this life, and on the Day of Judgment We shall make him taste the Penalty of burning Fire (Hareeq). (22:9)

Going further, after a few verses it is stated:

> Every time they wish to get away therefrom, from anguish, they will be forced back therein, and (it will be said), 'Taste ye the Penalty of Burning (Hareeq)!' (22:22) See also (85:10)

Due to the intensity of the 'heat', in another verse it is also called '*Azaab e Samoom*' - the literal translation of which is of a very hot strong wind which penetrates the body and results in the effects similar to that of a poison. In the deserts, such winds produce very severe destruction (52:27).

18.9 '*Azaab e Hameem*' – The Punishment of Boiling Water

In the same context there are some verses about the punishments in hell, in which it is stated that boiling water will be made available for drinking:

> ...they will have for drink boiling water, and for punishment, one most grievous: for they persisted in rejecting Allah. (6:70) See also (10:4)

In *Surah Dukhan* it is stated that boiling water will be poured over his head and it will be said:

> Then pour over his head the Penalty of Boiling Water, 'Taste you (this)! Truly you were mighty, full of honour!' (44:49)

You considered yourself as master of great power and status in the world. The end of false power is humiliating destruction.

18.10 'Azaab-un Ileem' – The Punishment of Extreme Grief

The Quran has comprehensively put together all the forms of extreme grief and pain in one word 'Azaab-un Ileem'. 'Ilam' is that pain which is extreme in its grief, anguish and sorrow. From this, the concept of Azaab-un Ileem becomes clear. This state of grief defines many types of deprivations, about which the Quran states:

> As for those who sell the faith they owe to Allah and their own plighted word for a small price, they shall have no portion in the Hereafter: Nor will Allah speak to them or look at them on the Day of Judgment, nor will He purify them: They shall have a grievous penalty (Azaab-un Ileem). (3:77) See also (2:10)

This also happens to those who realise their state of loss too late when they cannot rectify it– one can imagine the internal torment of such an individual (4:18, 5:36, and 10:4).

18.11 'Azaab-un Shadeed' – Very Severe Punishment

Pain to such a severe degree which then keeps increasing in intensity – such a tormented state is called Azaab-un Shadeed (10:70, 35:7). This is an automatic consequence of 'Shirk' i.e. mixing your own or other man-made laws with the Divine Laws (50:26), or for those who consider the aim of their life to be only the immediate material benefits of this life and who ignore the Permanent Values of the Quran (57:20).

The severity of the punishment in hell which has been described in these words can be imagined from the following verse:

> …death will come to him from every quarter, yet will he not die: and in front of him will be a chastisement unrelenting. (14:17)

Apart from this, it will be such a punishment in which all types of chastisements are concentrated and become focused in one place. In reference to this, the guardians of hell are called 'Ghilaz-un Shidad-un'[141]:

> O you who believe! save yourselves and your families from a Fire whose fuel is Men and Stones, over which are (appointed) angels stern (and) severe, who flinch not (from executing) the Commands they receive from Allah, but do (precisely) what they are commanded. (66:6)

These are the different forms of Allah's punishment (14:21) which are noted as metaphorical states which are the consequence of man's living a life based on wrong values. For all of these states, one comprehensive term is used - Jahannum - the detailed explanation of which is the topic of the next chapter and should provide the cause for

---

[141] 'Ghilaz-un Shidad-un' – those who unflinchingly carry out the commands of Allah (Ed)

learning thousands of salutary lessons.

(Intentionally left blank)

(Intentionally left blank)

19 'Jahannum' – Hell

In olden times, there was a valley located south of Jerusalem, in which there was a temple dedicated to a God called *'Maulook'*. There, human beings were burnt alive as a sacrifice to this deity. In Hebrew, a valley is called *'Jee'* and the person after whom this valley was named was called *'Hanum'*. Therefore, this valley in which human beings were burnt and sacrificed was called *'Jee-Hanum'* (or *Jahannum*)[142]. From this context, *Jahannum* means a place where humanity is sacrificed. The Quran has used this word in this context.

According to the Quran, the purpose of human life is that after development of the human self to live a pleasant life both in this world and after this, in the life of the hereafter to be enabled to develop in the further evolutionary stages of life. The life in which this aim is achieved will be called a life of paradise – in this world as well as in the hereafter. Contrary to this, the life in which development of the human self stops and as a result his life's achievements remain barren - that is a life of *Jahannum* or hell. For the development of the human self the following is necessary:

(1) The physical needs of his life are met without any worry and are met with great respect and dignity.

(2) Man, apart from the confines of the Permanent Values, is completely free in every respect. He should breathe in an environment of respect for human worth and dignity and be brought up in valleys where he receives the respect he is due. There, none should be a slave of another human being, nor be dependent on another, nor should he have any fear or grief. Such a society will be called paradise[143].

Contrary to the above, a society in which any human being is a slave (in any form), where humanity is humiliated and disrespected, and human beings are at the mercy of other fellow human beings to meet their basic needs and as a result are humiliated and ridiculed, where there is no regard for the Permanent Values and the Divine Laws are rebelled against, such a society will be called *Jahannum*. As far as the state of *Jahannum* in the next life is concerned, the Quran has explained this metaphorically – and this could not be explained in another way because man at his present level of consciousness cannot visualise that life's details which is beyond the perception of the physical life of this world.

The Quran informs us that those people in this life who have reached that level of consciousness, so that when they are presented with wrong and right can differentiate between the two, but despite this do not leave their wrong path to follow the right

---

[142] Some experts of lexicon think this word is Arabic and it means deep pit. But I think this is a Hebrew term as this very closely matches with the Quranic meaning.
[143] The next life of paradise will have this as a standard. (Ed)

path, will be among those who will be left behind in the progressive journey of life. In this life they do not realise this loss (as they consider the immediate material gains and conveniences to be the purpose of life and when they achieve these material benefits, they consider themselves successful), but when in the next life the veils over their eyes are lifted, and they see clearly that in the race of life, by lagging behind in this way, what a great loss it is to them. Due to this sense of loss, the inner turmoil and grief which will overwhelm them is called the punishment of *Jahannum*. And because there is no opportunity for compensation of this loss there, (because according to the law of evolution the species which does not evolve forward and instead stops at one place can then never progress forward), therefore this internal burning in their hearts will be permanent and their inner turmoil will be everlasting.

The criterion for differentiating between right and wrong is provided by the revelation. Till the time of the Quran, this criterion used to come to other people through the messengers of Allah. But with the departure of the last messenger of Allah, the continuity of messenger-hood ended. This criterion for right or wrong is now written in the folds of the Quran and is protected, and this duty to pass on this message to others has been passed on to Muslims. In previous centuries, the extent to which the Muslim Ummah has delivered this responsibility, we do not wish to go into details regarding this. But in our present age, the free availability and means of communication and resources and a questioning public has resulted in the Quranic message reaching the civilised world. And their intellect and consciousness has developed to such an extent that they can understand these criteria well. Therefore at least in the present time, the civilised people have no excuse to say they did not have knowledge about right or wrong, or that they were incapable of understanding it. In this respect, regarding those nations living a life of *Jahannum* which the Quran has mentioned as examples, I think in the present age this category also includes the so-called civilised nations of today.

As far as the use of reason and intellect is concerned, there are many verses in the Quran which make this clear. For example, in *Surah Araaf* it is stated that concerning this, we can have no difficulty in recognising as to which people will go to *Jahannum*. These are those people:

> ...*they have hearts wherewith they understand not, eyes wherewith they see not, and ears wherewith they hear not. They are like cattle, nay more misguided: for they are heedless.*
> *(7:179)*

About the nations of 'Ad and *Thamud* the Quran states:

> *(Remember also) the 'Ad and the Thamud (people): clearly will appear to you from (the traces) of their buildings (their fate): the Evil One made their deeds alluring to them, and kept them back from the Path, though they were gifted with intelligence and skill. (29:38)*

In Surah Ahqaf the Quran states that We had given them ears, eyes, hearts and minds but when they went against the Divine Laws their ears, eyes, hearts and minds were of no use to them:

And We had firmly established them in a (prosperity and) power which We have not given to you and We had endowed them with (faculties of) hearing, seeing, heart and intellect: but of no profit to them were their (faculties of) hearing, sight, and heart and intellect, when they went on rejecting the Signs of Allah, and they were (completely) encircled by that which they used to mock at. (46:26) See also (67:10)

In this and many other similar verses in the Quran, it is clear that responsibility and accountability for following the wrong path lies only with those people who have the ability to differentiate between right and wrong in the first place – those who are not at such an intellectual level are not held responsible.

The second condition was that they should have been made aware of the criteria defining right and wrong and regarding this there are also many verses in the Quran:

Who receives guidance, receives it for his own benefit: who goes astray does so to his own loss: No bearer of burdens can bear the burden of another: nor would We visit with Our Wrath until We had sent a messenger (to give warning). (17:15)

This reality is further clarified in another verse:

For your Sustainer would not destroy men's habitations for their wrong-doing, while their occupants were unwarned. (6:131) See also (26:208-209, 28:59)

This is because Allah does not destroy anyone who is in an uninformed state. Doing this is injustice. In *Surah Momin* it is stated that the guardians of hell will ask the occupants of hell whether they did not have messengers come to them with clear messages, and they will say:

'Yes'. (40:50) See also (67:8-9)

Allah Himself will address these criminals:

He will say: Dispute not with each other in My Presence: I had already in advance sent you Warning. (50:28) See also (5:19, 9:115, 30:9, 35:42).

From these facts, it is clear that to establish a crime the two criteria which must be met prior to declaring anyone a criminal is knowledge about the law, and the ability to understand it. In reality only those deeds leave an imprint on the human self which are knowingly and deliberately carried out by us through the use of our intellect and reasoning. Therefore, hell is the name of those effects on the human self which are the consequences of wrong deeds. For those individuals who have neither intellect nor intelligence and do not have the choice or responsibility to make decisions, for them the question of hell or paradise does not arise. The question of responsibility and intention only arises when the criteria for right and wrong are made clear to man. That is why the Quran has categorically stated:

Let there be no compulsion in Deen[144]: Truth stands out clear from wrong: whoever rejects evil and believes in Allah has grasped the most trustworthy hand-hold that never breaks. And Allah hears and knows all things. (2:256)

This is why the right and wrong paths have been made clear:

Say, 'The truth is from your Sustainer': Let him who will, believe, and let him who will, reject (it)... (18:29) See also (104:7)

19.1 Hell in This World

As previously stated, the results of crimes which manifest themselves during this life have been called *Azaab* (punishment) by the Quran. In many verses this is also called hell. It includes those punishments which criminals receive in the courts of an Islamic System and also includes the end of those nations which in this world appears in the form of destruction and ruin. This destruction and ruin can come to a nation at the hands of its own people or via a clash with other nations.

19.2 Hell Created Through the Hands of Leaders

In *Surah Ibrahim* it is stated:

Have you not turned your vision to those who have changed the favour of Allah, into evil and caused their people to descend to the House of Perdition, i.e. Hell. They will burn therein, an evil place to stay in! (14:28-29)

19.3 Life of Humiliation in Hell

Nations which do not use intellect and reasoning about the universe and as a result do not make use of the natural resources, pass a life of humiliation and deprivation. This life is called a hell of fire. In *Surah Al e Imran*:

Behold! in the creation of the heavens and the earth, and the alternation of night and day, there are indeed Signs for men of understanding, Men who celebrate the praises of Allah, standing, sitting, and lying down on their sides, and contemplate the (wonders of) creation in the heavens and the earth, (With the thought): 'Our Sustainer! not for naught Have You created (all) this! Glory to You! Give us protection from the penalty of the Fire. 'Our Sustainer! any whom You do admit to the Fire, Truly You have covered with shame, and never will wrong-doers Find any helpers! (3:190-192)

Even after exploiting the natural resources, if nations go against the Permanent Values, then inequities will develop in their societies and they suffer the consequences of this crime – this punishment manifests itself to them in the form of humiliation and degradation (10:27).

---

[144] The Quran calls its message *Deen*, and not religion. (Ed)

19.4 Cowardice and Absence of Perseverance Create Hell

Shirk means that man either recognises the forces of nature as superior to him and bows to them, or considers other men superior to him and becomes subservient to them[145]. In *Surah Al e Imran*, it is stated that people with such a mentality are extremely cowardly. In their hearts is the fear of others (3:150) and in this way their abode becomes hell.

19.5 Subjugation is also Hell

The Arab tribes vehemently opposed the last messenger's invitation to the guidance of the Quran. They tried their best to hinder the establishment of an Islamic System in every known way possible, but the Quran has declared in plain terms:

> *...at length they will be overcome: and the Unbelievers will be gathered together to Hell.*
> *(8:36)*

This was that hell which they encountered as a result of defeats in various battles against the *Momineen*. (The details of these will be covered later). Regarding the 'Hudaibia' pact, the *Momineen* were assured by Allah that with this agreement or peace pact (which seemingly looked like a defeat), they should not feel morose, and instead would soon see what opportunities, successes and prosperity lay ahead for them, and how these hypocrites and pagans (opponents) would be consigned to a life of hell (48:4-6).

19.6 Mutual Divisions and Animosity is Hell[146]

The Quran has warned Muslims:

> *And hold fast, all together, by the rope of Allah (the Quran), and be not divided among yourselves; and remember with gratitude Allah's favour on you; for you were enemies and He joined your hearts in love, so that by His Grace, you became brethren; and you were on the brink of the pit of Fire[147], and He saved you from it. Thus does Allah make His Signs clear to you: That you may be guided. (3:102)*

---

[145] The Quran states that man is the best of creation in the known universe and he should strive to subjugate the forces of nature and utilise them within the Permanent Values for the good of mankind in general (95:4). (Ed)

[146] There are two groups – the *Momineen* and the opponents. The divisions referred to are those within these groups. (Ed)

[147] Note the state to which the Quran refers – without this guidance you will always be in a pit of fire. Look at the history of human conflicts and fights at all levels. (Ed)

19.7 Hell in Family Life

The Quran has deemed it essential that the outlook and ideology (compatibility of ideas) in marital life should be the same. It states that if the same beliefs and values are shared by both husband and wife, then family life becomes a model of heavenly life. And if there are differences, then family life becomes hell. In relation to this ideology and outlook, the Quran illustrates it by drawing a comparison between *Eimann* and *Shirk.*[148] The Quran states that a *Momin* man's marriage to a *Mushriq* (pagan) woman and a *Momin* woman's marriage to a *Mushriq* man is not legitimate. The aim of this constraint is to:

> *Do not marry unbelieving women (idolaters or pagans), until they believe: A slave woman who believes is better than an unbelieving woman, even though she allures you. Nor marry (your girls) to unbelievers until they believe: A man slave who believes is better than an unbeliever, even though he allures you. Unbelievers do (but) beckon you to the Fire. But Allah beckons by His Grace to the Garden (of bliss) and protection, and makes His Signs clear to mankind: That they may reflect and pay attention. (2:221)*

19.8 The Life of Hell in a Corrupt Society

When the Islamic System was established in Madina, a general invitation was extended to Muslims living in other areas to migrate and come to Madina, and in this way live life in an Islamic environment. In this connection, the Quran states that those people who have the ability and means to migrate and do not do so and remain resolved to live in a non-Islamic society, these are those people whose abode is in hell both in this life and in the hereafter.

> *When angels take the lives of those who die in sin against their souls, they say: 'In what (plight) Were ye?' They reply: 'Weak and oppressed Were we in the earth.' They say: 'Was not the earth of Allah spacious enough for you to move yourselves away (From evil)?' Such men will find their abode in Hell, What an evil refuge! (4:97)*

> *Except those who are (really) weak and oppressed - men, women, and children - who have no means in their power, nor (a guide-post) to their way. (4:98)*

19.9 The Punishment for Crimes is Defined as Hell

When the Islamic System is established, those who rebel against the Permanent Values will be punished via the Islamic Justice System. The Quran calls this punishment hell in this life also. But this life of hell does not end here, for them will be hell in the hereafter also. Regarding this, the hell that the Quran refers to can therefore be applied to both lives. In *Surah Mujadila*, in relation to the hypocrites, it is said that they do not desist from conspiracies and intrigues against the Islamic System. And then regarding

---

[148] *Shirk* is associating other values with the Permanent Values, and as a consequence one cannot get those benefits which one can get by having *Eimaan*. (Ed)

themselves, they deceive themselves by saying that if this system is based on truth, then why do we not get punished for our wrong doings. In reply the Quran states:

> ... '*Why does not Allah punish us for our words?' Enough for them is Hell: In it will they burn, and evil is that destination. (58:8)*

It is clear that this hell could also mean that punishment which they received through the hands of the Islamic System.

In *Surah Nisa* it is stated that whichever individual deliberately murders a *Momin*, his punishment is hell and Allah's condemnation and severe chastisement. It is obvious that this punishment of hell includes the punishment in this life.

> *If a man kills a believer (Momin) intentionally, his recompense is Hell, to abide therein (For ever): And the wrath and the curse of Allah are upon him, and a dreadful penalty is prepared for him. (4:93)*

In *Surah Al Barooj*, it is mentioned that those troublemakers who cause distress and pain to believing *Momin*, men and women, and despite admonition do not desist from this, punishment is also meted out to these criminals in this life:

> *Those who persecute the Believers, men and women, and do not turn in repentance, will have the Penalty of Hell: They will have the Penalty of the Burning Fire. (85:10)*

In another verse:

> *Truly, if the Hypocrites, and those in whose hearts is a disease, and those who stir up sedition in the City, desist not, We shall certainly stir you up against them: Then will they not be able to stay in it as your neighbours for any length of time. They shall have a curse on them: whenever they are found, they shall be seized and slain. (33:60-61)*

There were many backward tribes which operated under the messenger Solomon, and regarding these it is said that among them, whosoever rebelled against the Divine Laws, was punished (34:12). In another place, such criminals are punished by being chained and locked up in dark cells (25:11-13). In another verse it is stated that for the criminals there are chains and shackles (76:4). In *Surah Ibrahim*, it is stated that the criminals will all be tied together in chains (14:49) and in this way they will be dragged and put into fire (40:71-72). In *Surah Muzzamil*, it is declared that the people who oppose the truth will be handed over to the grip of Our Law of Requital. With Us we have chains, and means of confining them and such food which sticks in their throats (73:11-13). See also (69:32).

19.10 The Outcome of the Opponents of the Islamic System

The last ploy of the opponents of the message of the last messenger was to resort to war with a view to ending the Islamic System. The Quran assured the *Momineen* that there was no need for apprehension, and if you remain firm and steadfast in your programme, then these opponents will be defeated –the condition of such defeated criminals is also called hell by the Quran. For example, in *Surah Al e Imran* it is stated that even though at present these people undoubtedly have control and power in the land, they are gaining benefit from this for but a short period:

Little is it for enjoyment: Their ultimate abode is Hell: what an evil bed (To lie on)! (3:197)

A little earlier it is stated, that these people in power should be warned that you will soon be overwhelmed and defeated:

Say to those who reject Faith: 'Soon will you be vanquished and gathered together to Hell; an evil bed indeed (to lie on)!' (3:11)

After this are given details of the battle of *Badr*. It is evident from this that this is the hell which the leaders of *Quraish*[149] encountered in the Battle of *Badr* in the shape of their defeat.

In *Surah Tauba*, the ultimate end of those who battled against the Islamic System is referred to in detail in many verses and their exemplary punishment is called hell:

Know they not that for those who oppose Allah and His Messenger, is the Fire of Hell, wherein they shall dwell. That is the supreme disgrace and humiliation. (9:63)

The punishment of disgrace and humiliation makes it clear what kind of *Jahannum* it is. The Quran has warned the hypocrites of this very fire of *Jahannum*, and declares that they should reflect, and learn a lesson from history about those previous nations that opposed truth (*Haqq*) and what was their end (9:68-69, 9:73). It is obvious that these past nations were destroyed in this world, so this reference is presented as an example for them to learn a lesson.

The messenger of Allah was told to engage in war against these opponents (*Kuffar* and Hypocrites) and suppress them firmly. And you will see how their end is hell (9:73).

There were many hypocrites in Madina, who outwardly were apparently with the *Momineen* but internally used to oppose them. During the times of war their hypocrisy used to be exposed. They did not give support to the Muslim armies and instead used to make all sorts of excuses. Regarding this, the *Momineen* were advised by the Quran to ignore them for the time being, but ultimately they will be punished for this and they

---

[149] This was the name of the tribe of opponents in Makkah at the time of the advent of Islam. (Ed)

Page **235** of 298

will be consigned to hell (9:95). That punishment was that the Islamic System was established and these hypocrites were destroyed and vanished.

In *Surah Anfal* various aspects of the Battle of *Badr* are mentioned in great detail. In one place, after smiting the necks of their opponents in the battlefield, it is stated that these opponents faced these consequences because they vehemently opposed the establishment of the Islamic System. Now they should taste this punishment and thus see the truth unveiled in front of their eyes. Those who oppose *Haqq* (Truth) will face the penalty of fire (8:12-14).

In connection with these battles, regarding the way in which the opponents spent wealth and resources, the Quran points this out and says that when they are defeated and overwhelmed then they will have immense regret for wasting so much of their wealth unnecessarily:

The Unbelievers spend their wealth to hinder (others and themselves) from the path of Allah, and so will they continue to spend; but in the end they will have (only) regrets and sighs; at length they will be overcome: and the Unbelievers will be gathered together to Hell. (8:36)

In *Surah Qamar* it states that these people say that in order to oppose *Haqq* we have established a common front, and who can defeat us. Say to them, you will see how your great army will flee with their backs turned from the battlefield. That revolution about which you are being warned will soon arrive. It will then become evident how the criminals are held accountable and punished. At that time they will be dragged into the fire and will be told to taste it (54:44-48).

In *Surah Tehreem* all these details are summarised in one verse:

O Messenger! Strive hard against the Unbelievers and the Hypocrites, and be firm against them. Their abode is Hell, an evil refuge (indeed). (66:9)

In *Surah Tauba*, regarding this hell it is stated that it is encompassing them from all directions and they cannot escape it (9:49). The pages of history are a witness how in a short time this truth became evident for all to see. All of the opponents were defeated and humiliated, and the Islamic System was established in all its valour and glory assuring the good of all humanity. They were repeatedly warned that they should not create such circumstances due to which the *Momineen* would be forced to engage in battle. But they were intoxicated in their power and were wont to ridicule these warnings and say, why do you give us empty threats, why do you not bring on this destruction with which you are always trying to make us fearful. In reply, it was said, alas, would that they knew that when the destruction comes, they will seek refuge from its flames in vain. At this time their eyes are veiled with self-deception so they cannot see this destruction, but they are not hidden from it, and it is encompassing them from all directions (21:39, 82:16 and 9:49).

The severest blow of the Islamic System is against the religious clergy and the capitalist junta, because due to it their vested interests and exploitation ceases. Therefore the most vehement opposition to the establishment of this System comes from these two lobbies (who serve as the vanguards of the political system) and after the Islamic System is established, these people are the foremost ones to be consigned to hell. This is the reason why the Quran declares regarding the religious clergy that they do not allow truth and reality to be shown and made clear to people, and in this way they earn their living. But they should know:

Those who conceal Allah's revelations in the Book, and purchase for them a miserable profit, they fill their bellies with naught but Fire... (2:174)

These are the same words to describe those who eat up the property of orphans (4:10).

In *Surah Tauba*, the capitalists are lumped together with the religious clergy:

O you who believe! there are indeed many among the priests and anchorites, who in Falsehood devour the substance of men and hinder (them) from the way of Allah. And there are those who bury gold and silver and spend it not in the way of Allah. Announce unto them a most grievous penalty - On the Day when heat will be produced out of that (wealth) in the fire of Hell, and with it will be branded their foreheads, their flanks, and their backs, 'This is the (treasure) which you buried for yourselves: taste you, then, the (treasures) you buried!' *(9:34-35)*

A few verses later the *Momineen* are addressed and asked to come out and fight against this system of lies and exploitation. If you do not do this, then Allah will bring another nation in place of you which will eliminate this inhuman system created by the capitalists and the religious clergy (9:38-39).

But if a nation after establishing a system of truth, then gives it up and establishes of its own accord a system based on political dictatorship, religious clergy and the capitalist system, which it had once upon a time eliminated, Allah says regarding such a nation that it will be subjected to the punishment of hell and in this punishment of theirs, there will be no decrease, nor will they be given any respite (2:86).

This is that punishment of hell to which we have been subjected for centuries. But self-deception is such that we are imprisoned in a belief that hell is for those others who are *Kaffar* and it is not for us.

19.11 *Jahannum* is the Name of the Inner Human State

The Quran has called human beings fuel of the fire of hell:

...then fear the Fire whose fuel is men and stones[150], which is prepared for those who reject Faith. (2:24) See also (21:98, 66:6, 3:9)

In another verse the Quran states that they kindle this fire themselves, stoke it and then burn themselves in it:

But those who swerve (do not do justice), they are (but) fuel for Hell-fire. (72:15)

(It is) the Fire of (the Wrath of) Allah, kindled (to a blaze), the which does mount (Right) to the Hearts (104:6-7)

A mosque is a place of gathering in an Islamic System, therefore its control should lie only with the governing authority of the system. But in Madina at the time of the last messenger, some people built another mosque with a view to creating dissension and conflict within the community of Muslims. This action of theirs was considered so dangerous, that Allah Himself made the messenger aware of it, and said do not put a single step in this mosque. According to history, the last messenger had this mosque dismantled. And as a consequence this conspiracy of these people was made futile. The Quran sums it up:

And there are those who put up a mosque by way of mischief and infidelity - to disunite the Believers - and in preparation for one who warred against Allah and His Messenger aforetime. They will indeed swear that their intention is nothing but good; But Allah doth declare that they are certainly liars. (9:107)

Never stand thou forth therein. There is a mosque whose foundation was laid from the first day on piety; it is more worthy of the standing forth (for prayer) therein. In it are men who love to be purified; and Allah loves those who make themselves pure. (9:108)

The Quran has described the inner state of those who built this second mosque:

The foundation of those who so build, is never free from suspicion and shakiness in their hearts, until their hearts are cut to pieces. And Allah is All-Knowing, Wise. (9:110)

As previously written, those people whose consciousness in this life is in a state of awareness, but they have not developed their self, they will have a profound realisation in the life after death that they are left behind in the evolutionary process of further

---

[150] Their own inner turmoil and unhappiness is the equivalent of fire which contributes to their agony and torture. The reference to stones could mean those human beings who do not pay attention to the Quranic Values for their own good and thus do not benefit from the guidance. (Ed)

development. The awakening of this realisation, but the deprivation of being able to move to a higher stage of life, is described by the Quran in the following verse:

...therein shall he neither die nor live. (20:74) See also (87:13)

...death will come to him from every quarter, yet will he not die... (14:17-18)

They will screech and wail and implore for death – they will be told even if you beg a thousand times over for death, it cannot come to finish you off (25:13-14). Neither will the penalty be such that they die, nor will it be reduced:

But those who reject (Allah) - for them will be the Fire of Hell: No term shall be determined for them, so they should die, nor shall its Penalty be lightened for them... (35:36)

The one who denied truth will say with intense anguish:

...Woe unto me! Would that I were (mere) dust. (78:40)

We have already written that man's every deed leaves imprints on his self continuously – wrong deeds will have negative effects and constructive deeds will have positive effects. Viewed from this angle, man's paradise and hell are being prepared for him during his life.

However, man's emotional desires cover his eyes in such a manner that he is unable to see this hell. In the life after death, these covers will lift and everything will manifest in its real form. At this time there will be no possibility of self-deception. So the *Jahannum* which is hidden from the eyes in this life will be uncovered. In *Surah Kahf* it is stated that We will expose hell before them:

And We shall present Hell that day for Unbelievers to see, all spread out, (Unbelievers) whose eyes had been under a veil from remembrance[151] of Me, and who had been unable even to hear. (18:100-101)

In another verse, hell will rise and appear before those who discard the right path for the wrong path of life:

... hell will be placed in full view... (26:91)

And hell-fire shall be placed in full view for (all) to see... (79:36)

Whoever has eyes to see it, to him it will be apparent. Currently, we can only know about hell at a conceptual level, but at that time in the next life you will see it with your own eyes (102:6-7). And you will know that it truly exists. This is why the reality is that

---

151 This means ignoring His Laws and the purpose of life. (Ed)

hell is even now encompassing the *Kuffar* from all directions. They do not see it, but hell keeps them in its sight all the time (82:16, 78:21).

In *Surah Al-Fajar* a great reality is noted in a very refined manner. Usually it is said that criminals will be taken towards hell, but in this *Surah* it states that on this Day, hell will be brought to them i.e. hell will spring forward and snatch man itself (89:23). And not just hell, but on that Day:

> *And your Sustainer will come, and His angels, rank upon rank... (89:22)*

In this verse, there is an indication about a great reality about '*Mahsher*' (the gathering on the Day of Judgment) i.e. that it is not a particular place or abode where men will be gathered: Allah and His angels will come themselves and in the same way, hell will also be brought there.

19.12 The Details of Hell (*Jahannum*)

This is actually the name of the internal state of man; however the Quran's method is to use daily examples from human life, so that those who possess knowledge and vision can understand these unseen abstract realities intellectually, whereas an ordinary man can take effect from it according to his own mental level of understanding. This method of expression is useful for people with both high and low levels of intellect and understanding so that both categories can benefit from this. Whereas a man of higher intellectual capability can deduce the deeper connotations from these visible examples of daily life, a man of ordinary mental status can still learn a lesson from these. And this is indeed the purpose of providing these details related to paradise and hell.

The Quran is revealed in a human language, so for the expression and comprehension of events, the methods adopted for expression by the Quran also follow similar terminology. According to these visible examples, the pain caused by burning in fire is given a central focal reality and the remainder of the details are built around it. Or by giving the examples of farmland and describing such elements which can destroy crops, the example is given how the efforts that man makes are wasted by not following the Divine Laws. In these verses, we present the literal meanings of the Quran. What their metaphorical meanings are, we leave to the intellect of the reader. Nevertheless, those who wish to find out what I have understood by these metaphorical interpretations can refer to the Exposition of the Quran, or the Lughat ul Quran. Following this introduction, we will present details of *Jahannum* in the words of the Quran.

19.13 Flames of Fire

In *Surah Takweer* it is stated:

When the Blazing Fire is kindled to fierce heat... (81:12) See also (10:90)

In another verse it is stated that whenever this fire starts to cool down, it will be made fierce again and that fire will burn the faces of the inhabitants of hell:

The Fire will burn their faces, and they will therein grin, with their lips displaced. (23:104)
See also (55:35)

Its smoke and flames will engulf from all sides (55:35). The inhabitants of hell will be placed into this and will be shut in from above (90:20). That fire will melt the skins, when one skin is burnt it will be replaced with another, and in this way they will remain in a state of continuous punishment (4:56). The clothes of the inhabitants of hell will be burnt, on their heads boiling water will be poured, in this way their skin and intestines will rot and they will be beaten with iron rods (22:19-21).

By no means! for it would be the Fire of Hell! Plucking out (his being) right to the skull!
Inviting (all) such as turn their backs and turn away their faces (from the Right). (70:15-17)
See also (77:30-33,101:9-11)

19.14 Boiling Water

- '...for the wrong-doers We have prepared a Fire whose (smoke and flames), like the walls and roof of a tent, will hem them in: if they implore relief they will be granted water like molten brass, that will scald their faces, how dreadful the drink! How uncomfortable a couch to recline on!' (18:29)

- '(Can those in such Bliss) be compared to such as shall dwell for ever in the Fire, and be given, to drink, boiling water, so that it cuts up their bowels (to pieces)?' (47:15)

- This boiling water will cause severe pain (6:70, 10:41).

- They will try to drink this water by sipping it, but will not be able to swallow it (14:16-17), see also (55:54).

- Being boiled in this water and burnt in this fire will be their treatment (56:93-94) see also (56:43-45, 88:2-5).

- In some verses, examples about farming in relation to very hot or very cold water are also mentioned: whether the water is hot or cold, the fields will be burnt by both. This is why along with very hot water, freezing water is also a punishment of hell (78:25, 38:57).

19.15 For Eating – '*Shajrat Al-Zaqum*' (Bitter and Unpleasant)

Such water for drinking and *Shajrat Al-Zaqum* for eating - this usually refers to a cactus, but in Arabic, this term is used for every bitter and unpleasant thing. In *Surah Al-Saffat* it is stated:

For it is a tree that springs out of the bottom of Hell: the shoots of its fruit-stalks are like the heads of cobra: truly they will eat thereof and fill their bellies therewith. Then on top of that they will be given a mixture made of boiling water. Then shall their return be to the (Blazing) Fire. (37:64-68)

In *Surah Al-Dukhan:*

Verily the tree of Zaqqum will be the food of the Sinful, Like molten brass; it will boil in their insides, Like the boiling of scalding water… (44:43-46)

They will try to swallow it but it will get stuck in their throats (73:13). What will be that food? This will be such thorns and bushes which are considered waste and thrown away. They will somehow swallow it but it will neither satisfy their appetite nor will it provide energy to the body (88:6-7). This is the metaphorical food of hell.

19.16 Like a Prison

(As previously stated), the image of hell has been drawn as if it is a horrible prison, in which prisoners are recognised by the numbers allotted to each; similarly the criminals in hell will be recognised by their foreheads (55:41). They will be dragged by the hair of their foreheads and by their feet (55:41). Shackles will be put around their necks and chains on their feet (40:71-72, 76:4, 69:31-32). Being chained like this they will be locked in dark cells (25:13) and they will be beaten with big iron rods (22:21).

19.17 Guardians of Hell

Just like prison, hell will also have security guards who will be terrifying and strict (66:6). There will not be one but many (74:30-31). The inhabitants of hell will request these guards as to whether there can be a reduction made in their punishments. They will reply, what, did messengers not come to you who warned you that if you do not leave your wrong path you will find yourself in a severe punishment. The inhabitants will say, yes, they did come but we did not listen to them (40:50, 67:8-9). The head guard of hell will be called '*Malik*' (master) – the inhabitants being fed up with the hardships of punishment, will say to him, can you ask Allah that He finishes this drudgery of ours, so that we can gain freedom from this punishment (43:77). He (*Malik*) will say, death cannot come here, you will have to stay here dragging your heels (this is the highest level of hopelessness).

19.18 Humiliating Punishment

Alongside these punishments, the inhabitants will also face humiliation – they will come towards hell in a state with eyes cast down looking furtively from side to side (42:45). If they resist taking a step forward, then they will be dragged into hell by their faces (25:34). Just as being a prisoner is in itself extremely degrading, in the same way entering into hell is also the cause of thousands of mortifications (3:191, 40:60). This is why it is called the hell of humiliating punishment (45:9, 39:40).

19.19 The Various Doors of Hell

Depending on the types of crimes, the doors of entry to hell will be different, but hell will remain one (15:44). It will have different doors, and for every door criminals will be allocated. It will be said to these criminals, enter into hell through your apportioned doors (16:29, 39:72, 40:76).

19.20 Howling and Shrieking

Having been gripped in this punishment, they will howl and shriek in such a way that it will not be possible to hear in hell (21:100). Being fed up there, they will plead for death, but death will not hear their cries (25:13-14). Hell itself seeing them will become enraged, and there will be a horrendous noise within it (67:7). The capacity of hell will be so massive that when it is asked, are you full yet, it will say:

One Day We will ask Hell, 'Are you filled to the full?' It will say, 'Are there any more (to come)?' (50:30)

19.21 Prayers for Protection from this Punishment of Hell

This is the metaphorical explanation of the punishment of hell from which no-one, not even the last messenger, can save another:

Is, then, one against whom the decree of Punishment is justly due (equal to one who eschews Evil)? Would you, then, deliver one (who is) in the Fire? (39:19)

This is why the *Momineen* were told to take heed and save themselves and their kin from the fire of hell. This is why at every moment the prayer of these *Momineen* is:

…and protect us from the torment of the Fire. (2:201) See also (3:15, 3:19, 25:65)

Since the balance of righteous deeds of the *Momineen* will be heavy, they will be protected from it (19:71-72, 39:61, 44:56, 52:18, 3:184). They will be kept so far from hell that they will not hear a rustle from it (21:101-102). Therefore the belief that criminals will be made to enter hell and once they have done their time for the punishments of their crimes, they will then be transferred into paradise, is against the Quran. The one who deserves paradise due to his deeds is never ever sent to hell. (The details of this will be made clear further ahead).

19.22 Who Deserves *Jahannum*?

Now we face the question as to who are those people who deserve to go to hell or which are the crimes which result in the fire of hell. This is a very important question which the Quran has answered in great detail, so that every individual becomes aware without any doubt as to which type of deeds will make him deserve hell, so that he can avoid such deeds. If these details are not provided in the Quran (Divine Laws), then the accused cannot be held responsible for his deeds. In the Quran in various verses there is mention of those actual deeds whose consequences are the punishment of hell, but mostly mention is made of the categories of human beings who will be consigned to hell. This is similar to stating as in a constitution, that death is a punishment of treason, or likewise can be stated as those who commit treason will be killed.

19.23 Man's Freedom to Choose and Responsibility

The fundamental difference between man and the other creations which includes all living creatures in the universe, is that man has been given the freedom to choose and responsibility, whereas the other creations do not possess this ability. This is the reason that this creation other than man does not go against the Divine Laws (because it cannot do this) as it has been created to live in accordance with these Laws. But man has been given freedom of choice so that he can choose to follow whichever path he wishes. His possession of this freedom to choose therefore makes him responsible for his deeds and due to this responsibility the question then arises of reward or punishment (i.e. for the results of deeds). If man, like the other creation of the universe, had been programmed to follow a particular defined path, then the question of right or wrong and the difference between hell and paradise would not have arisen for him. This reality has been explained very concisely by the Quran in various places e.g. in *Surah Hud*:

If your Sustainer had so willed, He could have made mankind one people: but they will not cease to dispute. Except those on whom your Sustainer has bestowed His Mercy[152] *(to those who follow His Laws): and for this did He create them: and the Word of your Sustainer shall be fulfilled: 'I will fill Hell with men (both urban and nomadic) all together*[153].' (11:118-119)

This is the Law for Allah's creation of man, the result of which is that hell will be filled with those men who elect to follow the wrong path through their own free choice.

In another verse it is stated, that if it were Our Will, We could have done this, and put every man on the right path, but by doing this his freedom of choice would have ended, therefore We did not do this, and gave him instead the freedom to choose his

---

[152] Mercy is a translation of *Rehmat*, and means getting results by following the Divine Laws i.e. it has to be earned. It does not mean blanket forgiveness (Ed).

[153] Those who do not follow the Permanent Values will as a consequence do wrong deeds with wrong effects and will thus earn hell for themselves. 'His Mercy' refers to the Quranic guidance. (Ed)

own path in life and by using his freedom of choice wrongly, man creates hell for himself.

If We had so willed, We could certainly have brought every self its true guidance: but the Word from Me will come true, 'I will fill Hell with men (both nomadic and urban) all together[154].*' (32:13)*

Through His Revelation, which Allah sent to different messengers, man was informed as to which was the right path and which was the wrong path. Then it was left to man to make his own decision to choose whichever path he wanted to in life. This is why the last messenger was told:

Verily We have sent you in truth as a bearer of glad tidings and a warner: But of you no question shall be asked of the Companions of the Blazing Fire. (2:119)

In the world of philosophy there exists such a concept according to which human nature is evil, and this is why man goes towards the wrong path. This doctrine in reality derives from the Christian belief that every human child is born with the original sin of his first parents (Adam and Eve) and enters this world with the burden of this sin on his back. And he cannot get rid of this blot of sin except by believing in the *Kuffarah* (atonement) of Christ. Whatever may be the belief or doctrine, both conclude that man does not have the ability to save himself from the wrong path. This means that man like other creations of the universe is created pre-programmed. And also that man is thus obliged to follow the wrong path[155]. The Quran has completely contradicted this false concept. The Quran has stated that man has been given certain inherent potentials and it is up to him how he utilises these potentials. When he uses them wrongly it is called 'Iblees-e-Tahreeq' - following the devil; but man is not helpless in this path, he can control and overcome it. The Quran has, using the allegory of *Iblees* and Adam, exposed this fact in various verses, and in every place regarding this challenge by *Iblees* that I will put the children of Adam on the path of *Iblees*[156] (the path of the devil), declared with great clarity:

As for My servants, no authority you will have over them... (17:65)

However, those who decide to follow you of their own accord, hell will be filled with them (38:85, 15:43). The Quran states that *Iblees* cannot misguide those who decide to follow the Permanent Values.

---

[154] Allah has made it very clear that the purpose of the human creation is to give man freedom to choose and this will result in differences and will have consequences which will lead to rewards and punishments for what he does in this life. (Ed)

[155] This concept makes a mockery of the justice system within this world, as why would you punish those who have no choice but to follow the wrong path and do wrong. (Ed)

[156] *Iblees* is the equivalent of *Satan* – this refers to our inner base desires. (Ed)

Therefore hell is for those who by exercising their own choice deliberately opt for the path of evil. If a man's intention and decision is not involved in an act, then responsibility for that action cannot be imposed on him. If one does not have any responsibility for a task, then the question of punishment or reward will not arise.

19.24 Those Who Do Not Make Use of Their Intellect and Reasoning

An insane person cannot be held accountable for any of his actions, because if one does not even have the ability to think and understand, he cannot be held answerable for any of his actions. But if a person has the ability to think and understand but he fails to make use of his reasoning and intellect and breaks the law under the influence of his emotions, he is declared a criminal. Similarly, the individual who does not use his intellect and reasoning and instead follows others blindly thus doing wrong, he will also deserve punishment. The Quran in very clear words states that those people who do not use their faculties of intellect and reasoning will go to hell:

> *Many are the men (Both urban and nomadic) we have made for Hell: They have hearts wherewith they understand not, eyes wherewith they see not, and ears wherewith they hear not. They are like cattle, nay more misguided: for they are heedless. (7:179)*

Those people who in this life do not make use of their hearing, vision and intellect, will on the Day of Judgment be resurrected blind, deaf and dumb (17:97, 36:62). In *Surah Al-Mulk* this reality is narrated in a very visionary and instructive way. It is said that when these people are admitted into hell, the guardians of hell will ask them, what! did the messengers of Allah not come to you, who could have informed you of the right and wrong paths by drawing a line of demarcation between them? They will say, yes, they did come and will then be asked, so what happened that you have landed in hell, and the reply will be:

> *...Had we but listened or used our intelligence, we should not (now) be among the Companions of the Blazing Fire. (67:10)*

So hell is the abode of those who despite having the ability of intellect and reasoning, do not make use of it. Those people are also included in this category who blindly follow the political leaders and religious clergy. In *Surah Ahzab* it is stated:

> *And they would say: 'Our Sustainer! We obeyed our chiefs and our great ones, and they misled us as to the (right) Path.' (33:67)*

They will say that since these leaders turned us from the right path, they should be given double punishment – firstly, because of being misguided themselves, and secondly because they misguided others (33:68). In *Surah Al-Safaat*, regarding the denizens of hell, it states that these are the people who with head down, ran along whichever wrong path they saw their forefathers following, without stopping to use their own intellect and reasoning (37:69-70).

Therefore, hell is the abode of those who do not use their intellect and reasoning. Either due to the influence of emotions resulting from their vested interests they keep following the wrong paths, or they follow in the footsteps of their forefathers by blindly following their religious leaders. This is indeed the other name of following emotive desires, because blind devotion is the product of human emotions and not of intellect and reasoning. The Quran demands that everyone in the light of the Revelation using their intellect and reasoning should select their own paths themselves. This so-called religious leadership which (in the words of the Quran), in order to get worldly benefits has created a kind of trade union, will itself land in hell; then how can those who follow them go to paradise?

19.25 Those Who Follow Their Emotions

The right approach for man is to keep his emotions under the direction and control of his intellect and to make use of this intellect and reasoning in the light of the Divine Revelation i.e. the Quran. But regarding those people whose aim of life is to satisfy their emotions and desires, there can be no doubt as to their being of hell. The Quran has called man's rebellious emotive desires or that intellect which follows the influence of emotive desires as '*Shaitan*' or *Iblees* (so-called devil). According to the Quran, those who follow *Shaitan* or *Iblees* belong to hell. In the story of *Iblees* and Adam, *Iblees* is warned:

> *...If any of them follow you, Hell will I fill with you all. (7:18) See also (15:43, 22:3-4, 38:58)*

In this category are also included those people who when they are told to follow what the Quran has revealed, say no, we will follow the path of what our forefathers did. After this:

> *When they are told to follow the (Revelation) that Allah has sent down, they say: 'Nay, we shall follow the ways that we found our fathers (following).' What! even if it is Satan beckoning them to the Penalty of the (Blazing) Fire? (31:21)*

In fact, even if *Satan* himself was calling them to the punishment of hell, they would follow him. Even though they were warned that he is your avowed enemy and will lead you to hell (35:6). In *Surah Yasin* this warning has been called the promise of *Bani Adam* (children of Adam) (36:60-64).

Among these people who follow *Satan*, those leaders are also included who first incite people to wrongdoing and then when the time comes for accountability, disown any responsibility in misguiding them in the first place[157]. Such people may escape in the courts of justice in this life, but they cannot escape the Divine Court, and will be

---

[157] This drama we see daily in the media when most political leaders never give a straight answer and never take responsibility for their previous mistakes. (Ed)

included among the criminals (22:3-4, 19:6). And it includes those who spread the net of spiritual holiness or saintliness, and claim they know of heavenly information and through mischievous ways try to impress people with 'miracles' (67:5).

19.26 Hell for Those Who Deny the Hereafter

The foundations of *Deen* are based on the functioning of the Law of Requital i.e. according to the principle that whatever constructive deeds a man does, his self should develop to such an extent that after this life he will enable himself to progress to the further evolutionary stages of the next life. The one whose balance of constructive deeds is light, his self will not be able to progress forward. That is called the life of hell. Now it is obvious that the individual who does not accept the human self and its future, i.e. the life in the hereafter, for him the issue of the development of his self does not arise - therefore, what question can there be about these people being owners of hell? The Quran has mentioned in several verses that those people who do not have conviction *(Eimaan)* in the hereafter are inhabitants of hell. The basic difference between an animal and a human being is that the life of an animal is only a physical existence, which ends with death, while the life of a human being continues forward after death. Therefore, the one who is not convinced about the continuity of life does not differentiate between a man and an animal. He lives his life at an animal level. But his not accepting the continuity of life does not mean that his life will finish with his death. Whether he accepts it or not, his life will still go forward after death and his abode will be hell. The Quran states this clearly:

> ...while those who reject Allah[158] will enjoy (this world) and eat as cattle eat; and the Fire will be their abode. (47:12) See also (13:5, 10:7, 78:27)

Since in this life the results of human endeavours are according to the physical laws, there is no difference therefore in the results between those who believe in the hereafter and those who do not. Both get results in proportion to their opportunities and efforts. However, those who do not believe in the hereafter do not have a share in anything good in the next life. Whatever the level of prosperity and success in this life, in comparison with the next life it is trifling indeed, because the life of this world is short while the evolutionary phases or stages of the next life are countless. This is the reason the Quran declares that that which deserves to be called life indeed, is the next one:

> What is the life of this world but amusement and play[159]? but verily the Home in the Hereafter, that is life indeed, if they but knew. (29:64) See also (3:196, 2:126)

---

[158] Rejecting Allah means denying the Law of Requital and not accepting that one is accountable for his deeds. (Ed)

[159] The Quran notes here the seriousness of this life and advises us to not to take it as mere entertainment and sport. (Ed)

Therefore, for the one who does not have a share in the good of the hereafter, what doubt can there be of his being in hell. In *Surah Bani Israel*, it is stated that those who work for the immediate benefits in this life as the aim of their life, they achieve these, but after this their end is in hell (17:18, 11:15-16, and 39:8). In *Surah Ahqaf* it is stated that these people will ask in the hereafter as to why they are being deprived of the pleasantries and conveniences of that life. They will be informed:

…You received your good things in the life of the world, and you took your pleasure out of them… (46:21)

In *Surah Kahf* it is mentioned that these are the people who wasted all their efforts in attaining the benefits of this life, therefore on the Day of Judgment no balance will be raised for them (18:103-105), because they preferred this life over the hereafter (79:38). There is nothing wrong with making efforts in this life to acquire benefits, but when there is a clash with this and a Permanent Value, the individual who at that juncture prefers the benefits of this life and turns his back on the Permanent Value, does not in reality believe in the life of the hereafter. These are the ones who 'buy this life over the next life' (2:175, 3:76).

19.27 Balancing of Deeds

But those people who despite accepting the life of the hereafter keep breaking some of the Permanent Values, in their cases it will be seen as to whether their constructive deeds are heavier or destructive. If the balance of their destructive deeds is heavier they will belong to hell:

But those whose balance is light, will be those who have lost their self, in Hell will they abide. (23:103) See also (101:8-9)

19.28 Different Categories ✔

Apart from the above, the Quran has also mentioned different categories of the inhabitants of hell:

(1) *'Kuffar'* – those who deny i.e. those who refuse to accept the Permanent Values. This also includes those who oppose the establishment of an Islamic System and rebel against it.

(2) *'Mushrikeen'*: Those who along with Allah's Laws, associate and include non-Divine powers and values. Along with the Divine Laws, they follow man-made laws as well.

(3) *'Mukazzibeen'*: Those who make efforts to falsify the Permanent Values given by the Revelation. This also includes those who say they accept these values, but deny it through their deeds.

(4) *'Murtadeen'*: Those who after accepting the truth of the Permanent Values, then deny them and take the path of *Kufr* (wrong). There remains no difference between them and the *Kuffar*, - even those people are included among them who despite calling themselves Muslims, in some matters obey the *Kuffar* (47:25).

(5) *'Munafiqeen'* – Hypocrites: those who in their hearts do not accept the truth but because it suits them due to the benefits associated with the system, include themselves among the *Momineen*.

(6) *'Mujrimeen'* – Criminals: those who disobey the Divine Laws and transgress against these. They are also called *'Zalimeen'*, *'Fasiqeen*, and *'Fujjar'*. (Those who avoid or side-step these Values are also included in this category).

In the Quran there are many verses about these groups, in which it is stated that these are among the inhabitants of hell. Due to paucity of space, is not possible to note down all the verses here, therefore a few will be quoted to illustrate this. But in relation to crimes, more details will be provided as to their nature and importance. (So that we can assess our own situation as to which crimes we are committing).

19.29 Hell for '*Kafireen*' (Those Who Deny)

In *Surah Bani Israel* it is stated:

> *And we have made Hell a prison for those who reject (Kafireen). (17:8)*

> *This is that hell about which you were warned. (36:64)*

In *Surah Fatir* it is stated that those who practice *Kufr* will enter into fire (35:36).
The Quran has clearly stated what the constituents of *Eimaan* (belief) are, and the denial of these is called *Kufr*. Regarding *Eimaan*, it is stated in *Surah Baqra*:

> *…but it is righteousness- to believe in Allah and the Last Day, and the Angels, and the Book, and the Messengers… (2:177)*

In another verse:

> *…Any who denies Allah, His angels, His Books, His Messenger, and the Day of Judgment, has gone far, far astray. (4:136)*

It has also been made clear about *Eimaan*, that it does not mean that whatever concept one wishes to have one can keep about Allah, the books, messengers, angels and the hereafter, and that this will be accepted as *Eimaan* - absolutely not, the Quran states in very clear terms that it must be in line with that which is revealed in the Quran[160].

So if they believe as you believe, they are indeed on the right path... (2:137)

If these people believe the way you (the last messenger) have believed, then it will be accepted that they are on the right path, otherwise not[161]. This is why the Quran does not accept even the People of the Book (Jews, and Christians, etc) as *Momin*. For *Eimaan*, a basic condition is to believe what has been revealed to the last messenger i.e. the Quran:

... and believe in the (Revelation) sent down to Muhammad ... (47:2)

19.30 Hell for *'Mushrikeen'* (Those Who Associate Other Values with the Quran)

In *Surah Qaaf*, it is stated:
Who set up another god beside Allah[162]. Throw him into a severe penalty. (50:26)

Those who consider other sovereigns besides Allah as Sovereign, will be consigned to severe punishment in hell and are declared to be *Mushrikeen* (9:17).

To make it clear, *Mushrik* are not only those who worship idols, but includes whoever follows man-made laws along with the Divine Laws (those noted in the Quran). They do *Shirk*. Even the ones who create sects in *Deen* are also *Mushrik* (30:31). About the Christians, the Quran has clearly stated that those who call Jesus as son of God or believe in 'trinity' they commit *Kufr* and also *Shirk* – for them Paradise is *Haram* (forbidden) and their abode is hell (5:72-73). The Quran includes all people of the Book, along with *Kuffar* and *Mushrikeen*, in this category (98:6). *Shirk* is the greatest crime from whose destructive effects there is no protection:

...one who joins other gods with Allah, has strayed far, far away (from the right path).
(4:116)

It is clear that all those who follow and practice pagan customs and traditions are also included in the *Mushrikeen* and will also earn hell (4:117-121). If *Shirk* is such a heinous crime, then for those who consider themselves as 'god' in this world, there is no doubt

---

[160] This is an important issue related to belief. This *Eimaan* as described in the Quran brings a change in our inner self by changing our thinking and thus our outer conduct which is not possible to achieve with any other religious belief. (Ed)

[161] The messenger believed in the Quran and accepted its guidance willingly, using his intellect and reasoning and so did his companions (2:285). (Ed)

[162] It is important to understand that associating other values with those of the Quran will not give those benefits which one gets by purely following the Permanent Values. (Ed)

in their being denizens of hell (21:29) – they will be in hell and their devotees as well (21:98).

19.31 Hell for *'Mukazzibeen'* (Those Who Falsify the Truth)

In *Surah Toor* it is stated that on this Day there will be great destruction for the *Mukazzibeen*, and it will be said, this is that fire of hell which you used to deny or falsify (52:11-14). In *Surah Araaf* it is stated:

To those who reject Our signs and treat them with arrogance, no opening will there be of the gates of heaven, nor will they enter the garden, until the camel can pass through the eye of the needle: Such is Our reward for those who are criminals. For them there is Hell, as a couch (below) and folds and folds of covering above: such is Our requital of those who do wrong. (7:40-41)

In another verse it is stated that hell is for those who falsify Allah's Laws and try to find ways to avoid these Laws (92:16)

19.32 Hell for *'Murtadeen'* (Reverting after Becoming a Muslim)

The individual who accepts *Eimann* and then denies it will have no benefit from his previous state of belief. He is also included in the inhabitants of hell (2:217). As noted previously, declaring oneself a Muslim and then following the *Kuffar* in some matters is also *'Irtadaad'* (equivalent of not being a Muslim):

This, because they said to those who hate what Allah has revealed, 'We will obey you in part of (this) matter'; but Allah knows their (inner) secrets. (47:26).

19.33 Hell for *'Munafiqeen'* (Hypocrites)

A hypocrite in this life too lives in hell with each breath. He is in a continuous state of inner conflict creating turmoil which is a state of continuous punishment. This hell is of this life, and this same hell going forward becomes the fire of the life of the hereafter. The Quran has included both *Kuffar* and *Munafiqeen* in the same category and told the messenger:

O Messenger! Strive hard against the Unbelievers and the Hypocrites, and be firm against them. Their abode is Hell, an evil refuge (indeed). (66:9) See also (9:73)

In another verse, regarding the hypocrites it is even stated:

The Hypocrites will be in the lowest depths of the Fire… (4:145)

This means that they will have a more severe punishment even when compared with the *Kuffar*. Regarding those who built a mosque in *Madina* to cause division among the *Momineen*, it is said in the Quran that this evil action of theirs will be a source of an inner tumult of silent fire which will cut their hearts into pieces and this mosque and its builders will all be consigned to hell (9·107-110)

19.34 Rebels against the Islamic System

Those people who are intoxicated by their wealth and power, and rebel against the Islamic System or try to create hurdles in the path of its establishment – their abode is also hell, both in this life as well as in the life of the hereafter:

> *Know they not that for those who oppose Allah and His Messenger, is the Fire of Hell, wherein they shall dwell. That is the supreme disgrace. (9:63) See also (4:14, 72:23)*

In *Surah Hajj* a reference is made to those who make an attempt to make the Divine Laws ineffective (not allow them to function), they are of those who belong to hell (22:51). In *Surah Momin*, regarding those people who are arrogant and do not accept Allah's sovereignty, they will be disgraced and humiliated and will enter hell (40:60). In another verse they are declared as enemies of Allah and their abode has been declared as hell (41:28).

19.35 Hell for Criminals

Before we go into the Quranic details about the criminals, there is a point of principle which requires clarification. The Quran has used the terms *Kafireen, Mushrikeen, Munafiqeen* and *Mujrimeen* not in such a way that whatever meaning one wishes to ascribe to these he is at liberty to do so. The Quran has used these terms preceded by the prefix 'al' which is a definite article in Arabic, so these are stated as e.g. Al-*Kafireen*, *Al-Mushrikeen*. This means that *Kaffur* are those who are declared as *Kaffur* by the Quran. *Mushrik* are those whom the Quran declares as *Mushrik*. *Mujrim* are those who are declared to be criminals according to the Quran. According to the definition of the Quran, criminals (*Mujrimeen*), are those who defy the Divine Laws and break them. In this respect, whereas the Quran has discussed details of some of these crimes, it has stated as a collective term that the abode of *Al-Mujrimeen* (the criminals) will be hell. Whether these crimes are committed by Muslims or non-Muslims, both will be declared criminals. Here we are mentioning the effects of those crimes which affect the human self and their result is in the next life. We are not discussing the punishments for those crimes which a worldly court will give to criminals in this life. (This issue has already been discussed, regarding the relation to the next life of those crimes whose punishment is received in this life). As an example in *Surah Qamar* it is stated:

> *The Day they will be dragged through the Fire on their faces, (they will hear:) 'Taste you the touch of Hell!' (54:48)*

In *Surah Rehman* it is stated:

> *This is the Hell which the criminals deny. (55:43)*

In *Surah Mudathar*, it is stated that the inhabitants of paradise will say to those in hell, for what crimes have you landed here (74:40-41)? In another verse, they are called '*Al-Fujjar*' (those who cause dissension) (82:14), *Al-Fasiqeen* (those who violate Allah's Laws) (32:20), *Al-Zalimeen* (those who are unjust) (21:29), and those who depart from justice and uprightness (72:15) and are declared the opposite of the *Muslimeen* (72:14)

19.36 Details of Some Crimes

1) Those who hide the conveniences of life which are bestowed from Allah. Those who spend in wrong places and hold back wealth. Those who transgress all bounds. The ones who doubt the truth of the Divine Laws – they will be in the grip of a severe punishment of hell (50:24-26).

2) The religious scholars and priests, who misappropriate others' earnings and due to their vested interests become a hurdle and prevent others from being guided to the path of Allah (9:34)

3) Those who hoard wealth only for their own benefit, and do not spend it for the good of mankind will earn a severe punishment of hell (9:34-35, 70:21).

The Quran states:

Who piles up wealth and lays it by, thinking that his wealth would make him last for ever! By no means! he will be sure to be thrown into that which breaks to pieces, and what will explain to you that which breaks to pieces? (It is) the Fire of (the Wrath of) Allah kindled (to a blaze), the fire which does mount (Right) to the hearts: it shall be made into a vault over them, in columns outstretched. (104:2-9)

This is the type of hell which is a consequence of the capitalist system – in this life as well in the hereafter.

4) Those who keep Allah's *Deen* as revealed in the Quran secret, or sell it as part of their business (2:174-175).

5) Those who eat up others' earnings by illegal means (4:29-30) – it is important to remember that all those ways which the Quran has not declared as allowed, are illegitimate. In this, those people who engulf the possessions of orphans are especially included (4:10).

6) Those who earn a profit on the Capital only – this could be earning interest on loans extended to others, earning extra money on money, or investing money to get so-called profit or in any other form, this is called '*Riba*' by the Quran. The consequence of such a system and practices is hell in this life and in the hereafter (2:275, 3:129-130).

7) Those who do not make arrangements for the sustenance of those whose running business has stopped or they are no longer able to work. Those who

talk a lot but practically do nothing for the welfare of others. These are the ones who despite being so-called *Mussaleen* i.e. observing their prayers, are in fact not *Mussaleen* (those who follow the Divine Laws) (74:41-45). People who block sources of sustenance by sitting on them like a cobra, and think by just saying empty prayers that they have become *Mussaleen*, for them destruction awaits in hell (107:4-7). The real *Mussaleen* are those in whose wealth and resources there is a known part for every deprived and needy person, and who have a right to this (70:22-25).

8) The one who does not respect those who are left alone in society, and does not encourage others to make arrangements for the sustenance of the deprived and poor. The one who receives wealth and resources through inheritance and considers himself the sole owner of it. The one who on the basis of the power of his capital, establishes such a system through which the earnings of others' toil and sweat from all four directions accumulates and makes its way to him (89:17-20).

9) If a correct Islamic System has been established in some place, then it is important that all those who live in a non-Islamic system should migrate to this place to spend their life under this system. If people have the means to do so and despite this, do not and sit satisfied in a non-Islamic system, their abode is hell (4:97-98).

10) Those who argue against *Deen* without knowledge and reason and without reference to the Quran (22:8-9).

11) Those who consider the Divine Laws to be a joke, that is, not taking them seriously (18:106), saying that the realities of the Quran are but the tales of the ancients (83:13-16); or those who find an excuse to escape from the Permanent Values - this is called *Al-Haad* (41:40); or those who mock about Allah (3:180).

12) Those who refer wrong things to Allah (16:62).

13) Those who do not respond to the call of the Islamic System in the name of some duty or assignment (13:10) or behave arrogantly against the Permanent Values (40:60). Those who turn their backs and run away from the battlefield (8:15-16).

14) The one who kills a *Momin* deliberately (4:93), even those who cause pain and grief to *Momin* men and women (85:10, 33:57).

Be aware that this is not a complete list of all the crimes which makes these criminals deserve hell as a consequence. This is just a list of a few prominent crimes. For this type of detailed list, a separate volume is required in its own right. As a rule, the Quran has declared that those with righteous deeds will be in paradise while those with evil deeds will be in hell (27:90). Both these aspects are referred to throughout the Quran.

19.37 A Few Specific Issues

The Quran has quoted Pharaoh as being the representative of political exploitation, oppression, slavery, and tyranny and because of this has specially declared both him and his nation to be inhabitants of hell. And further states that he, Pharaoh, while leading his nation, went to hell (11:90). He (Pharaoh) has been called leader of those people who invite others to hell (28:41) and it is stated that they are in a continuous state of hell (40:41, 40:46).

At the time of the last messenger, the staunchest opponent of the establishment of the Islamic system, the guardian of Kaaba and a very great capitalist, was his uncle Abu Lahb. The Quran mentions the defeat of his plots and specifically mentions the consignment of both him and the companion in his plotting, his wife, as being consigned to hell (111:1-5).

Similarly the wives of the messengers Noah and Lut (Lot) are mentioned in the Quran. The purpose of mentioning them is to relate that if the wife of a messenger does not believe in his message, then her being the wife of a messenger will be of no use to her. She will be in hell herself (66:10). In the Divine Balance, the weight is of deeds, not of who is related to whom, nor who is a friend of whom (37:51-55).

The Jews believed that paradise was made exclusively for them, the *Bani Israel.* These people would go to hell only for a few days due to their going against the Sabbath in the past. The Quran has rejected this belief and declared that belonging to any party, group, generation, family, caste, creed etc is of no consequence. Whoever commits evil deeds and is engulfed by their results will find himself in hell (2:81), regardless of which lineage he may be (3:23), and whether he belongs to the urban population (*Ins*) or is from nomadic tribes of the desert (*Jinn*) (41:25)[163].

19.38 Mutual Arguments in Hell between Leaders and Their Followers

This question that the cause for the destruction of a nation is its leaders or the people who follow these leaders and provide them with strength, has great significance in sociology. The Quran has referred to this aspect in a very interesting and striking manner as mutual arguments which take place between the leaders and their followers in hell. (This has already been referred to in Chapter 16. It has been considered necessary to add further details here).

In *Surah Ibrahim* it is stated that the leaders of a nation who are unappreciative of Allah's favours and do not utilise the resources properly, end up taking the caravan of their people to that market where they cannot find any buyer for their produce, and this is a punishment of hell (14:28-29). But the Quran does not absolve the people of a

---

[163] '*Ins*' – those people who live in urban dwellings. '*Jinn*' are those nomadic tribes who roam the desert. (Ed)

nation of their responsibility. It says, who told you to close your eyes and keep following behind others - had you made use of your intellect and reasoning, and not followed the path of destruction behind them, these leaders had no power of their own. You became the tool of their power and thus they created havoc and destruction in the world, so both they and you deserve hell. When a nation faces destruction, the people do not remain protected from its effects. This is the focal point of these exchanges, which are presented by the Quran in a metaphorical way. These leaders include politicians, capitalists and religious leaders.

In *Surah Saba* it states:

> The Unbelievers say: 'We shall neither believe in this scripture nor in (any) that (came) before it.' Could you but see when the wrong-doers will be made to stand before their Sustainer, throwing back the word (of blame) on one another! Those who had been despised will say to the arrogant ones: 'Had it not been for you, we should certainly have been believers!' The arrogant ones will say to those who had been despised: 'Was it we who kept you back from Guidance after it reached you? Nay, rather, it was you who transgressed.' Those who had been despised will say to the arrogant ones: 'Nay! it was a plot (of yours) by day and by night: Behold! You (constantly) ordered us to be ungrateful to Allah and to attribute equals to Him!' They will declare (their) repentance when they see the Penalty: We shall put yokes on the necks of the Unbelievers: It would only be a requital for their (ill) Deeds. Never did We send a warner to a population, but the wealthy ones among them said: 'We believe not in the (Message) with which you have been sent.' (34:31-33)

This excuse of theirs will not be acceptable and they will all be put into hell. In another verse it is stated:

> And they will turn to one another, and question one another. They will say: 'It was you who used to come to us from the right hand (of power and authority)!' They will reply: 'Nay, you yourselves had no Faith! nor had we any authority over you. Nay, it was you who were a people in obstinate rebellion!' So now has been proved true, against us, the word of our Sustainer that we shall indeed (have to) taste (the punishment of our crimes). 'We led you astray: for truly we were ourselves astray.' Truly, that Day, they will (all) share in the Penalty. (37:27-33)

In the next verse the Quran has declared them all equal as criminals. In *Surah Momin*:

> Behold, they will dispute with each other in the Fire! The weak ones (who followed) will say to those who had been arrogant, 'We but followed you: Can you then take (on yourselves) from us some share of the Fire?' Those who had been arrogant will say: 'We are all in this (Fire)! Truly, Allah has judged between (his) Servants!' (40:47-48)

In *Surah Shu'araa*, the leaders are called *Iblees* and their followers as the army of *Iblees*, and their mutual arguments are quoted while they are in hell:

And the whole hosts of Iblees together. They will say there in their mutual bickering: "By Allah, we were truly in an error manifest, when we held you as equals with the Sustainer of the Worlds; and our seducers were only those who were steeped in guilt. Now, then, we have none to intercede (for us), nor a single friend to feel (for us). Now if we only had a chance of return we shall truly be of those who believe!' (26:95-102)

In *Surah Baqra*:

Then would those who are followed clear themselves of those who follow (them): they would see the penalty, and all relations between them would be cut off. And those who followed would say: 'If only We had one more chance, we would clear ourselves of them, as they have cleared themselves of us.' Thus will Allah show them (The fruits of) their deeds as (nothing but) regrets. Nor will there be a way for them out of the Fire. (2:166-167)

In another verse, the Quran states that when the punishment of hell will be announced to this people, they will say, O our Sustainer! (*Rabb*), where are those leaders (urban and rural) and religious priesthood of ours who have ruined us. Show them to us just once so that we can trample them underfoot and at least release some of the rage in our hearts (41:29). Over here we have quoted those verses where the leaders and their followers dispute mutually. The Quran also states that in the world nations also copy other nations and adopt wrong paths, and this is referred in *Surah Araaf*:

He will say: 'Enter you in the company of the people who passed away before you - men (both urban and nomads), into the Fire.' Every time a new people enters, it curses its sister-people (that went before), until they follow each other, all into the Fire. Says the last about the first: 'Our Sustainer! it is these that misled us: so give them a double penalty in the Fire.' He will say: 'Doubled for all': but this you do not understand. Then the first will say to the last: 'See then! No advantage have you over us; so taste you of the penalty for all that you did!' (7:38-39)

At another place, among the nations entering hell, no nation will be pleased to see another nation, because every nation will accuse another nation, that it was responsible for creating this punishment for it. And in this way, every nation will say to Allah, O! Our Sustainer, the nation which has stirred this fire of hell for us, give it double punishment (38:59-61).

19.39 Inhabitants of Paradise and Hell – Their Mutual Conversation

In a few verses of the Quran this has also been noted:

> *The Companions of the Paradise will call out to the Companions of the Fire: 'We have indeed found the promises of our Sustainer to us true: Have you also found your Sustainer's promises true?' They shall say, 'Yes'; but a crier shall proclaim between them: 'The condemnation of Allah is on the wrong-doers; those who would hinder (men) from the path of Allah and would seek in it something crooked: they were those who denied the Hereafter. Between them shall be a veil, and on the heights will be men who would know everyone by his marks: they will call out to the Companions of the Paradise, 'peace on you': they will not have entered, but they will have an assurance (thereof). When their eyes shall be turned towards the Companions of the Fire, they will say: Our Sustainer! send us not to the company of the wrong-doers.' The men on the heights will call to certain men whom they will know from their marks, saying: 'Of what profit to you were your hoards and your arrogant ways?' Behold! are these not the men whom you swore that Allah with His Mercy would never bless? Enter you the Paradise: no fear shall be on you, nor shall you grieve. The Companions of the Fire will call to the Companions of the Paradise: 'pour down to us water or anything that Allah does provide for your sustenance.' They will say: 'Both these things has Allah forbidden to those who rejected Him.' 'Such as took their Deen to be mere amusement and play, and were deceived by the life of the world.' That day shall We forget them as they forgot the meeting of this day of theirs, and as they were wont to reject Our signs. (7:44-51)*

In *Surah Hadeed*, the hypocrites will call to the inhabitants of paradise and will ask:

> *One Day will the Hypocrites- men and women - say to the Believers: 'Wait for us! Let us borrow (a Light) from your Light!' It will be said: 'Turn you back to your rear (previous life)! then seek a Light (where you can)!' So a wall will be put up betwixt them, with a gate therein. Within it will be Mercy throughout, and without it, all alongside, will be (Wrath and) Punishment! (Those without) will call out, 'Were we not with you?' (The others) will reply, 'True! but you led yourselves into temptation; you looked forward (to our ruin); you doubted Allah's Promise; and (your false) desires deceived you; until there issued the Command of Allah. And the Deceiver deceived you in respect of Allah. (57:13-14)*

19.40 Only Two Categories

The Quran has divided people into two categories only – one category belonging to paradise and one belonging to hell (47:7). These two can never be alike (47:14-15). The owners of paradise will be very successful and elevated (59:20), while the owners of hell will be very unfortunate (87:11-12).

19.41 Inhabitants of 'Araaf' (Elevated Place)

As we mentioned above, in the Quran there are only two categories of people – the group belonging to paradise and the other belonging to hell. But in *Surah Araaf* there is mention of the 'people of *Araaf*. Regarding them, it is commonly said that they are those people about whom a final decision has not yet been reached as to whether they should be sent to paradise or hell. In other words, their case will be pending. According to the Quran, this is not a correct concept. The state of the Divine Court (Law of Requital) is not such where a case cannot be decided and a criminal is kept in suspension, as under the Law of Requital nothing remains undecided.

Araaf means an elevated place – therefore, the people of *Araaf* are those among the inhabitants of paradise, who in comparison to the rest, will enjoy a higher status. This is that category of inhabitants of paradise who are called '*Al-Sabiqun*' (foremost) and '*Al-Muqarabun*' (very close) (56:10-11). These people will come forward as witnesses of their respective groups (4:41) and this is why it is stated that they will be recognised from their foreheads (7:47-49).

The people about whom it is stated in (7:46) that they will not be in paradise yet but they will wish to be there, appears to refer to those people in this life who aspire in their hearts to join the *Momineen* and the Divine System. (More details will be provided in the last chapter under '*Jannat*').

19.42 Punishment in Hell is Forever

There is a commonly held view about hell that it is like a prison where prisoners (criminals) will go to serve their time. Once they have completed their tenure of punishment, then they will be taken out and sent to paradise. Those who do not consider the simile of a jail suitable, say hell is a hospital where (sinful) patients are sent. When they recover, they are then sent to paradise. In another example, hell is described as being like a laundry, where dirty clothes are washed, and when the dirt is removed and they become clean, they are then sent to the paradise.

Whatever the simile, according to the Quran, this very concept is wrong that the inhabitants of hell will at any time ever be able to leave hell and enter paradise. According to Quranic teaching, in this worldly life man is provided with the opportunity that through his righteous conduct he develops his self to such an extent that it is enabled to traverse through to the next evolutionary stages of life. Whichever human self has developed to such an extent, will after death be at the next higher plane of life. This has been compared to the life of paradise. The self which has not developed to such an extent will be stopped after death from going forward in the next life. This is compared to a life in hell. In paradise there will be further opportunities for 'action' for the human self to develop further, but in hell there will be no possibility of action, so the question will not arise of being able to redeem one's shortcomings and move forward. For example, like a university in this world, the student who fails his exams is not given another chance. And it is obvious that such a student cannot be promoted to the next class. This is the law of evolution according to which the species which has not developed itself further will remain in the same state of life forever. This law is also applicable to human life. Therefore hell is neither a prison nor a hospital. It is the name of the stoppage in the evolutionary process. This is why it is called *Jaheem*, which means to be stopped (56:94). From this it is made clear that *Jahannum* (hell) is therefore the name of stoppage forever. In the Quran this fact has been referred to in various ways, for example in *Surah Nisa*:

Those who reject and do wrong, Allah will not protect them nor guide them to any way - except the way of Hell, to dwell therein for ever. And this to Allah is easy. (4:168-169) See also (72:23, 33:64-65, and 41:28)

In *Surah Furqan*, hell is called such a punishment which sticks and never detaches (25:65). In other places it is also called a punishment which stays (39:40), and a punishment which stays forever (42:45, and 32:14). The denizens of hell will acknowledge their wrongdoings and will say, is there a way out of this (40:11). They will cry out and say - if we can once be taken out and given an opportunity to work then you will see what good works we do (23:108, 35:37). The reply will be given, do not talk so much, the time for deeds is gone, and you will now have to live this life of humiliation (4:121). In this way, they will find no escape from there:

Their wish will be to get out of the Fire, but never will they get out therefrom: their penalty will be one that endures. (5:37)

In *Surah Hajj* it is stated:

Every time they wish to get away therefrom, from anguish, they will be forced back therein, and (it will be said), 'Taste you the Penalty of Burning!' (22:22) See also (2:167)

Leaving aside being able to get out of hell, there will not even be a reduction in the punishment:

Nowise will the (Punishment) be lightened for them, and in despair will they be there overwhelmed. (43:75) See also (40:49, 70:30)

In this way, hopelessness will engulf them forever. This unending hopelessness is a very severe punishment, and as this increases, the intensity of this punishment will increase as well (70:30). Being fed up with this hopelessness, they will wail and say:

They will cry: 'O Malik! would that your Sustainer put an end to us!' He will say, 'Nay, but you will abide!' (43:77)

The punishment of hell on one side, on seeing their record of deeds also they will say, would that death had finished us and we would not have had to see these days (69:27) In this way they will repeatedly call on death there, but they will not die (25:13). They will see death coming from all directions but they will not be able to die. (14:17).

☞ 19.43 'Abde'at' (Living Forever) – What Does it Mean?

From these explanations it is evident that the punishment of hell is forever. (Similarly life in paradise is also denoted as being forever. Further details about paradise will be covered in the next chapter). The question is, what does 'forever' means?

One *Abde'at*, living forever, is the infinite existence of Allah which has no end. The concept of time in which there is no end or which has no beginning, we can never understand. Our mind with its limited understanding can only conceive of that period of time which is located between two points which have both a beginning and an endpoint. The concept of no beginning and no end regarding time is outside the scope of understanding of the human mind. This kind of no beginning and no end is applicable only to Allah – only for one Allah with whom none else can share. Other than that of Allah, this infinite existence for a non-divine entity will in any case come to an end at some point. The fine, but very important difference of *Abde'at* between Divine and non-divine has been defined by a term which describes Allah's infinite existence. This is called '*Sarmdiat*' (infinite), and in Allah's *Sarmdiat* none other can be included. Therefore the punishment of hell is not without an end. In the Arabic language and in the Quran itself, the term '*abada*' is used to denote a very long time and the term '*khalood*' means something which remains unchanged. The *khalood* of life in paradise is that it cannot change into hell and the *khalood* of life in hell is that it cannot change into paradise.

While mentioning the punishment of hell, the terms used are '*khalood*', '*abd*', '*muqeem*' etc. In a verse it is stated:

> *They will dwell therein for ages ('Ahqaaba'). (78:23)*

The meaning of *Ahqaab* (plural of *Haqab*) is a very long time i.e. they will remain there for a long period. From this the meaning of *Abde'at* becomes evident. However, it is elaborated even further in *Surah Hud*:

> *They will dwell therein for all the time that the heavens and the earth endure, except as your Sustainer wills: for your Sustainer is the (sure) accomplisher of what He plans. (11:107)*

As long as the heavens and earth exist, whatever conclusions we draw, it is clear that the *Khalood* and *Abde'at* of hell is not infinite like Allah. What the end of this universe will be, what will happen to the inhabitants of hell, even what will be the final destination of those who are in paradise, (as the same words are used for paradise) (11:108), these are those questions which cannot be answered at the level of our present consciousness nor can we understand them. From this it is important to state that this *Abde'at* is not like Allah's *Abde'at*.

But for 'hell to remain for a very long time', its meaning is not that the inhabitants of hell will one day come out and move to paradise – as long as hell remains the inhabitants will stay in it.

19.44 One Great Reality

We have seen that the individual who has not done such deeds which can lead to the development of his self, he will live a life of hell. And in hell there will be no possibility that man can change his state. From this you can imagine that for the future of man how important the present life is. You can understand it as a student whose whole future depends on passing his exam and this is the last chance to present himself in this exam. Now consider, if that student wastes even one moment of that year, how much loss he incurs in the long term i.e. such a loss which can never be redeemed.

This is the reason that the Quran in comparison to the life in the hereafter, has called every convenience of this life as short, and every attraction of this life is declared to be sport and entertainment. If the time in this life is being spent to put the future (including in the hereafter) right, then every breath of this life is more valuable than the life to come, and if the future is being ruined, then the most valuable convenience of this life is inferior to even a particle of sand.

Let us once again remind ourselves, that this is the only life we have to decide our future in the hereafter. After this there is no chance. If anyone wastes this opportunity then he will find himself forever in hell where there is no chance of release. With this keep in mind that no individual can know for sure how much worldly life remains to him. Therefore he cannot even say that he has enough time to sort out his future. In this case if he had wasted some time, it would not greatly matter. The chance is the last one, and there is no knowledge either of when the day for the examination will be announced. This is why the Quran invites us to:

Be quick in the race for protection from your Sustainer, and for a paradise whose width is that (of the whole) of the heavens and of the earth, prepared for the righteous. (3:133)

Now let us move on to the subject of paradise.

(Intentionally left blank)

(Intentionally left blank)

20 'Jannat' or Paradise

The way in which the Quran has compared a life of pain, turmoil, destruction and ruin with the punishment of fire and given it as an example of a life of hell, it has similarly (contrary to this), compared a life of peace and contentment, prosperity, success, achievement and certainty as an example of *Jannat*. The root of this word is *J-N-N* which means to hide, or something which is hidden from the eyes. Arabs used to call that orchard a *Jannat* whose soil was not visible due to very dense vegetation, because in the barren desert lands of Arabia where there was no sign of water and vegetation for mile upon mile, a garden i.e. water, greenery, trees and their shade and fruit was considered a great blessing. Therefore for them the greatest success and prosperity, happiness and pleasures in life, were expressed by this term. Indeed it is not only the Arabs, but every nation of the world, every country and in every time, considers a garden as a sign of peace, tranquillity, comfort and freshness. This is the reason the Quran has also used a garden as an example to refer to a successful life.

The Quran has mentioned three stages or aspects of human life. Stage one refers to that period when man's collective social life had not yet commenced, and there was plenty available for his use and needs, and man was not yet familiar with the words 'yours' and 'mine'. This was that period in which the word 'ownership' was not yet coined in the human lexicon. The concept was to use and obtain benefit from the available materials. The Quran has called this an example of 'Adam's paradise'.

After this man's social life started, and confrontations arose between the mutual interests of human beings due to which the first stage of life ended. For this man was given guidance from Allah through His messengers, so that he could make his social life a paradise on earth. Paradise on earth is the other name of the Quranic society, in which there will not only be means of sustenance but it will also lead to the development of the human self.

After death all materials required for physical life will be left behind, and the human self will proceed forward. The self that has become developed will enter a higher developed stage - the Quran has called this a life of paradise as well.

In the Quran, 'Adam's paradise' is referred to separately, but after this the right human society and the successful life in the hereafter (earthly paradise and paradise in the hereafter), are mentioned mixed together. But by careful examination the difference between the two becomes apparent. In this regard it is important to understand regarding the details given in the Quran of the rewards relating to paradise, that in earthly paradise it means material things (similar things or those which produce a similar state of feeling). But in relation to the paradise in the hereafter, these meanings should be understood metaphorically. We should understand that this is a state of feeling which we cannot appreciate at our present level of consciousness. This is why the next life will not be like our physical life in this world - so such details given in the Quran should not be seen like our physical existence. These should be understood as states of feelings. Like hell, paradise in the hereafter is not a place, but refers to a state.

20.1 *Jannat* is Explained Metaphorically

In *Surah Ra'ad'* it is stated:

The parable of the Garden which the righteous are promised! beneath it flow rivers: perpetual is the enjoyment thereof and the shade therein: such is the end of the Righteous; and the end of Unbelievers in the Fire. (13:35)

Similarly in *Surah Muhammed*:

(Here is) a Parable of the Garden which the righteous are promised: in it are rivers of water incorruptible; rivers of milk of which the taste never changes; rivers of wine, a joy to those who drink; and rivers of honey pure and clear. In it there are for them all kinds of fruits; and Grace from their Sustainer. (Can those in such Bliss) be compared to such as shall dwell for ever in the Fire, and be given, to drink, boiling water, so that it cuts up their inside? (47:15)

In *Surah Al e Imran*:

Be quick in the race for seeking protection from your Sustainer, and for a Garden whose width is that (of the whole) of the heavens and of the earth, prepared for the righteous. (3:133)

Be you foremost (in seeking) protection from your Sustainer, and a Garden (of Bliss), the width whereof is as the width of heaven and earth, prepared for those who believe in Allah and His messengers... (57:21)

It is clear from these verses that paradise is not the name of a particular place. For example, the Quran says about its springs:

A fountain where the devotees of Allah do drink, making it erupt thus flowing through their own endeavours. (76:6)

This fountain is one which they tear open from their insides, through their inner efforts, i.e. that fountain which flows from the depths of their hearts. This fountain is called '*Salsabeel*'[164] (76:18) i.e. which while asking its way, flows forward on its own accord. In another verse the Quran states:

Now no person knows what delights of the eye are kept hidden (in reserve) for them - as a reward for their (good) deeds. (32:17)

---

[164] This word has two parts '*Sal*' and '*Sabeel*' – *Sal* means asking a question, *Sabeel* means that which can meet a need. It will mean something which flows and also meets the needs of those who need it or ask for it. (Ed)

It is clear from this that we cannot understand the paradise in the hereafter. We can make a guess through the metaphorical examples. We should keep this reality in mind, that though the words are in Arabic, their meanings are metaphorical. The thorns of most doubts and suspicions arise when this fundamental reality is ignored.

20.2 Paradise of Adam

The parable mentioned in the Quran about Adam is not about one man or one couple, but is a narrative of mankind presented as an example in which Adam represents men, and his wife (Eve is not mentioned by name in the Quran) represents women. The Quran states that in the initial stages of humanity, human life was very simple and was free from hard struggle. Means of sustenance were plenty, and there was no conflict as to ownership. The one who was hungry could fill his belly from wherever he wished (2:35). The general term used 'wherever he wished he could eat' is a very important phrase. Food, dress and shelter i.e. the basic needs of life, were available for everyone without hardship or any worry. There were no mutual squabbles and there was no clash of interests. After this, there arose in man's heart the desire for personal interest and its basic motive was to cater for the future of his children. That is, in place of *Bani Adam* (mankind), everyone was filled with concern for his own children. This is why everyone started accumulating for himself. This is what the Quran terms as '*Ibleesy* Doctrine'[165]. According to the Quranic concept, *Satan* or *Iblees* is a simile which gives name to human emotions and desires which wish to be gratified by going against the guidance of the revelation. This affected the initial harmonious human life of community and cooperation, which transformed into conflicts and mutual rivalry, and thus that initial paradise was snatched from man.

Now in order to regain that paradise man needs to shape his society in the light of the Permanent Values of the Quran. This will result in turning the whole of mankind into one big community in which there will be a life of unity and cooperation. Since such a life will be established by man himself, it will therefore not only meet the physical needs, but will also help to develop his self. And when this developed self after death moves on to the next stage, there too it will have a life of paradise. This is the parable of Adam quoted in various verses in the Quran. Because the subject at this time under discussion is not to explain the story of Adam, but is only about the *Jannat* of Adam (Adam's paradise), this is why we will present only those aspects of the details which refer to this[166]. In *Surah Baqra* it is stated:

---

[165] In the Bible it is stated that God created Adam only originally, but when Adam became sad due to being alone, then woman was created from his rib, so that she could provide him with pleasant company. Then Satan misguided woman (Eve) and she in turn became the cause of man's slip – this is why in the world, woman is considered the source of all sins. The Quran has rejected both these concepts. It states that man and woman were created alike and declares that each has his or her own significance and both can commit errors. Therefore woman is not the source of sins.

[166] Further details are available in the book titled '*Iblees aur Adam*' ('Iblees and Adam' in English) written by the author.

We said: 'O Adam! dwell you and your wife in the Garden; and eat of the bountiful things therein as (where and when) you will; but approach not this tree (i.e. don't be divided like the branches of a tree), or you will run into harm and transgression.' (2:35)

After this it is stated that Satan misguided them, and as a consequence there were wedges of self-interest created between various people and this is how Adam lost his paradise (2:36). On this Adam was very regretful and repented, and Allah stated that a mistake has been surely committed by you, but this mistake is not such which cannot be remedied. From Us you will keep receiving Divine Guidance and whoever among you in the light of this guidance shapes their society based on its values will be protected from fear and grief (2:37-38).

These details are mentioned in *Surah Araaf* with this addition, that in reference to sexual attraction between man and woman, man was self-deceived into thinking that he could get indefinite life by having children. So in place of mankind, he started chasing the interests of his own progeny, as a result of which his paradise disappeared (7:19-25). It is made clear here that the Quran is not against family and children, in fact it recognises their attraction for human beings. It simply states that your society should be organised in such a way that everyone is concerned with the sustenance of everyone else. The desire to accumulate all for yourself or for your children should not overtake you.

In *Surah Taha* in reference to *Jannat* it is stated to Adam:

There is therein (enough provision) for you not to go hungry nor to go naked, nor to suffer from thirst, nor from the sun's heat (all basic needs will be met). (20:118-119)

If you succumb to the *Iblees* of individual self-interest, he will create such conditions in which you will be deprived of these basic necessities and to gain them you will have to go through extreme hardships and struggles[167] (20:117). After this it is noted how Adam became deceived and he lost his paradise. He was told that in order to regain this lost paradise, he would need to organise his society according to the guidance of Allah. Regarding this it is stated that you should always keep the following principle in mind:

But whosoever turns away from My Message (the Quran), verily for him is a life narrowed down (economic deprivation), and We shall raise him up blind on the Day of Judgment. (20:124)

---

[167] The inequitable distribution of wealth has created horrendous problems across the world. It is important to keep in mind that the Quran addresses the whole of mankind when it talks about the Permanent Values. The creation of nation states is against these Values, since every nation takes care of its own vested interests and this causes conflicts and wars across the world. (Ed)

This makes it clear that:

(1) By following the Permanent Values of the Quran man can regain his earthly paradise.

(2) The people who go against these values, their living will be affected.

(3) The one whose living is restricted in this life, his hereafter will be ruined.

20.3 Paradise in This World

As mentioned previously, for Arabs gardens and flowing water were signs of great prosperity and wealth in this life. This had such significance for them that the opponents of the last messenger used to say if you are truly the messenger of Allah, then you should have such an orchard of dates and grapes in which there are streams with flowing water:

Or (until) you have a garden of date trees and vines, and cause rivers to gush forth in their midst, carrying abundant water. (17:91)

In reply to this, the revelation answered that they speak of one orchard, Allah will according to his Divine Law bestow on you many orchards (*Jannat*). Underneath will be streams of flowing water and along with this there will be palaces for you as well:

Blessed is He who, if that were His will (as per His laws), could give you better (things) than those, Gardens beneath which rivers flow; and He could give you palaces (secure to dwell in). (25:10)

This is that paradise which a society with a righteous system (through *Eimaan* and righteous deeds) will achieve in this life.

To achieve such a *Jannat,* the degree to which the last messenger and his companions had to struggle and endeavour with persistence and perseverance, the Quran records this in its verses as evidence for posterity - this was the bargain (business) about which the Quran notes:

O you who believe! Shall I lead you to a bargain that will save you from a grievous Penalty? That you believe in Allah and His Messenger, and that you strive (your utmost) in the Cause of Allah, with your property and your persons: That will be best for you, if you but knew! He will provide protection on your mistakes, and admit you to Gardens beneath which Rivers flow, and to beautiful mansions in Gardens of Eternity: that is indeed the Supreme Achievement. (61:10-12)

In *Surah Tauba* it states that as a consequence of *Eimaan*, migration and *Jehad*[168]:

...give them glad tidings of a Mercy from Himself, of His good pleasure, and of gardens for them, wherein are delights that endure. (9:21)

As a result of these persistent efforts to establish the Islamic System, they were made owners of the lands and properties, and of the wealth and resources of their opponents (33:27). Whenever they gained a new victory, they would acknowledge:

They will say: 'Praise be to Allah, Who has truly fulfilled His Promise (as per His laws) to us, and has given us (this) land in heritage: We can dwell in the Garden as we will: how excellent a reward for those who work (righteousness)!' (39:74)

This is that promise of Allah which is referred to in *Surah Noor* – for those who believe and do righteous deeds Allah has promised them that He will surely establish them on earth as He established those who met these conditions before them (24:55). These were the promises made by Allah which the *Momineen* were later reminded of (5:11, 8:26). This cannot be acquired in one day, as sustained effort and continuous endeavour is required for this:

In the case of those who say, 'Our Sustainer is Allah' and, further, stand straight and steadfast, the angels[169] descend on them: 'Fear you not!' (they suggest), 'Nor grieve! but receive the Glad Tidings of the Garden (of Bliss), the which you were promised! We are your protectors in this life and in the Hereafter: therein you will have all that your self shall desire; therein you will have all that you ask for! a hospitable gift from one Who gives protection and is Merciful!' (41:30-32)

In another verse regarding the promise of *Jannat* it is stated that Allah will not let His messenger and his companions be humiliated (66:8). In *Surah Yunus* it is made clear that in *Jannat* there will be no humiliation and disgrace (10:26).

In relation to the famous agreement with the pagans of Makkah, called 'Hudaibia', which was a prelude to the Makkan victory, *Surah Al-Fatah* was revealed. In this *Surah*, the *Momineen* were reassured that you need not be discouraged with the apparent compromise in this agreement, as Allah will soon bestow victory on you:

That He may admit the men and women who believe, to Gardens beneath which rivers flow, to dwell therein for aye... (48:5)

---

[168] *Jehad* means to spend all energies to the full in order to achieve some goal. (Ed)
[169] 'Angels' here means the material and psychological forces which are required to exert sustained efforts and persevere for a righteous cause. (Ed)

So that Allah could admit those *Momin* men and women into gardens (*Jannat*) beneath which rivers flow, and their opponents could receive punishment in the form of their defeat (48:6).

From these explanations it is clear that the consequences of having *Eimann* and doing righteous deeds leads to achieving a life of *Jannat* in this world, and for the people who gain in this way, because their self is developed as well, they get *Jannat* in the next life as well. This is the reason that the Quran has mentioned two *Jannats*:

> *But for such as fear the time when they will stand before their Sustainer, there will be two Gardens. (55:46)*

For the one who is concerned that I have to stand in the Divine court and be held accountable in front of Allah for my deeds and character, there are two paradises - a paradise in this world and another in the hereafter. These are the most elevated places. Besides this, there are other paradises at another level and those are also two in number (55:62).

After these details, the Quran addresses those of us who wish to attain paradise by empty prayers only:

> *Or do you think that you will enter the Garden (of bliss) without such (trials and tribulations) as came to those who passed away before you, they encountered suffering and adversity, and were so shaken in spirit that even the Messenger and those of Eimaan who were with him cried: 'When (will come) the help of Allah.' Ah! Verily, the help of Allah is (always) near! (2:214)*

This is in reference to the paradise of collective life. The Quran has declared that the family in which the husband and wife's ideas, doctrines, beliefs and *Eimaan* in the truth of the Permanent Values leads to mutual compatibility and one vision, to be *Jannat*, and a family in which there are mutual clashes and conflicts as *Jahannum* (2:221).

A point needs clarification before we go any further. A verse of the Quran is quoted previously according to which it is stated that the one who avoids the Divine Laws, his life in this world will be of deprivation and humiliation, and the one whose life here is restricted, on the Day of Judgement he will be also be raised up as blind.
This raises the question that if a nation is poor and deprived, will its inhabitants just by being poor and deprived be consigned to hell? This is not the case, but it is as follows:

(1) If a nation for some reason has gone downhill (or is living according to a wrong system), and has become content with its existing condition, then it lives a life of hell in this world, and in the hereafter will also go to hell.

(2) But if this nation (or some of its people) are not satisfied with their present lot and make efforts to change it, even if they are not able to overturn this wrong system during their lifetime and transform their condition, their life in the hereafter will be bright and successful. In the time of the last messenger

himself, the *Momineen* who while engaged in the struggle before the Islamic System was established, left this life, their life in this world was undoubtedly one of hardship, but who can doubt in their being inheritors of paradise of the hereafter?

(3) Contrary to this, if a nation harnesses the natural resources and makes its worldly life prosperous and wealthy and achieves power and status, but does not follow the Permanent Values, though its life in this world will be prosperous, its next life will be of hell. So much so, that its prosperity in this life will not be long lasting, because the foundation of a wrong system in a society has the seed of self-destruction in it.

(4) For the nation which adopts the Permanent Values in this world and establishes a system based on these Values, its life in this world will be of paradise and the next life will also be of paradise. The prosperity and successes of this life will keep reaching them while it remains on this path.

Regarding paragraph (3) above, an illustration of this in the Quran is the state of the previous nations e.g. in the case of the people of Ad:

Will you be left secure, in (the enjoyment of) all that you have here? 'Gardens and Springs'...
(26:147)

The same words have been used in reference to the *Jannat* of the *Momineen* (15:46). But they rebelled against the Divine Laws and as a consequence they met their destruction (26:158). Similarly regarding the people of Pharaoh it is said they lived a life of *Jannat*, but when they rebelled against the Divine Laws they were turned out of their land and in their place *Bani Israel* were made their heirs (26:57, 26:59, 44:25-28).

This reality has been explained through a few examples in the Quran. In *Surah Al-Qalam* there is an example of the owners of Gardens whose trees were heavy with fruit and they were proceeding to pick it, but they took strict precautions that the poor and needy should not take any share of it. Then the Quran says that according to the Law of Requital, there was such a windstorm[170] that their gardens were razed to the ground. (68:17-26)

A similar example is given in *Surah Kahf* (18:32-44). In *Surah Baqra* it is stated, would any of you like it if he had a blooming orchard with trees heavily laden with fruit, and he becomes old and has young children, and then to this orchard should come such a storm leaving destruction in its wake and its trees are burned and left as ashes, and in

---

[170] This needs further research as to how these natural events have long term economic effects in this world. Historically there are numerous natural events which have contributed to the fall of nations and of peoples in the past. Such events have also affected the outcomes of battles and wars. (Ed)

this way in his old age he has no means of sustenance nor any way to support his family[171]! (2:266).

It is clear from these examples also that the prosperity and success of *Jannat* in this life is associated with a righteous system – in a wrong system one can gain this temporarily, but ultimately such a system will be destroyed. That which is sustainable and long lasting is only for that *Jannat* which is based on the righteous deeds and a righteous system.

20.4 Details of *Jannat*

We now move on to the details of *Jannat* as referred to in the Quran. Before this it is important to understand a few issues in this respect:

1) The details of this *Jannat* are related to this life also. As far as the life in the hereafter is concerned, these details should be taken metaphorically and not as literal meanings.

2) As far as the *Jannat* of this life is concerned, the meanings of these words can be taken literally. However, it does not mean that all the comforts and adornments and wealth and status of civilisation and culture mentioned under this subject will remain the same throughout all ages. At the time of the revelation of the Quran, around the Arabian Peninsula there were two great civilisations i.e. the Persian and Roman empires. Arab merchants used to visit their towns and thus were familiar with their items of luxury and comfort etc. The Quran has referred to these things for the Arabs of that time and the fact is that all these 'comforts of *Jannat*' were also acquired by them within a short period of time. It is not necessary that in every age these 'comforts of *Jannat*' will remain the same. As life progresses the nature of these things will change as well, therefore their explanation will then be considered metaphorical. In *Surah Baqra* it is stated that the *Jannat* which will result as a consequence of *Eimaan* and righteous deeds will be the same, but the means of sustenance within it will not remain the same (2:25).

3) One characteristic of *Jannat* is such which makes it paradise. It is that all its blessings will be equally shared by all its inhabitants. It will not be the case that one class enjoys all the comforts, and the rest are dying of hunger. There will be no division into classes, e.g. upper, middle or working class etc. It will have categories according to the abilities to carry out certain work, but no class difference in relation to facilities and prosperity. This is that *Jannat* which the

---

[171] Through these examples the Quran points to the economic issues of mankind as a whole, and asks us to solve these problems on a global basis. (Ed)

Quranic system wishes to shape in this world. The *Jannat* of this life is the mirror image of the *Jannat* in the hereafter.

After these introductory premises, a few more points also need elucidation:

a) '*Azwaaj*[172] – This is generally taken to mean wives, so much so that *Zauja* is taken to mean a wife but not a husband. But in the Arabic language and according to the Quran its meanings are very wide. When two things are such that one cannot be complete without the other then each one is called the *Zauj* of the other e.g. two wheels of a vehicle are called *Zauj* of each other because if one wheel is missing or faulty the other becomes useless. From this meaning, *Azwaaj* means those companions who have similar thinking, values and outlook. This includes both men and women. According to the standard of the Quran, a husband and wife have to be the most close in thinking and outlook, therefore a husband is the *Zauj* of his wife and the wife is the *Zuaj* of her husband. But because the concept of paradise in the hereafter is non-physical, that is why in this paradise *Azwaaj* means that the companions will be of the same values, thinking and outlook, which will include both men and women. We cannot say whether in that life the present difference in nature of man and woman will be the same or it will be of another form. From *Azwaaj*, we should not infer that it relates to any kind of sexuality in the next life. As previously mentioned, the form that life will take there, we cannot comprehend or grasp at our present level of consciousness today.

b) '*Hoor Ain*' – Regarding *Jannat* there is also mention of this term *Hoor Ain*, which our mind also relates to relations (e.g. marital or sexual) between a man and woman. Keep it in mind that sexual relations between man and woman are not a bad thing, and if this condition is continued in the next life, we should not feel any reticence. But when we cannot even ascertain the state of our consciousness in the next life, then we should not try and imagine the details of it in present material forms. However, the life of paradise in this world will be expressed in material forms.

c) *Hoor* is a plural word which is used for both masculine and feminine. One of its meanings is such people (man or woman) who have very clear white eyes with a very black iris - among Arabs such an eye was considered very beautiful. But after this, among them this word began to be used for those people who were of very pious character and visionary outlook. Therefore in their lexicon, the word '*Ah warun*' (the plural of which is *Hoor*), means of 'pure and clean intellect'- i.e. the intellect which is not dishonest or cunning and is instead very pious and transparent and which does not teach any to deceive.

---

[172] In some Muslim cultures this refers to wives e.g. '*zauj*' is taken as meaning a wife while a husband is not called '*zauj*'. According to the Arabic lexicon this term has far wider meanings.

Ain is similarly a plural form of *Ayanu*, which is used for someone who has beautiful eyes and is used both for both male and female.

Therefore the *Hoor* of *Jannat* does not mean beautiful women, but people of very pure character and very sharp intellect but who are not cunning or deceptive. This includes both men and women. If it has any reference to physical beauty, then it will mean people with beautiful and clear eyes.

d) *'Asawara'* - This word means a bracelet made of gold. During the Persian Empire, those who were in the inner circle of the emperor, and whose status was considered very important, used to get a gold bracelet from the emperor as a mark of their eminence and would wear these bracelets as a sign to indicate their elevated rank. The Quran has used this term as a sign to indicate the successful and eminent status of life in paradise.

e) *'Anhaar'* (Canals) - In the Quran there is reference to canals of honey and milk which means abundance and prosperity - in Arabic the word *'nehr'* (singular of *Anhaar*) is used for flowing water, which is not necessarily a canal.

f) *'Sharab'* (all types of drinks) – We use this word to refer to wine or liquor. But among Arabs this denotes any kind of drink. The drinks in *Jannat* are differentiated by stating that in them there will be nothing to cause intoxication or to give rise to any debility.

Principally, we should keep in mind that *Jannat* is the name of the society of the *Momineen*. So everything which is declared *'haram'* or prohibited in the Quran, cannot be legitimate in *Jannat*. Nor can those things whose use is allowed in *Jannat*, be considered *haram* or disallowed now.

We now come to the details of *Jannat*, and need to bear in mind this reality, that this is a metaphorical representation of a luxurious, respectable and dignified life and its first audience were the nomadic Arabs of fourteen centuries ago.

20.5 General Depiction

The climate is neither very hot nor very cold, streams flowing with clean water, shaded greenery all around, fruit trees whose branches are bent heavily laden with fruit. In the shades of these trees, on the banks of the streams - there are spread carpets of very high quality with couches, and there will be companions of similar temperament, colour, one outlook and values gathered together having virtuous discussions. Meat of fowls (roast meats) to eat, extremely delicious drinks, everything beautiful to behold and hear, and such luxuries in it whose effects do not debilitate human potentials but instead promote development of human abilities. On the other side, there are grand palaces with chandeliers, hanging curtains of pure silk, beautiful carpets, carved tables and chairs, crystal ornaments, gold and silver utensils and crockery - all types of conveniences and comforts and also peace and tranquillity – and this is the reward of their own hard work – and in which all members of society, far above the distinction of 'yours' and 'mine,' will be sharing equally.

Now let us look at these particulars in the words of the Quran.

20.6 Dress, Utensils, Decorations and Sustenance

Gold ornaments and dresses of silk, seated high on thrones (18:31), prized pearls to wear (35:33). The following is another scenario in the Quran referring to *Jannat*:

(They will be) on Thrones encrusted (with gold and precious stones), reclining on them, facing each other. Round about them youths of perpetual (freshness), With goblets, (shining) beakers, and cups (filled) out of clear-flowing fountains: No after-ache will they receive therefrom, nor will they suffer intoxication: and with fruits, any that they may select: and the flesh of fowls, any that they may desire. (56:15-21) See also (37:42-47)

They will all be sitting in front of each other as 'brothers' (companions) and there will be nothing in any of their hearts which they wish to keep hidden from the others. No jealousy, vengeance, meanness, prejudice, nor hardship or tiredness (15:47-49).

Orchards, springs and fruit (44:52-55). Climate such that there will be neither extreme heat nor severe cold. Trees with branches bent low and fruit so close that everyone's hands can reach it[173]. Silver crockery and glass goblets, utensils, silken dresses, bracelets denoting achievement (76:13-22, and 69:23).

In another verse the following is outlined:

In a Garden on high, where they shall hear no (word) of vanity: therein will be a bubbling spring: therein will be Thrones (of dignity), raised on high, goblets placed (ready), and cushions set in rows, and rich carpets (all) spread out. (88:10-16) See also (22:23, 55:54-75, and 78:32)

Alongside the flowing streams, beneath the shades of trees, companions of similar taste and their picnic parties, and each according to his preference will have sustenance available according to their desires (36:55-57). Fruit trees which have no thorns, long shadows, water from springs which does not have to be dug up with hard work, abundance of fruit available all year round and available to everyone – no-one to prevent their access, no-one to hinder or stop them (56:28-33, 77:41-43).

---

[173] This is the biggest characteristic, that its fruit will be within the reach of everyone i.e. everyone will have access to it. In fact it can be said that it falls of its own accord into their laps. Pay particular attention to the term 'everyone' – this is the characteristic of *Jannat*, that it is for everyone.

The following verse covers another aspect:

> *On Thrones (of Dignity) will they command a sight (of all things): You will recognise in their faces the beaming brightness of Bliss. Their thirst will be slaked with Pure Wine sealed: The seal thereof will be Musk: and for this let those aspire, who have aspirations[174].*
> *(83:23-26)*

Sustenance will be available on a continuous basis (19:62) and will be plentiful (38:51) and everyone will have knowledge of it i.e. the stores of sustenance will not be hidden or concealed and everyone will get it with respect and dignity (37:41-44, and 52:19).

20.7 Drinks

1) Streams of clean water whose taste will not alter. Streams of honey and milk whose taste will not go sour. (47:15)
2) Pure cups full to the brim. (78:34)
3) Sealed bottles full of drinks[175] (83:25-26).
4) In these meetings such drinks will be served which will be white like ice, and the taste will be very delicious and its effect will be so good that it will neither intoxicate nor will there be any reduction in its delightful effects (37:45-47, 52:23, 56:19).

Now let us look at the properties and effects of these drinks.

In *Surah Al-Dahr* it is mentioned:

> *As to the Righteous, they shall drink of a Cup mixed with Kafur, a fountain where the devotees of Allah do drink, making it flow in unstinted abundance[176]. (76:5-6)*

Later in the same *Surah* it is mentioned:

> *Crystal-clear, made of silver: they will determine the measure thereof (according to their wishes), and they will be given to drink there of a Cup (of Wine) mixed with Zanjabeel.*
> *(76:16-17)*

The effect of 'Kafur' is known for reducing a raised body temperature while the effect of 'Zanjibeel' is to increase the lowered body temperature. Therefore the drinks in *Jannat* will create balance in the human character i.e. where the temperature is high it will be

---

[174] This points to the fact that it is up to man to aspire for the higher values of life i.e. life is about going forward with a developed self or lagging behind by not following the Permanent Values. (Ed)
[175] These are drinks which are free from impurities and provide nourishment for the self. (Ed)
[176] This is that spring which the *Momineen* will have 'brought out of their own hearts' through their own endeavours.

reduced and where there is a deficiency it will be compensated and in this way a balanced personality will emerge.

Then this spring (the origin of this drink) in *Jannat* is named '*Sal-Sabeel*' – *Sal* and *Sabeel* means flowing forward while asking directions; as will be explained later, *Jannat* is not the final destination of the evolutionary journey. It is just one of the destinations from where the journey of life has to move forward. This is why the water of *Jannat* is named as ever flowing and there is mention of springs which never stop (88:12). It is characterised by the name *Sal-Sabeel* – i.e. progressing forward and to keep progressing.

A little later this drink is called '*Sharab e Tahoor*' (76:21), free from all types of impurities, that is such a drink in which there is respect for humanity and dignity for mankind.

In *Surah Tatfeef*, there is mention of a source of springs located at a height, called *Tasneem*:

> *With it will be (given) a mixture of Tasneem: a spring, from (the waters) whereof drink those Nearest to Allah. (83:27-28)*

Tasneem means heights i.e. the sources of the springs of the life of *Jannat* will be at great heights[177]. Obviously, that spring source which is at a height, its water will flow forward under its own momentum.

Through these metaphors it is evident that in the life of *Jannat* there will be balance and equilibrium in the human self and the source of its abilities will be at such 'heights' as a result of which, without any external support, it will keep progressing forward. There is the desire for competitiveness within man (83:25). This means that whoever wishes to progress should move forward in this field and develop his self, so that having acquired equilibrium and balance, he can under his own momentum keep progressing forward. The purpose of the challenges and endeavours of life is:

> *To any of you that chooses to press forward, or to follow behind. (74:37)*

The desire to get ahead of each other produces jealousy in the hearts but in the life of paradise this desire to exceed each other will not produce jealousy and envy, instead the reality will be the following:

> *And We shall remove from their hearts any lurking sense of injury... (7:43, 15:47)*

---

[177] Water flowing down from heights has an aesthetic aspect as well. (Ed)

20.8 'Azwaaj um Mutahrat' - Righteous Companions

We have already discussed the term *Azwaaj* as meaning companions with similar values and beliefs, and this includes husbands and wives. According to the Quran, the relation between husband and wife is of a companion. In the paradise in this world, *Azwaaj* and *Hoor Ain* will include husband and wife. In the paradise of the next life, from the metaphorical interpretation, we cannot say what shape the companionships will take. These are those righteous companions about which the Quran has spoken.

The Quran has stated that the following people will be in this:

Gardens of perpetual bliss: they shall enter there, as well as the righteous among their fathers, their spouses, and their offspring: and angels shall enter unto them from every gate (with the salutation) (13:23) See also (40:8, 52:21)

These are called *Azwaaj um Mutahrat* – see (2:25, 3:14, 4:57). In some places only the term *Azwaaj* is used (43:70) and elsewhere *Hoor Ain* (44:54, 56:42, 52:20).

In the age of ignorance (before the advent of Islam), the condition of a woman was such that she had no status and she was kept ignorant and uneducated to such an extent that (in the words of the Quran) she could not stand up in court and give her opinion or evidence in her own case (43:18). The Quran gave women a new elevated status of respect and dignity in society and through education and training such a transformation took place that she became articulate and confident. In a society of paradise, these are the characteristics of women about which it is stated:

And on status raised high. We have created (their Companions) of special creation. and untouched - pure (56:34-36) See also (78:33)

We provided them with such education and training and gave them such an upbringing, that they were transformed into a seemingly new creation. They became such as if their seed was of the same source and they came out of the same mould.

Having similar outlook and values, skilled and competent, fluent and articulate, and possessing a high degree of self-respect and self-esteem (38:51). Guarding their chastity and not allowing their gaze to roam (37:48).

In *Surah Rehman* it is stated:

In them will be (Maidens), chaste, restraining their glances, whom no man (urban or nomad) before them has touched. (55:56) See also (55:58, 55:70-72, 37:48-49)

Before moving forward, this is a point at which to pause and reflect on this reality that in a society at the time of marriage, every young man or woman who wishes to get married has full certainty that his or her potential companion i.e. the chastity of their future partner, is such that he or she has not looked at another with any bad intentions.

Then this certainty and contentment is maintained throughout their lives. What doubt can there be of such a society not being *Jannat*!

20.9 Variety and Diversity in Paradise

In *Surah Rehman* it is stated about paradise in this world and in the next life:

> *But for such as fear the time when they will stand before their Sustainer, there will be two Gardens- then which of the attributes of your Sustainer will you deny? Containing all kinds (including knowledge, sustenance and delights). (55:46-48)*

These two paradises will be based on various interests and pursuits. Human life desires variety, and for the development of its (creative) abilities and their expression and use, there are many aspects. For these aspects, the Quran has called this paradise '*Zawata Afnan*' [178]. After this, in this *Surah* there is mention of various aspects of comforts and conveniences. Therefore, the life of paradise is not such in which eating, drinking and sleeping are the only activities. That life will have branches upon branches of various subjects and technical skills, so this life will be full of all types of comforts and pleasures, successes and achievements (56:89). So much so, that this will include beauty and aesthetics, adornments, creativity, art and very high quality music as well (30:15, 43:70).

20.10 Getting Whatever You Wish

The life of *Jannat* has been comprehensively summed up by the Quran in one verse by stating:

> *…they will have therein all that they wish: thus does Allah reward the righteous. (16:31) See also (21:102, 25:16, 42:22)*

Whatever they wish for, they will get and whatever they want will happen, in this world and in the hereafter (41:30-31).

In another verse:

> *…there will be there all that the self could desire, all that their eyes could delight in … (43:71)*

In another place is stated an aspect even beyond this:

> *There will be for them therein all that they wish, and more besides in Our Presence. (50:35)*

---

[178] *Zawata Afnan* means various branches, in other words, *Jannat* is a place where different sciences and art forms are found. According to the Quran, one aspect of the heavenly society is that it would be the centre of knowledge and arts. (Lughat ul Quran). (Ed).

There is a great reality implied in this verse. At the level of our present life in this world, no matter how elaborate human desires and wishes are, and according to his thinking these may be unlimited, these will remain confined to the concepts which can be formed in this physical world and its environment only. But the life in the hereafter will be many times more elevated. In that life what human desires will be, we cannot sense or even conceive of. This is why it is stated that they will get whatever they wish and even more beyond that. That is, that which they cannot even desire at present will also be made available. This is why it is stated that whatever their Sustainer bestows on them, they will accept (51:16, 52:18).

20.11 They Will Have No Fear or Grief

In the life of *Jannat* there will be no kind of fear or grief (6:48, 7:49, 41:30, 43:68, and 46:13). Fear arises from external threats and dangers, while grief is the name of the internal state of distress of an individual. In a society of *Jannat* there will be no worry about external dangers and threats, nor will there be grief or uncertainty, even the greatest terror will not produce any heartache (21:103). Their faces will be bright and peaceful (83:24) and they will be very pleased at seeing the rewards of their deeds (88:8, 84:9). Because of their protection from any grief and sorrow, they will enjoy inner peace and contentment and for this they will bow in gratitude to Allah (35:34).

In this there will not be wearisome efforts and tiresome activity (15:48, 35:35) and neither sadness nor disappointments (37:47). They will have a life of bliss (69:21), life will be successful and prosperous (101:7), and they will have a great state with all amenities and with that, success and achievements (76:20).

20.12 A Society with Peace and Security

With all these amenities and energies, society will be such where there will be no vanities:

They will not there hear any vain discourse, but only salutations of Peace... (19:62) See also (56:25-26, 88:11, 78:35)

The angels will welcome them with praiseworthy and good wishes (13:24, 16:32, 39:73). Everyone among them will wish peace on the others and will desire to establish a system of sustenance as proposed in the Quran (20:10), with peace and security (15:45). *Jannat* is but a place of security (44:51-55) and home of peace (6:128), in which there will be good wishes for everyone, which will provide pleasure to hearts and minds (14:23, 25:75).

20.13 Pleasure from Allah

With all these benefits and above all the pleasure of Allah (3:14). This means life conforming to the Divine Laws and (within human constraints) adopting the Attributes of Allah (5:119, 9:100, 58:22). And this is the greatest success and achievement of whoever attains it (9:72). This is the *Jannat* which is spread over the whole of the universe (3:132, 57:21) and which is the best place of rest and abode (25:24, 25:76).

20.14 Recompense of Deeds

A voice will be heard in paradise:

> *…Behold! the garden before you! You have been made its inheritors, as a consequence of your deeds of righteousness. (7:43) See also (43:72)*

This *Jannat* cannot be gained by requesting it, nor as a charity, nor by intercession, nor as a free prize; it is the natural consequence only of man's deeds. It is embedded in his own endeavours and accomplishments.

20.15 *'Has'unat Murtafaqan'* - Righteous Deeds which Rise

Through a life of prosperity and comforts, man becomes lazy and becomes less hard working. However, regarding the life of *Jannat*, the Quran sheds light on a reality due to which the nature of prosperity and comfort changes. In *Surah Kaaf*, regarding life in hell, the Quran states, *'Sa'at Murtafaqan'*[179] (18:29) - *Murtafaq* is that through the support of which something rises up. The Quran states that in a non-Quranic society (hell), the comforts and conveniences which are available cannot help to raise humanity. Contrary to this, it states that in *Jannat*, *'Has'unat Murtafaqan'* (18:31), these pleasantries and niceties of life will help man to rise higher through balanced support. That is as a consequence of this, the life of these people will not descend to an animal level and will instead be able to develop further.

To what extent these comforts are an indication of success and accomplishment which take human life to new heights – this is the characteristic of a society of paradise both in this life and in the life of the hereafter.

---

[179] *'Sa'at'* means evil or hell, while *'Murtafaqan'* means to raise up, so being raised up in this way (*Sa'at Murtafaqan*) means leading up to hell. *'Has'una't'* means righteous deeds, so *'Has'unat Murtafaqan'* means those good deeds which enable man to rise higher in self-development.

20.16 Who Deserves this *Jannat*

A man regularly goes for a walk every morning, and day by day his health improves, and what is this good health of his a consequence of? Due to his persistent efforts. The same is applicable to *Jannat* when a group of people who, having strong belief in the Divine Laws (which is called *Eimaan*), endeavour to establish a society according to these Values, then as a consequence *Jannat* emerges in this world. The positive effect of this effort is imprinted on the self of an individual, and the sum total of these effects result in the emergence of *Jannat* in the hereafter as well. Therefore *Jannat* is the name given to the results of sustained efforts along the right lines. The Quran has presented this reality in different ways.

20.17 *Jannat* is the Consequence of Your Deeds

In *Surah Nahl* it is stated that the angels will address the *Momineen* saying:

> ... enter you the garden, because of the good deeds which you did (in the world)[180]. (16:32)
> See also (56:24)

In another verse it is stated:

> Such will be the Garden of which you are made heirs for your (good) deeds (in life). (43:72)
> See also (7:43)

In one place after mentioning *Jannat* the Quran states:

> For the like of this let all strive, who wish to strive. (37:61) See also (3:135, 29:58)

In one place, regarding the owners of paradise, it is stated that these are those people whose righteous deeds have materialised in good results (46:16). In another verse it is confirmed that whatever you did in the days gone by, this is its result (69:24). Your efforts came to fruition in this way (76:22). And in another place, that the inhabitants of paradise seeing the results of their deeds will be much pleased (88:9).

20.18 The Results of *Eimaan* and Righteous Deeds - '*Amal e Saleh*'

If we look at the Quran from beginning to end, the theme of *Eimaan and Amal e Saleh* is described as the central characteristic defining a *Momin* and its unalterable outcome is *Jannat*. The Quran states:

> Verily Allah will admit those who believe and do righteous deeds, to Gardens beneath which rivers flow... (47:12) See also (23:10-11)

---

[180] Similar words i.e. this is because of your deeds, have been used in other verses e.g. (52:19, 46:14, 6:128, 77:43).

The places where *Eimaan* and *Amal e Saleh* are mentioned in the Quran are so numerous that it is not possible to note them all.

20.19 *Jannat* for '*Mutaqeen*' (Paradise for the Righteous)

One of the terms in the Quran is *Mutaqeen* – this means those people who guard themselves against those dangerous paths in life which go against the Permanent Values of the Quran, and follow the Divine Laws. They are declared heirs of paradise:

Verily, for the Righteous, are Gardens of Delight, in the Presence of their Sustainer. (68:34)
See also (51:15-19)

These verses are also numerous and are not quoted here.

20.20 *Jannat* for '*Mohsineen*' (Paradise for Doers of Balanced Deeds)

In some places the righteous people are declared to be *Mohsineen*, which refers to those who live their life with balance and equilibrium within the confines of the Divine Laws:

Taking joy in the things, which their Sustainer gives them, because, before then, they lived as Mohsineen (Righteous). (51:16) See also (10:26)

In *Surah Mursalaat* both *Mutaqeen* and *Mohsineen* are referred to and it is declared that for both is *Jannat* (77:41-44). These are all characteristics of the *Momineen* i.e. those who follow the path of guidance as defined by the Quran (7:43). In some places they are also called '*Abrar*' i.e. those whose self through righteous conduct has developed to the extent where it encompasses a breadth of outlook and expansive vision (82:13, 83:22). The inhabitants of paradise are also called '*Ashab ul Yameen*' (the companions of the right hand) i.e. the possessors of respect and piety (74:39, 69:19, 56:27, 38, 90). Obviously what else can be greater than this respect and piety, that a man's life in this world be full of success and achievement, and the life of the hereafter also be one of pleasure and eminence.

20.21 *Jannat* is Earned Through Sustained Effort

Whoever accepts Islam (i.e. becomes a Muslim), 'signs' an agreement in which he agrees to 'sell' his life and material possessions to Allah and in return Allah commits to provide them :

Allah has purchased of the believers their persons and their goods; for theirs (in return) is the garden (of Paradise)… (9:111)

According to this agreement, the state of these people is that, they are ever ready in time of need to fight in battle in the path of Allah and then they are either victorious or lay down their life:

…they fight in His cause, and slay and are slain… (9:111)

In this way they earn paradise. This is stated earlier in the following verse:

But the Messenger, and those who believe with him, strive and fight with their wealth and their persons: for them are (all) good things: and it is they who will prosper. (9:88) See also (61:11-12)

This is why for those people who according to their own standards, proclaim to be the owners of paradise, it is stated clearly in the Quran that you cannot get paradise by doing nothing. For this, you need great patience and have to pass through very difficult and challenging stages (2:214, 3:141). Only those who persevere in these dangerous phases get the benefits of paradise (47: 4-6). For this, everything has to be abandoned which is needed to be left behind, even your homes. And every kind of hardship has to be faced with a willing heart (3:194). *Eimaan*, and with it perseverance, are two essential requirements to obtain *Jannat* - both in this life and in the hereafter (41:30, 46:13-14). Its practical method is to obey this System which was established according to the Divine Laws by the last messenger and after him, his followers continued it (and whoever re-establish it) - this will be called the obedience of 'Allah and messenger' and this is a fundamental requirement in the achievement of *Jannat* (4:13, 48:17). Therefore, obtaining *Jannat* is not an individual matter, but a collective programme, for which forming a team is essential. This is why the Quran states:

Enter you, then, among My servants! Yea, enter you My Heaven! (89:29-30)

In order to be among His people it is necessary that man should rise beyond his personal benefits, and keep his emotions and desires under control and in obedience of the Divine Laws (79:40-41). If on this path, a wrong step is taken then it is necessary to immediately retrace your steps and go back onto the right path – this is called *Tauba* (66:8). These are the people who are true in the proclamation of their *Eimann*, and they deserve *Jannat* (5:119). Because of this programme, their self develops to such an extent that they are capable of going from this life to the evolutionary stages of development in the next life. This is what is called self-development ('*Tazkia Nafs*'). This cannot be obtained in monasteries, but is obtained in a society of paradise (20:76). This was that society which was established by the last messenger and his companions (9:100). These people did not foster friendships with those who opposed the Islamic System (58:22). This is the reason the Quran has declared the companions of the messenger as owners of *Jannat* (9:100).

20.22 *Jannat* for Mankind

The doors to this *Jannat* are open to the whole of mankind for all times – whoever becomes included in this category of *Momineen*, he has a right to *Jannat*, whatever may be his origin of birth or religion.

In *Surah Baqra* this point is made clear:

And they say: 'None shall enter Paradise unless he be a Jew or a Christian.' Those are their (vain) desires. Say: 'Produce your proof if you are truthful.' Nay, whoever submits His whole self to Allah (i.e. follows the Quran) and is a doer of good, He will get his reward with his Sustainer; on such shall be no fear, nor shall they grieve. (2:112) See also (5:65, 5:85)

20.23 *Jannat* for Men and Women

And in this there is no differentiation made between men and women – the doors of *Jannat* are open equally to all:

If any do deeds of righteousness - be they male or female - and have conviction (through intellect and reasoning), they will enter Heaven, and not the least injustice will be done to them. (4:124) See also (40:40, 3:194, 16:97)

The promise of *Jannat* is for *Momineen*, both men and women[181]. (9:72, 48:5) and the paths to self-development are equally open to both (57:12). This is that *Jannat* whose desire swells the heart of every *Momin*, so much so that even the messengers of Allah in their purified hearts wished for it (26:85). And those *Momineen* who are trapped among wrong people also have this desire (66:11).

20.24 Miscellaneous

(1) One who commits 'Shirk' i.e. along with the sovereignty of Allah obeys other powers and observes their laws (and goes from this world in this state), for him *Jannat* is declared *Haram* (forbidden) (5:72).

(2) The people who verbally accept the Divine Laws but practically go against these Laws, and also those who rebel against these Laws – they can never enter *Jannat* (7:40).

(3) Human beings are divided into two groups only - one deserves *Jannat* and the other meant for *Jahannum* (42:7). And these two groups can never be alike (59:20). The life of the inhabitants of *Jannat* is successful and prosperous (59:20, 3:184). This is a very great achievement i.e. it is not only the name of the place to protect oneself from *Jahannum*, which is called salvation, as this is a negative characteristic, but from a positive aspect *Jannat* is the name of achieving the best results. This means to spend a better life than the existing one, and whatever man is at this present time, to become better than this. To reach a higher plane than this current life.

---

[181] Men and women are equal at the level of the self – physically they are different because of their different roles in this life. They have the same thinking abilities which help to create a self. (Ed)

(4) Between the inhabitants of *Jannat* and the inhabitants of *Jahannum* there is a fine screen. This screen of differentiation is between the human self and their inner state (7:46). This is such a partition within which there is mercy, and on the other side is hell (57:13).

(5) In the Quran, there is mention of mutual exchanges between the inhabitants of paradise and those of hell, and the details have been noted in the chapter on *Jahannum*. See (7:44, 7:50, 37:50-51, 57:14, 74:40-46).

20.25 *Jannat* Forever

One *Jannat* was the one in which Adam resided, which was not the result of his own deeds. It was bestowed on him free. The result was that Adam committed one error of judgment and he was banished from there. And another *Jannat* is that which the children of Adam earn through their own toil and sweat, (i.e. it is the natural consequence of their own righteous deeds). From this no-one can expel them:

> ...nor shall they (ever) be asked to leave. (15:48)

This is the difference between a free and an earned *Jannat*.

No man can snatch from another his health, education, ability, experience and character - if he wastes it himself then it is different. Whatever belongs to a man others can snatch it or cause harm to it, but whatever a man has become, none can take that away from him nor cause harm to it. What man is himself, its name is *Jahannum* or *Jannat*. Therefore no one can turn someone out of a paradise achieved like this. This is why it is said that the inhabitants of paradise will stay in it forever:

> ...they will dwell therein for ever... (98:8) See also (8:119, 9:22, 9:100, 64:9, 65:11)

This promise of Allah is firm and true and whose promise can be more true than that of Allah? (4:122). Its reward will never stop, and neither would they themselves wish to leave it (41:8, 84:25, 95:6). Nor will death come there to anyone (37:58-59, 44:56).

This is about the inhabitants of *Jannat* (who will not be turned out of it). About *Jannat* itself, it is stated that its spring times will be infinite. In the Quran, the best characteristic of *Jannat* described is:

> ... beneath which rivers flow... (2:25)

A garden without water becomes dry whereas the garden in which flowing water is always present underneath the trees, can never alter in its freshness and greenery. This will be the state of the trees which will stay fresh and evergreen forever. Regarding the fruits of these trees, it is said that these will be unaffected by changes in climate and in every season these trees will always bear fruits (13:35, 14:25). These are those very tall trees of human righteous deeds whose roots are very deep and whose branches are touching the heavens (14:24). Therefore, in *Jannat* there will be no break in its sustenance nor any decrease (19:62, 38:54) - fruit in abundance which will not be discontinued, nor will any be prevented from it (56:32-33).

20.26 *Jannat* is Forever – What Does this Mean?

As was explained in detail in Chapter 19, the duration of the next life is not infinite like Allah - infinity is only for Allah (57:3), this why about *Jannat* it is also stated:

> And those who are blessed shall be in the Garden: They will dwell therein for all the time that the heavens and the earth endure, except as your Sustainer wills: a gift which will never end. (11:108)

The same words have been used for *Jahannum* as well (11:107). But the final words –'*a gift which will never end*' - used at the end are only mentioned in the case of *Jannat*. From this, another reality is presented to us, and which is discussed next.

20.27 *Jannat* is a Station – Not an End

As we have seen, that life after journeying through various evolutionary stages of development has reached the current human form. After this it has further evolutionary stages to go through. This evolution will now be of the human self. The individual whose self will have reached the requisite level of development so that it has become capable of moving from this life to the next stage, it will be said about him that he has entered *Jannat*. (The one who does not have this ability, he will stop, and this is called the life of *Jahannum*.) The ones who stop, stop at one point.

But for those progressing forward, the landscape will be vast. This is why for the inhabitants of *Jannat* there will be opportunities to go on to further evolutionary stages of development. This is the reason why various grades within *Jannat* have been referred to:

> And those Foremost (in conviction) will be Foremost (in the Hereafter). These will be those Nearest to Allah. (56:10-11) See also (56:27)

Then it is stated about the inhabitants of *Jannat*:

> One Day you will see the believing men and the believing women - how their Light runs forward before them and by their right hands: (their greeting will be): Good News for you this Day! Gardens beneath which flow rivers! to dwell therein for aye! This is indeed the highest achievement! (57:12, 66:8)

In this verse, the plural form is used for *Jannat*. The light of the righteous conduct of the inhabitants of *Jannat* will brighten their paths, and thus they will progress from one *Jannat* and arrive in another *Jannat*.

In *Surah Zumr* it is mentioned:

...that lofty mansions, one above another, have been built: beneath them flow rivers (of delight): (such is) the Promise of Allah, never does Allah fail in (His) promise. (39:20)

The word used for a lofty mansion is *'Ghuraf'*, and the term used is *'Ghuraf above Ghuraf'*. This word has many connotations. It includes speed of movement, water flowing in abundance in a stream, and a mansion over another mansion and of its height; all these are in its meanings. Therefore, it is said about the inhabitants of *Jannat*, for them will be all kinds of opportunities and prosperities, eminence and elation, and rising ever higher by progressing stage by stage. As they progress through various evolutionary stages, their state of development will be ever increasing in elevation. Therefore, the life of *Jannat* is not one of inertia and suspension. It is in itself a dynamic arena of activity - with this difference, that in the life of this world (of hell - if it is not based on these Values), a man's energies and abilities are spent in obtaining the sustenance of the physical body. In the life of *Jannat*, man will be completely free from this aspect. Therefore, he will direct all his abilities to further enhancement of his self.

Regarding the arena of this worldly life, the Quran has declared:

To any of you that chooses to press forward, or to follow behind. (74:37)

This life is a world of deeds, in which man has been left with various potentials so that he who wishes can go forward, and he who wishes can remain behind. About paradise in the next life, the Quran makes it clear:

...and for this let those aspire, who have aspirations. (83:26)

The individual who wishes in his heart to go forward, should progress in it, which can take him to higher stages of development in the next life – as already noted this will also make this life beautiful, peaceful and free from grief. This is how human life will go further forwards – and ascend stage by stage (84:19). What will be its ultimate end, we cannot say. Nor at our present conscious level can we conceptualise it.

But its beginning will be from our present life. Fortunate are those who view this opportunity as invaluable and commence laying down the foundation of their 'palace' brick by brick, through the hands of their righteous deeds without hesitation or delay, as this opportunity will never come again. And they should never overlook this fact, that the life of the hereafter will only be successful for the one whose life in this world is based on righteous conduct.

But those who were blind in this world, will be blind in the hereafter, and most astray from the Path. (17:72)

(Intentionally left blank)

21 Appendix 1: Some Permanent Values from the Quran

Permanent Values do not change with time and are applicable both at the individual and collective level. The following is not an exhaustive list.

- **Concept of God:** The concept of God as revealed in the Quran is an external objective standard for us to follow as far as it relates to the development of the human self. '*...don't be like those who forgot Allah and He made them forget their own Selves....*' (59:19)

- **Equality as a Human Being (unity in humanity):** At birth we are equal and the same is true when we die. The Quran declares: '*Mankind was one community....*' (2:213)

- **Respect as a Human Being:** Every human being possesses a self which has the attribute of free will. This entitles every human being to equal respect, so that there can be no discrimination due to reasons of family, tribe, race, community, nationality, religion, gender, colour, language, culture, tradition, ... '*Verily, We have honoured all children of Adam.*' (17:70)

- **Freedom:** Since every human being is born free, then he or she should remain free. According to the Quran, freedom means that no-one can extort obedience from another human being. Only the Quranic Values should be followed as it is only by operating within the confines of these Values that the self can develop. See verses (3:78), (5:44), 10:15) and (82:19)

- **Freedom to Choose (no compulsion):** Responsibility for the act of a human being is determined by his own volition and intent. It is our choices in life which define us. The Quran invites us to use the power of our intellect and reasoning to acquire evidence to then make informed decisions. '*Those who, when they are reminded with the signs of their Lord, droop not down at them as if they were deaf and blind*' (25:73)

- **Righteousness as a Criterion:** The level of development of the Self and individual conduct should be the criterion for higher responsibility within a society. The Quran declares: '*The noblest of you in the sight of Allah is the best in righteousness*' (49:13)

- **Tolerance:** Freedom to choose means that we need to be tolerant and accept the choices made by others in their lives. The Quran asks us to understand this at a fundamental level i.e. by being in possession of a self with freedom to choose, we need to recognise this state exists in others and accept it. (22:40), (2:256)

- **Existence of the Human Self:** We all have a strong sense of identity and are aware of our existence. We have self-consciousness and the ability to make decisions. Our inner attributes of emotions, thinking, memory etc help us to live our lives and in the process we gain experiences which helps to develop our self-concept. *(39:41)*

- **Accountability (The Law of Requital):** Human beings possess free will, emotions, and the ability to think about thinking, and memory. Our thinking and decisions leave an impact on our self i.e. it changes our personality and the way we think and act. The Quran declares that every cause has an effect in human daily living. This is called the Law of Requital. The purpose of human creation is that none of our deeds remains unaccountable and none of us is dealt with unjustly. *(45:21)*

- **Responsibility cannot be shared at the level of the self:** At an individual level each one of us is a complete unit therefore none can share our responsibility at this level. The Quran asks us to follow this value in our interactions as well. *(53:38)*

- **Free Will:** The use of this value is up to us as individuals to use by exercising our freedom to choose. However our choices have consequences and we are accountable for these. The Quran tells us that this is your world and you can live your life as you wish. '....*do what you will: verily He sees what you do*' *(41:40)*

- **Warning/Admonition:** We need to warn each other about the consequences of what we think, say and do in our lives. The Quran asks us to think of the consequences of every action we take in our lives both in the short term and the long term. The Quran calls its message a warning to mankind - to be accepted or rejected and then to live with the consequences of those choices. '*that it gives warning to any who are alive*' *(36:70)*. *(6:70)*, *(7:51)*. The Quran asks us to keep reminding each other about the purpose of life. (103:1-3)

- **Justice:** When dispensing justice, no distinction is allowed between friend and foe, us and others: '*and let not the dislike of a people incite you not to act equitably. Be just: that is nearer to observance of responsibility*' *(5:8)*. See also (2:283), (4:135), (4:105), (4:135). The changing of Allah's laws is declared to be injustice by the Quran: *(50:29)*

- **Good deeds replace the effects of bad deeds:** *The Quran declares:'.. for those things that are good remove those that are bad..' (11:114). 'Repel bad with that which is good..' (23:96)*

- **What is Good for Mankind remains on Earth:** *'..while that which is for the good of mankind remains on the earth....' (13:17).*

- **Knowledge:** The Quran has referred to both perceptual and conceptual knowledge and asked mankind to explore both the visible and the invisible worlds to understand the Truth and the purpose behind human creation. *'Taught man that which he knew not' (96:5). 'He taught Adam the ability to characterise....' (2:31).*

- **Science:** The Quran asks us to make efforts to discover both the physical and the psychic worlds and bring them into use for the good of mankind at large. *'and He has made subservient to you whatsoever is in the heavens and whatsoever is in the earth, all from Himself'. (45:13).*

- **Aesthetic Sense**: As human beings we have an aesthetic sense, an appreciation for beauty. The Quran acknowledges and respects this and considers it as a necessary element in the growth and development of human personality: *'Say: who has forbidden the adornment of Allah, which He has brought forth for His servants and the good things of His providing...' (7:32).* However, the pursuit of the aesthetic sense should be within the confines of the Permanent Values.

- **History as a Model:** The Quran asks mankind to study history and the rise and fall of civilisations with a view to learn lessons. This helps us to study the Permanent Values and see that violations of these values leads to wars and conflicts and leads to a waste of valuable human time. *'Do they not travel through the earth and see what was the end of those before them? They were more numerous than these and superior in strength and in the traces they have left in the land. Yet all that they accomplished was of no profit to them.'(40:82). (10:39)*

- **Subsistence:** Basic necessities[182] for all human beings must be met and an environment should be created for the development of the human Self. Meeting the physical needs of the human body is essential before intellectual reasoning and creative activity can be brought into play. This is the reason why the Quran declares that the aim is to establish an economic system in which there is no accumulation of wealth – *'and they ask you as to what they should give for the benefit of others. Say: whatever is surplus to your requirements...' (2:219)*

- **Reward is for the Work and not the Capital:** This value defines the economic system proposed by the Quran. Life is a journey and not a destination. The capital must remain in continuous flow and must not be accumulated. Reward for work must meet the necessities of life. *(53:39); (59:7).*

- **Patience and Perseverance:** Since the self takes time to develop, as it has to gain knowledge and overcome the challenges of life, it therefore needs time to

---

[182] Basic necessities will include food, shelter, security, medical treatment, education, job, freedom of expression, freedom to practice religion, etc. (Ed)

build up its inner conviction and strength. It needs guidance as an external criterion of reference to signpost its progress towards its development. *'..follow the revelation... and be patient and constan...' (10:109).* An analogy is a seed which needs to be nurtured to grow to its full potential

- **No Restriction on Human Movement:** The world is available for each one of us and is open for the use of anyone within the remit of the Permanent Values. No human being owns this world – the fact that with death we leave it all behind proves this. The world is 'loaned' to human beings to use it for a short time only. The Quran declares: *'....and brought forth therewith fruits for your sustenance; then set not up rivals unto Allah knowingly' (2:22).* (29:56), (39:10).

- **Relationships**: Human beings need the presence of other human beings within individual relationships and at the level of community in order to function, grow and develop the Self. *'...was but one nation, But it differed'. (10:19)*

- **Marriage:** A contract between two equal individuals to live their lives within the confines of the Permanent Values *(2:221).* Chastity is one of the permanent values within this context and the Quran demands observance from both men and women *(24:30-31).*

- **Freedom from Fear:** For free will to operate effectively, there has to be freedom from fear as this constrains it. The Quran declares that living within the Permanent Values will eliminates all fears. *(2:38)*

- **Freedom from Grief:** Grief is caused by events affecting human beings within a society. Most events causing grief can be linked directly or indirectly to human actions e.g. economic, wars, oppression, exploitation, slavery etc. The Quran recognises this and refers to it in many verses. *(2:38), (3:138), (12:84), (15:77).*

- **Death:** This is a deadline to remind us that we have a finite time to live in this life and our conduct here in this world will define the status of our next life after death. When we consider the event of death at the level of the self, the Quran declares: *'every Self shall have the taste of death...' (29:57).*

- **Hereafter:** The life of the 'emerged' human self continues beyond death. The 'emerged' human self is one that has reached a minimum threshold as per the Quran, when on balance the effects of the good deeds exceed those of the deeds which have negative effects. *'....let every Self look to what he has sent forth for tomorrow.....' (59:18). '...then shall each Self know what it has sent forward and what it left behind' (82:5)*

(Intentionally left blank)

22 Appendix 2 – Other Works by the Author

1. Exposition of the Quran
2. Islam: A Challenge to Religion
3. The Book of Destiny
4. The Quranic Laws
5. Reasons for the Decline of Muslims
6. Letters to Tahira
7. *Iblees* and Adam (Devil and Man)
8. Man and God
9. *Lughat ul Quran* (Dictionary of the Quranic Words) – Volume I and II (Available from Amazon)
10. The Quranic System of Sustenance (Available from Amazon)

These books are available free online at:
http://www.islamicdawn.com/
http://www.toluislam.com/

These books are also available from:

Tolu-e-Islam Trust
25 – B Gulberg 2
Lahore – 54660, Pakistan
Email: *tolueislam@gmail.com*
Phone: 00 92 42 35753666

(Intentionally left blank)

Printed in Great Britain
by Amazon